T0316727

Aspects of Real Estate Theory and Practice in Zimbabwe:
An Exploratory Text

Edited by

Innocent Chirisa and Mike Juru

Langaa Research & Publishing CIG
Mankon, Bamenda

Publisher:
Langaa RPCIG
Langaa Research & Publishing Common Initiative Group
P.O. Box 902 Mankon
Bamenda
North West Region
Cameroon
Langaagrp@gmail.com
www.langaa-rpcig.net

Distributed in and outside N. America by African Books Collective
orders@africanbookscollective.com
www.africanbookscollective.com

ISBN-10: 9956-551-12-0

ISBN-13: 978-9956-551-12-5

List Contributors

Emma Maphosa is urban and regional planner who graduated with a BSc Honours Degree in Rural and Urban Planning with the University of Zimbabwe in 2018. In 2017, Emma was employed with Gutu Rural District Council in Masvingo Zimbabwe her research interests are in real estate property management, urban management and transport planning.

Geraldine Usingarawe is a student at University of Zimbabwe currently studying BSc Honours in Real Estate Management. Her research interests are focused at on-going changes in property valuations, various disposal methods of Real Estate and how they can be improved and maintained to withstand harsh global environment of competition in the industry and ultimately continuous professional development.

Chipo Mutonhodza is a lecturer in the Department of Urban Planning and ~`Development at Great Zimbabwe University. She holds a MSc Development Studies (Women's University in Africa) and a BSc Rural and Urban Planning from University of Zimbabwe. Currently she is studying towards an MSc Rural and Urban Planning at University of Zimbabwe. Her research interests are in spatial planning and disaster risk reduction, cultural heritage and urban planning as well as transport planning. She has six years' experience working as a Town Planner in the Ministry of Local Government, Department of Physical Planning.

Innocent Chirisa is a full professor at the Department of Rural and Urban Planning, University of Zimbabwe. Currently is the deputy dean of the Faculty of Social Studies at the University of Zimbabwe and is a Research Fellow at the Department of Urban and Regional Planning, University of the Free State, South Africa. He holds a DPhil in Social Studies, MSc (Planning), BSc Honours in Rural and Urban Planning all from the University of Zimbabwe and a post-graduate Diploma in Land Management and Informal Land Resettlement from the Institute of Housing and Urban Development

Studies, Erasmus University, and the Netherlands. His research interests are systems dynamics in urban land, regional stewardship and resilience in human habitats.

Knowledge Murenje is a part-time lecturer at the Department of Rural and Urban Planning, University of Zimbabwe. He is employed at the District Development Fund (DDF) as a Chief Planning Officer and has been with the organization for 23 years. He holds a professional master's degree in geo-information science for urban planning from International Institute for Aerospace Survey and Earth Sciences (ITC), the Netherlands, BSc Honours in Rural and Urban Planning from University of Zimbabwe. Currently he is pursuing a post graduate PHD in urban planning, focussing on suburban dynamics, sustainability, urban development and GIS applications. His other area of interest includes land market, land administration and management systems.

Margaret Marewo is a student studying towards honours in BSc Rural and Urban Planning at the University of Zimbabwe. Her research interests are in transport planning and management, urbanisation and property rights and land tenure.

Mike Eric Juru is the founder and Chief Executive Officer for Integrated Properties an ISO certified Real Estate and Sustainability Consultancy Firm. He has over 20 years' experience in the Real Estate Sector in both corporate and private practice. He is the current President of the Real Estate Institute of Zimbabwe and a Council member at the Marondera University of Agriculture Sciences and Tech and also a non-executive Director at ZimTrade. A graduate from University of Zimbabwe, he is a registered practising Valuer and Estate Agent.

Motive Baloyi is a Master's student at the Department of Rural and Urban Planning, University of Zimbabwe. She holds a BSc Honours in Rural and Urban Planning from the University of Zimbabwe. Her research interests are governance, sustainable human settlements and development issues.

Patience Mazanhi is a student studying towards honours in BSc Rural and Urban Planning at the University of Zimbabwe. Her research interests are in project planning, policy and project evaluation, land rights and social research.

Ruvimbo Makurira is currently studying BSc in Real Estate Management with the University of Zimbabwe. Her research interests lie in real estate finance and investment, property valuation and behaviour of land markets in regard to regulations.

Tinashe Natasha Mujongonde–Kanonhuhwa is currently a Graduate Teaching Assistant and a Master of Science in Rural and Urban Planning student at the Department of Rural and Urban Planning, University Zimbabwe. She holds a BSc. in Rural and Urban Planning and an Executive Certificate in Programme and Project Monitoring and Evaluation, all from the University of Zimbabwe. Her research interests are in environmental planning and management, sustainability and poverty alleviation, housing and city development as well as blue and green issues.

Wendy Tsoriyo is a Lecturer in the Department of Urban Planning and Development at Great Zimbabwe University. She has lecturing experience in Zimbabwe as well as well as training experience in community capacity building and development in Zimbabwean marginalized communities. Wendy is currently studying for a PhD in Urban and Regional Planning. Her research interests are in areas of spatial transformation of urban areas, participatory planning and urban design and management. Wendy enjoys volunteering her services for the betterment of her community and spending time with her children who are also her source of inspiration.

Zebediah Muneta is a student studying honours BSc in Real Estate Management at the University of Zimbabwe. His research interests are in land management, property valuation and management of real estate investments.

Zvikomborero Denzel Mwashita is a student studying honours in BSc in Rural and Urban Planning at the University of Zimbabwe. His research interests are in land management, urban planning and design.

Table of Contents

Chapter 1

The context of real estate development and markets: An overview

Innocent Chirisa, Ruvimbo Makurira and Mike Juru

Setting the tone

Rental housing markets in many African countries are represented by a wide variety of shelter locations, with differing conditions and tenure statuses. Many of these countries are filled with informal housing which lacks the proper standards, security and expected quality of an average property (World Bank Group, 2015). In Ghana, the largest population resides in multifamily units which were converted into single household dwellings on given stand sizes. This means that in such areas or places, rental housing is only a form of occupancy provided in the owner-occupied homes. The cost of developing buildings is generally very high. This is due to the high prices of construction materials. As a result, housing becomes the most expensive asset that one will ever buy. This influences the supply of accommodation in the housing and real estate markets. There are limited options on the demand side to help the households in purchasing fully completed residential housing units. The majority of people in many African countries, particularly Zimbabwe, have irregular incomes and are exposed to limited financial options as most of them may not have the collateral security needed to acquire mortgage loans. This reduces borrowing and limits finance for rental housing, thus reducing demand on the housing market (World Bank Group, 2015). There is need for free flow of information about buyers and sellers on the market and this would also enhance the price mechanism to determine the prices using the forces of demand and supply. There is also too much speculation in the housing markets and high demand leads to price influx in real estate which may lead to inflation in the country. Overall, it is important to increase the supply of new residential properties in order to meet the existing demand as this would regulate prices (Ndiritu *et al.* 2017).

At the attainment of Independence, Zimbabwe experienced high economic growth. However, in the recent periods, the country is classified among the poorest nations in the African continent. The nation has been struggling from high inflationary conditions and this has had an impact on the property sector as well (Hanke and Kwok, 2009). Many of those who survive from the economic crises that so besets the country would invest in real estate property as its value is not easily wiped away. With the upbringing of the multi-currency system in the country, there has been some revival in the real estate sector and other facets of the economy (Tichaona, 2013). The country's economy experienced deindustrialisation from 1999 due to an economic contraction. This has led to lower economic growth which also affected the country's chances of accessing finance. As a result, many developers resorted to the general development of their own plots for rental purposes. The economic crisis has affected the real estate as many developments were brought to a standstill. This was more evident during the inflationary periods as money to purchase building materials had become valueless (CAHF, 2016). Therefore, amidst the challenges, there is need for the country to analyse how other nations are faring in the real estate sectors in order to upgrade Zimbabwe's housing industry. Due to dollarization, the country has been faced with challenges to support building and construction projects. There is also high risk in putting trust in the financial sector for the purposes of property developments. This has deterred the functionality and viability of the real estate in the country (CAHF, 2016). However, despite the existing challenges in the economy, there is still hope in the real estate sector as much effort can be done to cope up with the economic environment and at the same time promote development.

Even amidst the economic crisis in the country, construction and property development do not cease to increase in some parts of the nation though at a given pace. This is because, people still need shelter. The production of real estate properties in the country depends much upon the producers themselves. Due to the conditions of austerity in the country, there tends to be limited housing stock on the market. This is also due to the general increase in demand by the urban population which is putting pressure on the existing building structures. Some of the factors in consideration of construction and development in the economy include the availability of enough and even spare capacity to expand the production, the tenure as well as the administrative systems in the country. There is a lack by the service provision agencies to increase supply and be able to meet the existing high demand for infrastructure facilities. Also, the constraints in the accumulating of capital have been the hindrance to the development of infrastructure in the country (Mutizwa-Mangiza and Rakodi, 1990). Urban dwellers in most of the country's cities are grappling with the rising prices of properties as well as rentals along with the limited supply. The resulting effects have been the increase in overcrowding and the mushrooming of slums in towns as well as a general deterioration in the overall standards of the cities. Due to financial challenges in the economy, the bulk of developments have since been abandoned, thus creating many white elephants (Madichie and Madichie, 2006). Property development is the process of improving land-uses in a bid to produce more buildings for occupation. It involves large sums of money to execute a project and with the existing economic conditions in the country; it becomes difficult for many developers to erect their structures as available capital amount determines the feasibility of the project (Wilkinson and Reed, 2008).

Facilities management can be done through integrating the architecture, administration and engineering sciences. This helps in keeping the properties such as complexes in operation, in a safe state and at the same time keeping it more appealing to the clients. It is the duty of a facility manager to influence productivity at the workplace in meeting the government mandates as well as standard requirements. Management of facilities involves much of the janitorial and technical services that keep the property working efficiently. Van der Voodt (2017) explains that facilities management involves the monitoring of utilities, mitigation of impacts that may be resulting from the regulations by government as well as the formulation, execution and management of budgets. Facilities management is said to effective when all those factors and many other important variables increase efficiency are implemented and affirms an organisation's status and core business which enhances its overall success. The management of facilities at an organisation is more than just the application of a rolodex of management when the need arises. Nevertheless, it plays a crucial role in the maintenance of the property which; at the same time, links the core business of the organisation with the reliability of the utilities for the general users in the day-to-day running of business for the organisation. Therefore, there is an imperative need for proper planning and the coordination of the services on the organisation rather than just reacting to pop up issues that arise periodically. This requires proper planning, coordination and strict reliance on the maintenance procedures. It helps in saving the business and increasing reliability to the outside world and the stakeholders too. The way to achieve this is through implementing both corrective and preventative maintenance at the organisation (Van der Voodt, 2017).

To effectively carry out property valuation, the categorization of markets according to customer price behaviours and other differentiating market characteristics is a critical requirement. This segmentation would help in isolating market data from the one that is less relevant and thus removing possible distortions of calculations. In the property market or cluster, transactions made should be specific to the given characteristics of the market (Lawson, 2008). In Zimbabwe, property valuation is influenced by guidelines of many Acts; one of which include the Valuers Act. Various codes of conduct are required in the valuation of any property. As highlighted by Tichaona (2013), the valuation of commercial and Industrial properties requires the utilisation license and certified plan from the local planning authority among many other details. It is therefore necessary to get adequate information before acquiring any property. There are various laws that regulate the activities of the real estate agencies in the country. These rules require one to use official and government licensed agents in order to avoid chances of fraudulence on the part of the client during the process of valuation (Tichaona, 2013). Valuation in the real estate sector is the fulcrum of all activities. There is need for regulation on the activities as the final outcome of the property value is not standardised. Various methods are used in the valuation of properties in Zimbabwe and these include the Sales Comparison Approach, the Profits Method, the Contractor's method as well as the Residual method. Property valuation is very important in that it underpins a larger proportion of the financial decisions in any economy or property market as it also serves as collateral for loans (Ishaya *et al.* 2012). Therefore, there is need for proper management in the sector as the property and real estate is becoming the major contributor of revenue in the country since the properties withstand any harsh economic conditions such as inflation.

Statutory valuations are undertaken in terms of an Act of Parliament that is referred to as a statute which lays down the parameters to which the process of valuation must follow. In the execution of the real estate duties and processes, it is an important thing to know the value of the assets that are involved in the transactions. Generally, it is difficult to determine the value of a given asset. Therefore, in the valuation of the properties it is therefore necessary to follow a set of given procedures and standards in determining the value. Valuation is done on a legal basis by following an institutional set of rules which are generated within a given economy and the various forms of property transactions that are carried out. The given framework for the valuation of properties gives a variety of ways that are applicable to the valuation process. This, despite giving choice options to the valuer, is also a difficult task to the appraiser in the calculation of the value that is appropriate to a given entity. The valuation standards tend to work hand in hand with the legal order and as a result, this leads to challenges in the valuation process. Examples in the Zimbabwean context include valuation for compulsory land acquisition, statutory undertakers which are for electricity, water, roads and housing schemes, death duties, valuation for compensation, rating, taxation, stamp duty, income tax and capital gains tax. The rules or the set standards in the valuation procedures are there to minimise conflicts and the elimination of doubts between the involved parties. This also enhances cooperation and certainty among individuals. However, the standards followed in the valuation procedure may not be very rational as they just emanate from the set rules which may have been affirmed from continued or repeated use. The standards in the practice of property valuation in any given country differ and as such tend to follow the dictates of legislation of a country (Krabec, 2014).

In every growing urban set up, it is imperative to apply the principle of sustainability in all facets be it in the areas where there are low-income properties or not. The existing trend that there is lopsided sustainable development in many cities, has affected the public spaces which are being heavily used towards real estate investments. Green urbanism promotes sustainable development and growth. It is a model that encourages zero-emission and zero-waste in the urban environment. It ensures energy efficiency in the urban set ups (Apanaviciene, 2015). There tends to be an opportunity in the real estate sector when sustainable development is designed and promoted. There is need for sustainable properties in the construction world today and in the real estate industry in general. As the trends towards achieving sustainable growth and development in the cities increase, the real estate has a mandate to become flexible and adapt to the changes. This is because requirements in the development of sustainable properties need the real estate industry to have necessary changes, especially by owners and developers. It is initiated by modern requirements for energy consumption and environmental protection as well as the social corporate responsibility obligations. Sustainability is becoming an important factor as well in the determination of property value. Therefore, in order to create more value in the real estate environment for the benefit of the clients and future generations, there is need for new thinking and the implementation of better approaches by real estate society, planners and developers as well in order to accommodate new urbanism and sustainability approaches (Nassar, 2013).

In every economy, the evaluation of real estate is of uttermost importance as a result of the increasing requirements for quality structures and realignment of the real estate market. There is now need therefore, for field works in carrying out of the evaluation process in the real estate sector. However, this requires more time and is also costly as the data would then need to be compiled on a database. Therefore, in such a scenario, it then becomes critical to create a proper database that shuns repetitions and at the same time is cost-effective. This requires the adoption of technologies in the real estate valuations. GIS (Geographical Information Systems) has proven to be a good supporting system for the real estate sector as well as other various fields at large. When applied in real estate, GIS technology would be of greater benefit due to its advantages which include objectivity, accuracy as well as its reliability in determining evaluations. Real estate and property management is a field in which there is large involvement of social assets and as such, it is of much importance that every stakeholder gets the actual value of his or her property. GIS is a tool that helps in providing position based complex planning, at the same time solving organisational and management problems through the carrying out of transactions such as storing, processing and monitoring of data about geographical spaces. Real estate evaluations that are aided by GIS technology have the advantages of producing accurate and more rapid solutions in various transactions. For example, in renting, purchase sale, taxation as well as expropriation, it provides abundant data to do with positions and variability from the national economies. The use of GIS in the real estate discipline as well as urban planning provides updatable, accessible and analysable solutions and opportunities which result from fast, accurate and efficient decision-making process in the determination of real estate values (Sesli, 2015).

Negotiation is a day-to-day aspect in the carrying out of various duties in life. It is part of life which is most evident in the real estate environment. In order for every party to benefit in the real estate transactions, negotiation has to take place. As such, negotiation is an important aspect in day-to-day business; hence it requires adequate preparation of information and time. The accumulation of superior knowledge of any particular transaction gives a competitive edge in any particular transaction during negotiations. In carrying out negotiations, it is good and even more proper not to use emotions as they tend to be associated with unethical behaviour, cause impasses as well as desperation in value claiming. Emotions of anger emanate from selfish interests as an angry negotiator often chooses to reach impasse or even to commit unethical acts. Negotiations have to result in sustenance of positive business relationships between the client and the agent as this would enhance the overall success of the business (Schneider, 2016). Successful negotiation outcomes are a

7

result of proper planning and preparation. Any aspect that may be considered a defect or weakness to the other party has to be minimised. It is important to be very flexible in negotiation and to make one's offer as strong as it can be. There is need to know current information on real estate market pertaining to sales, lending rates and general market trends (Hale, 2017). Some of the key information which is required before engaging in a negotiation is to know the average cost per square foot within the comparable properties and also to assess the comparability of the properties (Hale, 2017). Every successful negotiation must be a win-win situation, where every party benefits, rather than one feeling a sense of loss after the process.

The reason for property maintenance is for the benefit of the property owner. This is achieved through constant and timely improvements and repairs of the property. Through maintenance of the property, the value of an asset would also be increased. Properties which the owners require to lease for a long term need very careful attention to prevent deterioration, damage and system failures. This may be achieved through the use of modern technology as well as materials. Types of buildings such as historic buildings may require the use of the original construction materials and design in order that the historical character is maintained or preserved. When the work pertaining to the maintenance of a building structure is properly done, the owner must get full satisfaction at the lowest possible cost (Oyedele, 2015). Proper maintenance of a building has to be achieved through creating good relations with the tenant who would be using the property. It is important that routine check-ups and maintenance on the property should be done by the tenants. This may be through handling emergency repairs and carrying out long improvements to the building. When properly maintained, the property may gain or maintain its value rather than lose it with time. The maintenance of a property is not a simple job of just supervising employees, it is a complex process. There is need to establish good communications with the tenants, their associations as well as the employees that are assigned to carry out the tasks. Therefore, the active participation of everyone in utilising the building properly is important. In order for easy follow ups and monitoring, it is therefore of importance to formulate a repair and maintenance committee with the primary responsibility of maintaining the structure (Oyedele, 2015).

Structure of the Book

Chapter 1 provides an overview of the structure of the book will be as follows: gives the context of real estate development and markets.

Chapter 2 is titled 'Urbanisation trends and urban land development in Zimbabwe' it seeks to shed light on how the land development process has been done; that is in the present and past, dating back to the pre-colonial era. Literature has been reviewed in this chapter about the topic at hand and critical analysis is made. Some of the issues that have been raised in the chapter include the problems that have been brought about by urban land development on the natural, social and economic environment. Adding on to that, political influence on the field of planning as well as development of urban areas is a hotspot for debate in this chapter as this has hindered the planning process. Recommended in this chapter are the solutions that can be implemented now or in the future so as to deal with the problems that have been brought about by politics, poor planning as well as to make urban planning and development be on a straight lane to re-establish the glory of our country's cities. Some of the solutions include devolution which will give the cities autonomy to plan what they want without political interference, improving the transport network, participation of the locals in the planning phase only to mention a few.

Chapter 3, 'Zimbabwean real estate finance since 1980', seeks to provide a descriptive analysis of the real estate finance in Zimbabwe beginning from the year 1980. It describes the challenges facing the real estate financing in the country. It also explains the state of the economy as well as the existing sources of finance for the real estate. The chapter further reviews the existing opportunities in the sector as well as the practices and options. Various sources of finance for the real estate sector are explored and analysed. Many of the challenges which are hindering the development of the real estate sector are centred upon the issue of finance. From the study, it is observed that finance is a pivotal factor in the success and viability of any development in the real estate sector and as such needs to be made available easily. Finance has been seen as the one factor which is at the core of any viability of a development project. Its importance is seen at the initial stages up to the completion stages of a project. Finance for the real estate development determines the viability of the project

Chapter 4, 'Understanding rental housing markets in selected African' countries', is the chapter that develops a theoretical framework to analyse the rental housing market in Africa. Basic models of demand and supply, rent controls and rent reviews give motivation to the rental housing market. The models are then extended in a number of ways to examine a variety of factors such as population growth and urbanisation that are important for developing countries when focusing on rental housing markets. A rental housing market is presented as a leasehold estate in which a person has an ownership of a temporary right to hold land or property of a landlord. The main focus of this chapter is on accessing trends and performances of rental housing markets in Africa after 2000 and experiences from other continents. Housing markets in African countries such as Ethiopia, Nigeria, South Africa and Angola have introduced market mechanisms into a previously welfare-oriented housing system. The chapter explores the challenges faced by landlords and tenants in formulating lease agreements and rent reviews, as the government ventures in formulating policies.

Chapter 5 is about 'Construction and property development under austerity in Zimbabwe. It expounds on the economic difficulties Zimbabwe has faced since the late 1990s to date and explores certain problems in the construction and property development industries that existing theories on their improvements did not consider. This chapter focuses on the impact of the financial crisis and public debt crisis management policies on construction and development of property.as it suggests that the industries need to be rescued and enable to help the on-going adjustment of the economy and to develop the capability to adapt future changes. Emphasis is put on what the industries themselves can do, as experience shows that it is naïve for governments to shield the industries from the effects of the unfavourable economic conditions. Zimbabwe's construction industry is in a precarious position, with operators living on the margins as they try to deal with underlying productivity, profitability, performance and sustainable challenges. This sharply contrasts with mature markets like South Africa where mortgages take up significant proportions of bank balance sheets, affording reasonable activity and liquidity on the property market. The mortgages are sufficient enough to influence more predictable and sustainable long-term yields. Although development and construction methods such as design-build, private public partnerships are being adopted, problems are still being faced due to low barriers to entry and exit in the property sector. Austerity implies the difficult economic conditions that are created by the government to reduce public expenditure; hence the chapter explores such matters.

Chapter 6 is entitled 'Facilities' management in Zimbabwe.' It examines the meaning and dimensions of facilities management in Zimbabwe. It has been regarded as a great management tool that integrates people and technology, property and processes experts to provide important services which support operations of the organisation. Many organisations view facilities management as a strategic facility planning, space management and services outsourcing. The purpose of this chapter is to help people to recognise the actual meaning, importance, categories and core values of facilities management to an organisation. At the same time, the chapter is helpful in having a detailed knowledge of how facilities can be managed and all the roles it plays to achieve organisational goals since it integrates people, work processes and physical assets to serve strategic objectives. This chapter represents theoretical view based on other countries practices on facilities management since it is a discipline that involves a variety of non-core operations and maintenance services to support the main goals of organisations which are both in public and private sector. The other important area of this research is to provide a clear meaning of facilities management in conjunction with real estate management.

Chapter 7 explores 'The institution and practice of property valuation in Zimbabwe.' It examines the institutionalisation of the real estate industry and the practice of property valuation by the practitioners known as the valuers. Property trade is highly regularised and the transaction cost is not simply negotiated like other goods. Therefore, the valuers should be governed by rules and regulations to reduce discrepancies. Missing in literature is the institutional content in the neoclassical theory and the application thereof. The study used the qualitative approach of secondary data and case studies of global, regional and local countries. Evident from the study are the challenges being faced by Zimbabwean valuers which include information asymmetry, lack of property data banks, lack of national valuation guide and also poor performance of the economy. The chapter concludes that the valuers rely on their professional networks to carry out their valuation and they tend not to specialise in one area of the property business like valuation only but other assignments such as property management. The Zimbabwean government should therefore try to implement new technology models in the property sector which are being applied globally thus minimising discrepancies and also implement the Continuing Professional Development campaign to increase the valuers' skills and knowledge.

Chapter 8 deals with 'Statutory valuation in Zimbabwe.' It examines the practice of statutory valuation in Zimbabwe. In more detail, the chapter sets out what valuers encounter when undertaking valuations. Property valuations are subject to a rigorous code of practice set out in the RICS Appraisal and Valuation Manual commonly known as the Red Book (RICS, 1995). Real property constitutes a substantial portion of the world's wealth. If the operations of property markets are to be established on dependable valuations there must be generally agreed upon standards by which Market Value and other value types are determined and reported by valuers. Correct understanding and proper application of these standards will inevitably promote the viability of international and domestic transactions in real property. It improves the relative position of real property among other investment alternatives and reduces the instances of fraud and abuse. Statutory valuations are used for revenue generation purposes by applicable authorities such as local governments or the Office of State Revenue. The lack of valuation standards in the property market has resulted in subjective practices in residential valuations. Unavailability of information databases has added to much variability in valuer performances. In the context of residential properties valued for current market valuations, real property valuers recognise the complexities of markets and the real estate bought and sold therein. The chapter explores how differences in real estate markets and between individual properties are reflected accurately and reliably where Generally Accepted Valuation Principles (GAVP) is followed.

Chapter 9 centres on 'Real estate, green urbanism and environmental sustainability.' It provides an overview of real estate, green urbanism and environment sustainability in the case of Zimbabwe. It addresses the questions of how to improve and meet better standards in terms of marking Zimbabwean cities to be recognised and to sustain them. An analysis of sustainable development and environmental planning is regarded as the spot light to green urbanism. This chapter focuses specifically on the links between real estate, green urbanism and environmental sustainability. Although sustainability addresses economic, social and environmental concerns, an emphasis on its environmental aspects serves as a first step in understanding this critical area. The analysis explains several sustainable design concepts which relate to urban development. They include compactness, sustainable transport, and density, mixed land-uses, diversity, passive solar design and greening. Moreover, there are other sustainable urban forms such as traditional development, urban containment, compact city and the eco-city. Finally, this chapter proposes favourable polices which support the growth of the real estate industry whilst promoting green urbanism and environmental sustainability in order to have smart cities which helps planners in assessing the contribution of different urban forms.

Chapter 10 is about 'GIS as a tool in real estate and urban planning'. It is argued that urban planning involves many different and interrelated municipal functions done at different scales, sectors and stages. Generally major functions of an urban or town planning include development control that is normally statutory, strategic plan making (subject plans, development plans and master plans), policy and research, project planning and real estate, housing and community services and the general municipal administration. The scale within which these functions operate may be at city, sub region of a city (e.g. decentralised Harare municipal offices) neighbourhood level and street block level. Sectors of town planning may include real estate, planning and research, transport, housing, land development and environment. Within these scales and sectors there are different stages of planning that involve planning objectives, analysis of the prevailing situation, modelling and projection, selection of planning options available, plan implement, monitor and evaluate and feedback. GIS can be used in these different stages of urban planning to achieve the desired goals. Different stages, scales and sectors of urban planning require different GIS uses. However, the purpose of this chapter is to give a general overview of the application and use of GIS in some of these sectors in urban planning in general with reference to Zimbabwe, giving as much as possible, Harare City as an example and then showing GIS urban applications by way of a pilot project.

Chapter 11 explores 'Negotiation in real estate.' This chapter provides an overview, definition and rationale of negotiation' with particular reference to the theory and practice of real estate. It discusses the models of negotiation including the substance and process in real estate, the players involved and strategies used. Reference is given to the laws that govern negotiation in real estate in the Zimbabwean real estate industry.

Chapter 12 expounds on 'The scope and issues of property maintenance.' This chapter seeks to unveil the scope and issues concerning property maintenance in Zimbabwe. Maintenance work is said to be done to restore, keep or improve every facility of the building. This is mainly done by the owner of the property upon letting it for investment to provide his clients with the best value for their money. The way maintenance is done in Zimbabwe is not properly accounted for in the literature, as most of the management companies are not performing well in the economic meltdown. New unregistered companies are entering the market despite the existing real estate companies. To discover empirical evidence the study uses secondary sources of data and reports from different maintenance managers with different perspectives on the management. Evidence from the sources shows that the property market in Zimbabwe is being greatly impacted by the current economic austerity and there is an increase of informal traders and huge occupational void levels. It is recommended that if the local government can facilitate the informal traders by providing them with premises and funds, they may be able to pay rent for the premises they will be using and boost the property markets' performance.

Chapter 13 provides insight into 'The role of real estate practitioners in the financial market.' It explores and assesses the contribution of realtors in the financial market, particularly given the financial change in most economies against the background that the financial markets are the backbone of an economy. There is an opportunity to address finance market challenges using the realtor services in Zimbabwe particularly given the infancy nature of real estate education and practice in Zimbabwe. The aim of chapter is to explore the role that a realtor could play in improving performance of financial markets in Zimbabwe.

Chapter 14 is entitled 'Urban graffiti: epitome of place-making, property value enhancement or socio-political resistance'. It argues that graffiti as part of the urban fabric in cities has become a worldwide spatial phenomenon which can be considered to be both an art and crime. As an art, graffiti can be utilised to become a place making tool. However both concepts of graffiti as art and the place making concept are fairly novel in the Zimbabwean context. The chapter examines the complex relationship between graffiti and the place- making concept in Zimbabwean urban public spaces. The study adopted a case study method that is based on extensive literature and document review. Observations and unstructured interviews with city council officials from Bulawayo and Harare were also instrumental data collection techniques used in the study. Results show that the adoption of graffiti as an art is still in its infancy stages, although the practice is common in the two major cities. Graffiti artist are not visible in the mainstream national art events such as the Harare International Festival of Arts. The chapter recommends harnessing graffiti as a place making tool is collective process which requires various stakeholders' participation to shape public urban spaces through shared values of a community, revisiting the legal framework for graffiti so that it becomes an art which is clearly defined and acknowledged in the urban spaces. The support of the business community in funding graffiti artists' initiatives will further refine their artistic skills and improve their global competitiveness.

Chapter 15 is entitled 'Factors influencing property values: the case of Harare.' It explores the different factors that influence property values. Property values are estimates of the market value by which a property can be traded on the market. These values are influenced by different factors, taking into account the type of property. Phenomena such as NIMBY (Not in My Backyard) also influence the property values if they are not decided carefully by the planners. NIMBY is defined as an attitude of opposition by local residents against certain risk-generating facilities that have been chosen to accommodate either government or industry. The search was done through the use of secondary data sources, which involve data collected by another person. Evidence from the source indicates that the values are influenced by factors such as locational factors, availability of services (water, roads, sewer and schools), proximity to the central business district (CBD), locally unwanted land-uses (LULU) which affects adjacent neighbourhoods among others. It is recommended that the Government of Zimbabwe should venture into public private partnerships because of lack of capital outlay to carry out housing construction projects, as its backlog is large due to rapid urbanisation. It should also decentralise some of its powers to local authorities.

Chapter 16 explores 'Resilience and sustainability in the real estate sector: issues and options.' It aims at discussing the various dimensions which Zimbabwe's property sector has adopted in improving adaptability and sustainability. The study aimed to have an appreciation of how sustainability issues are being tackled in relation to economic, social, environmental and climate change parameters. This is an attempt to reveal drawbacks and improvements made in Zimbabwe with regard to resilient and sustainable building. The desktop archival review method was engaged, to give appreciation of the global and regional trends on the evolution and improvements which has characterized the sector throughout ages. Lessons from the developed world shall be given in coming up with the best option for a more improved face of real-estate in Zimbabwe. The reason being, each situation is unique and solutions for each scenario are usually area-specific. This chapter goes an extra mile to analyse developments made in the built-environment with regards to selected towns and cities in Zimbabwe.

Chapter 17 outlines the conclusion and gives direction for future action and research.

References

Apanavičienė, R., Daugėlienė, A., Baltramonaitis, T and Maliene, V. (2015). Sustainability aspects of real estate development: Lithuanian case study of sports and entertainment arenas. *Sustainability*, 7(6), 6497-6522.

Centre for Affordable Housing Finance in Africa (CAHF). (2016). Understanding Zimbabwe's Housing Financial Market. CAHF.

Hale, J. P. (2017). Negotiating a Real Estate Contract. Long and Foster Real Estate, London: University of Westminster.

Hanke, S. H and Kwok, A. K. (2009). On the measurement of Zimbabwe's hyperinflation. *Cato J.*, 29, 353.

Ishaya, D.A., Dabo, D., and Makama, B. (2012). Clients Influence on Property Value in Valuation Report. *Empirical Evidence from Abuja*, Nigeria.

Kibunyi, D., Ndiritu, S. W., Carcel, H and Gil-Alana, L. A. (2017). Real estate prices in Kenya: is there a bubble? *Journal of Housing and the Built Environment*, 32(4), 787-804.

Krabec, T. (2014). Asset Valuation Standards: A Functional-Institutional Approach. *Prague Economic Papers*, 23(4), 531-540.

Madichie, N. O and Madichie, O. A. (2009). A theoretical review of the property development challenges in Nigeria. *International Journal of Business and Emerging Markets*, 1(3), 296-311.

Mutizwa M., and Rakodi, N. D. (1990). Housing policy, production and consumption in Harare: A review Part II. *Zambezia*, 17(2), 111-131.

Nassar, U. (2013). Principles of green urbanism: The absent value in Cairo, Egypt. *International Journal of Social Science and Humanity*, 3(4), 339.

Oyedele, O. A. (2015). Assessment of Property Management Practices in Nigeria. Nigerian Institute of Estate Surveyors and Valuers, Lagos State.

Schneider. (2016). Emotions in Real Estate Negotiations. *Scholarly Commons*. University of Pennysyvania.

Sesli, F. A. (2015). Creating real estate maps by using GIS: A case study of Atakum-Samsun/Turkey. *Acta Montanistica Slovaca*, 20(4), 1-12.

Tichaona, T. (2013). Real Estate and Property Management Challenges in the City of Beira, Mozambique. Harare: Zimbabwe Open University.

Van der Voordt, T. (2017). Facilities management and corporate real estate management: FM/CREM or FREM? *Journal of Facilities Management*, 15(3), 244-261.

Wilkinson, S. J and Reed, R. G. (2008). Property Development. 5th Edition. Routledge Taylor and Francis, New York and London.

World Bank Group. (2015). Stocktaking of the Housing sector in Sub-Saharan Africa: Challenges and Opportunities. World Bank Group, Washington DC.

Chapter 2

Urbanisation trends and urban land development in Zimbabwe

Zvikomborero Denzel Mwashita and Chipo Mutonhodza

Introduction

Development has been a major feature of Zimbabwe both in the urban and rural areas, though it takes various forms. This chapter will take development as the sustainable use of the available resources in trying to improve people's lives in all aspects that are social, economic and political. Urban land development has been a hotspot for scholars over the past few years and a lot has been documented on this topic. Development is a continuous process and paradigms always shift due to the advancements in technology, methods as well as information that can be found. When it comes to development, there are certain procedures that have to be followed both in Urban and Rural land development. This chapter will focus more on urban land development with emphasis on the processes, issues and future prospects of the topic in question. Urban land development is a technical and political process concerned with the use and development of the land and the environment. It involves the protection, the public welfare and design of the urban environment, including air, water and the infrastructure passing into and out of urban areas, such as transportation, communications and distribution networks (Wekwete, 1989). It is all aided by sustainable development and this is influenced by the state of political affairs in the country as well as the legal framework that prevails.

The topic at hand is not an issue that has emerged in this modern era. Urban land development dates back to the colonial era. Due to urban influx controls in the 1960's such as the Vagrancy Act of 1960, there was limited rural-urban migration into major cities such as Harare and Bulawayo. This meant that only a limited number of the population was allowed to live in urban areas because they were reserved mainly for the white population constituting only 3.5% of the country's population (Patel, 1988). The government affected urban inflow controls for the black population (Gadgett, 1977) thus limiting the overall rate of urbanisation, Rhodesia had thus counter-urbanised. During this period urbanisation depended on the availability of employment and accommodation in the city. However, in the same, period, industrial development followed transport and communication development as well as the introduction of the Hut and Poll tax which forced the black and the white population to flock into the monetary market. These developments stimulated the rise of towns such as Harare, Gweru, Marondera, Kadoma and Bulawayo among others. The establishment of rail transport at mining extraction points such as Zvishavane and Hwange marked the increase of the urban population in Rhodesia. Moreover, migration of the urbanised white population increased the urban population from 78.3% to 79.8% (Patel, 1988).

However, there are some loopholes in the existing present-day literature as to how the process of urban land development in Zimbabwe has been done in the pre-independence era due to the dominance of political decisions over planning decisions. As mentioned above, planning paradigms changed. This resulted in planning and development processes changing as well in order to match up to the modern trends of planning. Conversely these changes have resulted in issues that have arose over the past few years concerning urban land development globally, continentally as well as in Zimbabwe. To that end, there is need for the embracement of future prospects which will aid in solving the arising issues in the field of urban land development as that will help to smoothen out what seems to be a difficult task in this timeline, as shall be documented in the study. Planning functions in Zimbabwe have been mainly performed by the government through local authorities. Certain laws and legislations have also been put in place so as to protect this field. This chapter is to be structured in a way that will show the review, the introduction to the topic, theoretical framework, literature review, methodology, results, discussion and synthesis and a conclusion.

Theoretical framework

Urbanisation is the population shift from rural to urban areas which involves a lot of processes. One of the key processes is urban planning which is a technical and political process that controls the development and use of land (Mutondoro, 2017). As such, urban planning and politics are always an intertwined process. Therefore, one cannot really separate the two and this has been a major challenge that Zimbabwe is facing. There is need to deal with these problems immediately as this has resulted in a lot of chaos within the field of urban planning. Politics has taken over the role of planning in the name of diplomacy at most, trying to build relations with foreign nations and in the process taking for granted the consequences of such actions. During the colonial era, the land development process was indeed technical as stages of land development were taken and valued, not overlooked due to political reasons.

Over the years, planning in Harare has become poor. There has been a rise in the illegal settlements and the city fathers have also completely lost control due to the complete collapse of the rule of law. According to the Implementation Guide of 2014 to the National Housing Delivery Programme that was launched by the Ministry of Local Government, Public Works and National Housing, blame falls on the government whose overall responsibility of supervising the management of state land has failed in respect of; acquisition of private land, developed or undeveloped for urban state purposes , coordination of development controls on urban state land reserved or allocated to local authorities and user ministries, planning, designing and approval of layout plans on state land and facilitation of boundary extensions by local authorities. Power has been centralised in the above-mentioned bodies and local authorities have in due course become ineffective in finding new land to house people on their waiting lists.

The legal framework and urban development process in Zimbabwe

Physical and spatial planning in Zimbabwe are directed by the Department of Physical Planning (DPP), a technical arm of the government that is in charge of managing the spatial planning system and providing technical advice for the implementation of the development planning systems (Toriro, 2007; IBRD/WB, 2012). The department has oversight of the country's local authorities, who must adhere to the provisions of the Regional, Town and Country Planning Act (RTCPA) (Chapter 29:12) and related legislation. In addition, the DPP advises the Minister of Local Government on the interpretation of planning provisions and the execution of planning functions under the reserved powers of the Minister, in accordance with the RTCPA. The department is also involved in facilitating sites for the development of government, state enterprises, as well as parastatal activities and the detailed planning of housing estates on state land. In addition, it carries out technical evaluation of plans (master plans, local plans and layout plans) originating from local planning authorities to aid the Minister in making decisions on the plans, mediating in stakeholder conflicts arising from spatial planning decisions that interfere with other people's land rights. Furthermore, the DPP provides technical assistance relating to the planning of preparation structures for the development planning system which the Provincial Councils and Administration Act of 1984 prescribes to manage urban public transport and carries out tachometric survey and pegging of State land.

Physical planning embraces aspects of environmental planning, building codes (Cote and Grant, 2008) and balancing between land-uses to avoid incompatibility and conflict in land-use. Williams (2000:8) has pointed out that conventional planning "… is about nudging and accommodating prevailing trends, but ecosystem planning is about choosing and pursuing a desirable future." Overall, in physical planning terms, construction is an intervention in a natural environment that brings about development, in the form of improvement and value addition to land (Alexander, 1987). Land-use planning is a critical determinant in the siting of any facility. Such provisions are specified in the master, local, structure and subject plans of a given local authority. In Zimbabwe, Section 22 of the Regional, Town and Country Planning Act (RTCPA) provides for the meaning of development with regards to planning. Master plans can be sector specific (i.e. water or transport) or generic (covering a combination of developmental factors). The general master plan of an area takes into account the various aspects of a settlement. Section 14 (2a) defines a master plan as an instrument through which a local authority lays down its "general proposal for a planning area with respect to coordinated and harmonious development and other uses of land." This includes measures for the regulation of land-use, improvement of the physical environment, economic development of the area and movement of traffic in that area. Specific master plans may be for water, housing, industry, commerce, or tourism development, to name but a few. It is important to ensure that there are no conflicts between the master plans and the local plans, as sometimes expected from the development of physical plan products like houses and roads, in keeping with Section 21 of the RTCPA. Sections 17 and 18 of the RTCPA provide for the preparation and management of local plans. It is an instrument to ensure coordinated and harmonious development and re-development of land-use in a given area. Sometimes the development proposed is incompatible with existing and proposed uses of land. Existing local development plans assist in showing the different land-uses in different areas in the country.

The City of Harare has flimsy public infrastructure and this limits its capacity to incorporate the land to be under control (Chirisa *et al.* 2014). Political dynamics are also at play because with ZANU-PF having lost most urban seats to the opposition (MDC), it is trying to gain political mileage by allowing disarray in the housing system. According to the Combined Harare Residents Association, there is haphazard allocation of residential stands and this is mainly done for political convenience while entirely ignoring proper land-use and management. Housing cooperatives have emerged in peri-urban Harare with the majority of them being purported to be ZANU-PF supporters (Chirisa *et al.* 2014).

Literature review

Urban planning and related legislation created racial segregation until independence in 1980. The new government set about investing in new infrastructure aimed at redressing the imbalances of the colonial past (Wekwete, 1989). This included a focus on urban centres thereby bringing about the development of the contemporary urban areas in Zimbabwe.

In a broader sense, urban development suggests the transformation of the spatial pattern configuration of urban areas vertically, laterally, economically and demographically (Pacione 2005: 71). Williamson, Enemark *et al.* (2010: 200-201) defines urban development in general as "wide range of activities of different scales, from establishing new urban area or town, such as new residential areas, commercial or business centre, industrial complex, down to just building a new house or its extension." On the level of city, urban development can be understood as "the process of production of urban places." A simple model expresses this process as "the creation of built environment, with its physical, social and psychological features, as the results of the operation of the development agents, public and private sector organizations, using physical and social environment through their development factor such as resources, rules and ideas" (Madanipour 1996: 135-137).

Urban planning and development in Zimbabwe have been nurtured by the colonial political economy, which was centrally focused on a racial division of society between Europeans and Africans (Wekwete, 1989). Urban planning as an activity was designed to control and regulate land-use activity in emerging settlements and ensure the adequate provision of social and physical infrastructure. However, this ideology has been abandoned due to corruption and politics taking over the field of planning. In contrast to West Africa where there was significant indigenous urbanisation before colonisation, Zimbabwean urban patterns have been determined largely by the incoming settlers and indigenous participation in their design has been limited (Patel, 1988). This has been because of the limited access the black majority had on the planning matter. Moreover, this was due to our lack of expertise in the field of planning.

Early settlement planning in Zimbabwe was influenced by the settlers who arrived with the British South Africa Company. The first town planning exercise for Harare was carried out by Captain Thomas Ross, with a grid of streets aligned to the magnetic north (Wekwete, 1989). A segregated environment was also created early when the sanitary board promulgated regulations in 1892 to establish a native location which was later developed on a 25-hectare site about four kilometres from the Centre. In all the emerging towns a physical and cadastral framework was adopted which became the basis from which municipalities regulated and controlled land and building development. Town planning was closely linked to the emerging municipal administrative framework, which was in turn linked initially to the sanitary boards and later to the municipal law (1897). which increased municipal councils' powers to regulate their affairs.

There are a lot of statutes that underpin the process of urban land development and these help in guiding planners on what is required within the field. Wekwete (1989) observes that urban land development is and has been mainly practiced by the state and its organizations that are parastatals that have been entrusted with the planning and development process in Zimbabwe. However, this has been compromised over the past few years. In addition to this, urban development is also determined by the type of state ideology. An economically focused nation will try by all means to promote the private sector but here in Zimbabwe, the mixed economy allows for development of the land to be both public and private sector oriented (Wekwete, 1989), Due to the state of affairs now, one cannot tell if development is public or private sector oriented or whether it is now for personal gains of the ruling elite. Therefore, since the development is determined by the state of affairs, a lot of issues have rose due to this as the unstable economy of Zimbabwe makes urban land development not easy as there is no clear course on how things are to be done. Some of the issues are the bias and disorder that has been brought about by the political atmosphere within the nation, the work of property and land developers and the field of planning

25

rendered powerless or rather useless. All this disorder has been put on the shoulders of the planners.

Wekwete (1989) alludes that laws are created and used by the state apparatus (including the judiciary and administration) to legitimate state power. Planning law has therefore no ideology of its own, but that of the state, laws which is created to reflect state powers. However, one can also notice that these laws have been abused over the years. Some of them have been by passed due to the issue of politics taking the matters of planning into its own hands. Magwende (2015) is of the view that urban land development is a political, economic and social phenomenon. He takes the stance that the element of urbanisation in most African countries has been influenced by post-colonial policies with industrialisation in mind focusing on a few towns. Evidence can be very much be taken from Zimbabwe as Harare and Bulawayo are the major cities that have been industrialised through development of urban land.

Methodology

Data in this chapter was gathered from secondary sources of information such as books, journal articles and newspapers. Qualitative data analysis was one of the techniques used to analyse information. This involved identifying and analysing data so as to come out with a strong brand of valid and valuable information. Secondary information refers to information that has already been provided (Kothari, 2004). The data were obtained from various published sources such as publications and report from the state and various parastatals and international organisations research scholars.

Issues of urban land development in Zimbabwe

Urban land development has resulted in a lot of problems arising due to a number of reasons. Some of them include poor planning, political influence over planning decisions and corruption. Due to the facts stated above, this has led to a number of problems that are to be discussed in this section.

One of the fundamental problems confronting Zimbabwe is that of little or no employment creation at all. Over the past two decades, employment has been difficult to come by causing the educated populace in the country to improvise by means of vending and flooding of the informal markets. The closure of industries and companies in the country is a result of the underperforming economy and has caused joblessness for majority of the educated persons, leading to the blooming of the informal sector in Zimbabwe. Political influence in Zimbabwe has worsened the poor planning process and affected employment directly or indirectly. The construction of buildings and roads has a direct impact on employment creation as manual labour is required. Both semi and skilled labour are needed for the task at hand, so companies in the construction create a market. This will then magnetize other sectors like real estate and the food industry and might as well attract foreign direct investment. All this can be dealt with if planning and politics work hand in hand towards achieving great things for the society.

Considerable demands are placed on the urban social and physical infrastructure by the increasing urban population. One such example is in the area of housing where a critical need for accommodation is reached and manifests itself in spontaneous settlements. In the past, the existing housing stock has been able to absorb more people than planned for until recently; this was done to avoid squatting. Additionally, squatting was avoided through the implementation of control measures, which were designed to limit population movement to urban areas (Patel, 1988). Now, overcrowding has reached a state where existing housing stock cannot absorb additional people.

Overcrowded high-density housing schemes in areas such as White Cliff and Epworth or Sally Mugabe heights generally correlate with poor health. Therefore, conditions such as are malnutrition, acute respiratory infections, communicable childhood diseases, tuberculosis, digestive problems, inflammatory and no inflammatory diseases of the skin and mental illness are common (Zimbabwe 1986b). Co-existing with overcrowding are the problems of inadequate refuse collection, insufficient water supplies and sanitation, which create further health hazards. With increasing urbanisation, general environmental pollution becomes a problem. Water, noise and air pollution as well as solid wastes all contribute to deterioration of the environment not only in the urban areas but also in the surrounding rural areas. This has resulted in some areas being vulnerable to diseases such as cholera, typhoid as well as other water and air borne diseases.

Transport is an increasing problem as new low-income housing schemes are sited at the periphery of cities. Since independence conventional buses have failed to cope with the peak hour demand (Zimbabwe, 1982), hence the use of commuter Omnibuses which carry 12-15 passengers per vehicle which only but increases the number of vehicles in a single carriageway. Due to the increase in the use of private modes of transport over the few years, there have been some traffic problems around Harare (Zinyama, Tevera and Cumming, 1993). Initially, the capital was designed to accommodate about 1.5 million people but over the years, the population has increased threefold, making the area over populated and overcrowded. There have been initiatives to improve the transport system in Harare but due to politics, the funds have been redirected to where who knows (Muronda, 2008). This has resulted congestion which leads to accidents, injuries and fatalities.

Furthermore, the provision of recreational facilities has been inadequate in the past so old and new housing schemes require an increased provision of such amenities. Urban growth means there is acquisition of good farming land in peri-urban areas for further development (Muronda, 2008). This, in turn, leads to conflict over urban and agricultural demands on natural .resources or arable land, water and forests. Simultaneously, increasing urbanisation accelerates the need to increase food production per agricultural worker, because it raises the proportion of the population not producing its own food (Muchadenyika and Williams, 2016).

Adding on to the issues above, the concept of urban land development has brought about a lot of pollution. Taking a look at the capital of Zimbabwe, once called the sunshine city is a diaspora. The area is heavily polluted and there are a lot of eyesores in the vicinity. The City Council of Harare has abandoned its mandate of keeping the city clean. Areas along Chinhoyi Street, Mbuya Nehanda and Jason Moyo amongst others look like dump sites to the extent that one cannot see the essence of being in the capital. Due to the flooding of vendors as well, this has resulted in land pollution. Government and the City Council ought to do something about pollution and restore the legacy of the once so-called sunshine city (Muzondi, 2014).

Moreover, high juvenile delinquency has become one of the problems that have escalated Zimbabwe. A lot of people came to the capital with high hopes of employment only to be disappointed. This has resulted in high crime rates due to the lack of employment creation. During the peak hour in overcrowded places with in the CBD, pickpockets are rampant. In addition to that, this has also resulted in a lot of children living in the streets doing all kinds of mischief especially prostitution and drug abuse. This has resulted in the mushrooming of squatter camps especially along Mukuvisi River, as the homeless people built own shelter against the harsh weather conditions.

The case of Harare

Harare is Zimbabwe's capital and largest metropolitan city with a total population of more than 2.8 million people (Chirisa *et al.* 2015). Harare evolved out of the colonial system and as such, its present-day outlook and governance reflect the colonial legacy (Mutondoro *et al.* 2017). Munzwa and Jonga (2010) argue that in most Sub Saharan countries, one cannot discuss urban land development without making reference to colonisation and its impact as it brought about many changes in the outlook and shape of towns and cities, bringing with it a new socio political and economic dispensation. This section of the chapter will trace the history of urban land development of the City of Harare from the colonial times.

The Pioneer Column, a colonial force formed by Cecil Rhodes, founded Harare in 1890 as a fort. Once named Fort Salisbury, it was declared a city in 1935 and became known as Salisbury until 1982 (Mutondoro *et al.* 2017). Zinyama *et al.* (1993) alludes that, Harare is that type of colonial city founded on the philosophy and practice of separate development. As in many other African cities, Harare was specifically built to host the influx of people, which were moving to the city as labour force for the growing economy during the colonial period (Mlambo (2009) as cited in Wania *et al.* (2013). Wekwete (1994) states that, the era which spans between 1890 and 1939 was the establishment phase of colonial domination where the settlers speculated about the investment opportunities around Salisbury, now Harare.

As argued by Patel, (1988) the white settlers came up with methods and schemes for urban land development that excluded the black majority from being part of this philosophy (Patel, 1988). As such, the city planning at that time was done considering the racial division of the Rhodesia community comprising of native black Africans and the white settlers. The fertile Highveld was earmarked for white settlement and a system of railways and roads were constructed to facilitate development of mining and agriculture (Patel, 1988; Mutondoro 2017). All key investment and development of industry was concentrated in the white sector, which constituted about one third of the country's population in all the major towns taking up 50 per cent of the land and contributing around 90 per cent of the GNP (Rhodesia, 1969). The entire arrangement was prudently protected by legislative measures concerning land apportionment, crop-marketing, industrial relations and created a society of gross inequalities (Patel, 1988).

The first settlement for African workers was established in 1892 and legislation in 1906 allowed the designation of separate black residential areas and made it compulsory for all African workers not living at their place of work to live in these locations (Brown, 2001). In 1907, some 20 ha was allocated for the first African township at Harare (now Mbare), 3 km south of the city centre. However, one must be able to notice that the city was not only designed based on racial superiority but also on gender bias as women were not allowed into the city but were forced to stay in the rural areas. Brown (2001) highlights that the shortages of African housing was becoming acute and by 1935, an increase in squatters living just outside the city led the government to identify a second township for 2500 people on the state-owned High field Farm, about 8 km south-west of the City Centre. By 1935, Salisbury obtained city status though it had a population of below 20 000 (Muronda, 2008). The period after 1940s saw some changes in the outlook of the city of Salisbury, in the legal and policy framework regulating land and urban development as well as the changing demands of the colonial economy inspired by the end of the 2nd World War. Brown (2001) notes that, the pace of development increased after the Second World War. Mlambo (2008) argues that the white population grew slowly but steadily in the first 50 years of colonisation. In 1891, a year after the arrival of Cecil John Rhodes' Pioneer Column, there were approximately 1 500 Whites permanently resident in the country.

To accommodate the growing white population, new suburbs were designed according to imported planning fashions of the time, illustrating the garden city, neighbourhood and Radburn design concepts (Davison 2000 as cited in Brown 2001). Resultantly there was the establishment of settler populated suburbs such as Malbereign based on the Radburn garden city concept. The economic demands of the settler community have been well documented by Wekwete (1994) who is of the view that, the period between 1940 and 1952, was an era of Salisbury expansion and intensification. During the post-1945 epoch, Zimbabwe witnessed the development of its manufacturing industry and the state was in support of this agenda. Hence, the manufacturing industry lured high urban expansion reminiscent of the British industrial revolution.

In terms of the policy and legal framework, there was the introduction of the Land Apportionment Act and the Urban Areas Accommodation and Registration Act. Patel (1988) notes that; the amendment of the Land Apportionment Act in 1941 gave local authorities the mandate to provide housing for the black population. There followed an introduction of the Urban Areas Accommodation and Registration Act (Number 6 of 1946) which stipulated that blacks who were employed could be permitted into towns and cities and this allowed local authorities to set aside urban land to accommodate the workers (Musekiwa, 1993). Estimates of the Africa population in Salisbury place the figure at 22 126 in 1936, 28 119 in 1941 rising to 45 993 in 1946 and to 75 249 in 1951 (Yoshikuni, as cited in Raftopulous, 2014). The increase in population witnessed an expansion of the town size and this resulted in experts flying in to aid the process of land development (Muronda, 2008).

Discussion and synthesis

The Government of Zimbabwe has prioritised 8 goals dealing with poverty, hunger, energy, infrastructure, water and sanitation, health, education, gender equality and women empowerment. However, the decision to leave Sustainable Development Goal (SDG) 11 is not only problematic but also catastrophic. The majority of the 8 selected goals largely depend on how human settlements (rural and urban) are planned and governed. Hence, to achieve the selected 8 goals requires addressing the plight of cities and human settlements. Second, at the time of evaluating the SDGs in 2030, half of Zimbabwe's population will be living in cities (UN-Habitat, 2012). In other words, this means that issues of poverty, education, water and sanitation, hunger and food security, health, climate change, employment and decent work among others will be core priority issues in cities.

Urban land development should be distributed evenly across city regions for it to be inclusive. The distribution of cities across regions and distribution of land-uses within cities is a key defining feature of inclusive urbanisation. It avoids planning failures such as less sensitivity to low-income groups, too much separation of land-uses and slow and cumbersome housing delivery among others. Urban primacy in Zimbabwe has led among other things to urbanisation being concentrated in one region – metropolitan Harare. Such an approach is non-inclusive and unsustainable. The future of urbanisation in Zimbabwe pivots on developing cities like Bulawayo, Mutare and Masvingo to the size and level of Harare (Barnett, 2016). Furthermore, the internal development of cities should prioritise both areas for the rich and poor. Regeneration and redevelopment of shrinking towns is a vital strategy of resuscitating decaying mining town. Inclusive municipal governance 'emphasises on administrative arrangements that, promote the inclusion of the people in particular the poor and marginalized' in the management of city affairs (Muchadenyika, 2015: 2). The way cities are governed determines the nature of inclusivity. In this regard, the governance of cities should include the poor and marginalized through incorporating their needs and aspirations. Rather, these should be conceived as vital stakeholders in urban governance. Other than providing municipal services to the poor, city authorities should plan and manage cities with the poor in perspective (Earle, 2016). Here, key issues of regularisation and formalisation of informal settlements should be mainstream in urban governance agenda as opposed to demolitions and evictions (elements of a non-inclusive city). The pricing of municipal services should also depict the economic challenges such a constituency faces.

The impacts of climate change are more severe in cities as compared to rural areas. This is mainly because of the concentration of the built environment, people and the reliance of urban dwellers on urban infrastructure systems. As such, climate change should be a cornerstone of the planning and management of cities. In this regard, cities should prioritise the following: research on vulnerability of cities, development of climate change mitigation and adaptation plans, design of resilient city infrastructure (energy, water, sanitation and storm, water and transport), design and use of energy-efficient and climate sensitive city energy systems, and internalising national policy statements and strategies on climate change.

The conduct and proposals of planners' manifests in city designs and the actual structural developments, planning is a professional activity that requires professional and academic training. As such, in order to build cities that are inclusive, the profession of planning requires regulation. Regulation is a way of standardising and ensuring that the built environment adheres to principles of inclusivity and sustainability (Earle, 2016). Non-regulation as the current situation portrays is resulting in the built environment that is haphazard, non-inclusive and unsustainable.

Land is a vital resource for urban development. As such, a credible and transparent land institutional and regulatory system is fundamental in promoting city development. However, an unclear land institutional and regulatory system often provides unnecessary costs to land developers in particular the urban poor. This is normally through demolitions and evictions in instances where people are allocated and build houses on privately owned land (Barnett, 2016). The key argument here is that Zimbabwe ought to invest and develop a transparent land information system where actors can easily see land ownership arrangements. Without such a system, there is a tendency of land hoarding and proliferation of land barons which both militate against an inclusive city.

The provision of title deeds to the urban poor is a vital aspect of building the resilience of the lower class. The majority of the urban poor are allocated either council or state land. However, the present title deeds system is centralised and is skewed towards facilitating title to people who buy land via private developers. This has resulted in the majority of the urban poor having no title deeds despite accessing land from city councils and government (Muchadenyika, 2015). Such is an indicator of non-inclusion in cities. Based on this, I propose that major cities should perform title registration functions. This facilitates easy title access to the urban poor – which title is vital in reducing urban poverty.

Most Zimbabwean cities are characterized by an unsafe and unreliable public transport system. The system uses incidental termini which are not meant for and designed to cater for loading and offloading of passengers. As such, there exists immense contestation among public transport users, operators and local authorities on the management of public transport in cities (Muchadenyika, 2015). Further, women are vulnerable to abuse by 'mahwindi' in cities. Therefore, Zimbabwean cities should invest in mass transport systems with defined transport interchanges, loading and offloading bays. More so, the road networks have to be improved as well, potholes have been a major feature of Zimbabwean roads and this has to be addressed as it has resulted in a number of accidents over the decade. The existence of commuter Omnibuses within the CBD has also made the area unsafe to both motorists and pedestrians as they roam around freely. Careless driving is what they are well known for. There has to be some sought of policy or rules or rather the development of routes that divert them away from the CBD.

To add on, cities must be given the autonomy to run their own affairs. According to section 276 of the Constitution of Zimbabwe, rural and urban local authorities have the right to govern their own affairs. Such constitutional mandate is premised on devolution of powers and functions. In this regard, devolution is one strategy of promoting sustainable cities planned and governed by autonomous entities. However, the government of Zimbabwe has refused the idea of devolution because it wants to retain the overall power of decision-making. This has resulted in poor planning over the past few years as politics always takes precedence over the planning profession. Hence forth, there is need to abide by the constitution so that urban land development can take a clear lane towards re-establishing the city's glory.

There is no one top-down solution to urban sustainability but a wealth of bottom-up approaches to face challenges and way map the forward in the urban sector instead. One of the strengths of cities in both poor and wealthier countries is the initiative and inventiveness of their citizens. Seizing this opportunity requires critical rethinking, application of innovative non-market solutions and the active involvement of all those concerned. One-way information does not fulfil the contemporary requirement for the quality standards of citizen involvement. People have to be given the possibility to become the key resource of cities. Citizens need a supporting infrastructure, places for people to meet and get organized, an attentive media to communicate their concerns and tools, processes and channels to create initiatives and communicate. Some cities are fortunate to have visionary leaders for one or two electoral periods, while most cities cannot wait for enlightened leadership but have to establish permanent solutions of public participation. Methods and processes already exist which are very similar in developing and developed countries and are ready to be applied: participatory budgeting, stakeholder forums, popular votes on urban issues, user concretions of basic services, e-participation, or kiosks for basic services, information and internet access (Earle,2016). The right to participate is not linked to the home address only and does not concern only geographical communities but also communities of old or young people, pedestrians or bus drivers, street vendors and restaurant owners.

The urban agenda has further to democratise sustainable development. This can only happen at the local level. At some point the sustainability agenda has been hijacked by civil servants as if it was only a matter of finding the most appropriate technical solutions and cornered to the cities' environmental departments (Mutondoro, 2017). The next urban agenda has to be more inclusive, both in terms of participants and issues. Social and budgetary issues have to be integral parts of it. Economic questions must not be left to economists only and the financial decisions have to fulfil sustainability criteria, too. Cities all over the world need inclusive pro-poor strategies and guidelines enabling innovative local solutions. If the city is good for its weakest citizen such as a child, an aged person, a new immigrant and a handicapped person, it is going to be good for everyone else, too (Barnett, 2016). Integration and inclusion have to be on top of the urban sustainability agenda. Sustainable development has to be democratised at the local level in every country. Existing methods of citizen participation, such as participative budgeting, should be used in every city, selecting the most locally appropriate tools and most urgent issues. New methods of inclusion should be developed and disseminated among cities.

An integrated approach is the only way to avoid decisions being prepared under wrong assumptions. The prevailing preference of an "economic" view has to be replaced by a sustainable one, which includes ecological and social considerations and mid- and long-term thinking. Only if potential impacts of decisions are broadly assessed, will the development of cities become sustainable step by step. It is important to renew the city with energy-efficient and more flexible buildings of long-term value and longevity. Functional flexibility leads to a longer life for buildings, because they can be adapted to the changing needs. Technical systems and services that have a shorter life-cycle than the structure of the building have to be installed in such a manner that it is easy to renew them. This means applying technical aids sparingly, maintaining them and making the most of all passive means. Buildings should generate more energy than they consume as well as collect and purify their own water. Many cities have started with retrofitting their own public buildings with enormous success to serve as good examples within and outside the city. Experience in northern European markets indicates that low-income housing stock can be successfully retrofitted for profit, as well. Monitoring tools are necessary to measure building performance and progress. Criteria are also needed as assessment tools in all procurement, investment and subsidy decisions. Some of the indicators can be used worldwide, but when the rating system is developed within a specific region, it can contain assumptions about appropriate performance benchmarks and the relative importance of issues such as selection of site, water and energy resources, risk of earthquakes or flooding, local climate, solar hours, cultural aspects, availability of materials amongst other issues.

Conclusion

When considering the future development of the urban sphere especially in the Zimbabwean context, one key strategic aspect has to do with sustainability considerations such as the systemic interplay between environmental/ecological, economic and socio-cultural factors. When discussing these issues in connection with urban challenges, the starting points are sustainability challenges connected with the urban space itself. However, one would also find highly relevant considerations when dealing with what the urban development implies for other activities distributed in geographical space as mirrored by the urban-rural connections in the form of the connection between urban space and its natural resources.

References

Barnett, C., and Parnell, S. (2016). Ideas, Implementation and Indicators: Epistemologies of the Post-2015 Urban Agenda. *Environment and Urbanisation*, 28(1), 87-98.

Brown, A. (2001). Cities for the urban poor in Zimbabwe: urban space as a resource for sustainable development. *Development in Practice*, 11(2-3), 319-331.

Chirisa, I., Dirwai, S. O., and Matamanda. A. (2015). A Review of the Systems Approach for Solving the Complexity of the Environmental Problematique of Cities in Africa. *Future cities and Environment*, 1(11), 1-10.

Earle, L. (2016). Urban Crises and the New Urban Agenda. *Environment and Urbanisation*, 28(1), 77-86.

Kamete, A. (1999). 'Restrictive control of urban high-density housing in Zimbabwe: deregulation, challenges and implications for urban design'. *Housing, Theory and Society* 16(3), 136-151.

Mangwende, P. (2015). Urbanisation and Its Impact on Sustainable Development in Harare. A Case of Harare South, Gweru: Midlands State University Faculty of Arts Department of Development Studies

Mlambo, A. S. (2008). From the second world war to UDI, 1940-1965. *Becoming Zimbabwe: A history from the pre-colonial period to*, 75-114.

Raftopoulos, B and Mlambo, A. (Eds.). (2008). *Becoming Zimbabwe. A History from the Pre-colonial Period to 2008: A History from the Pre-colonial Period to 2008.* African Books Collective.

Moyo, W. (2014). Urban housing policy and its implications on the low-income earners of a Harare Municipality, Zimbabwe. *International Journal of Asian Social Science,* 4(3), 356- 365.

Muchadenyika, D and Williams, J. J. (2016). Social Change: Urban Governance and Urbanisation in Zimbabwe. *Urban Forum,* 27(2016), 253–274

Muchadenyika, D. (2015). Slum upgrading and inclusive municipal governance in Harare, Zimbabwe: new perspectives of the urban poor. *Habitat International,* 48(1), 1–10.

Muronda, T. (2008). Evolution of Harare as Zimbabwe's Capital City and a major Central Place in Southern Africa in the Context of by Byland's model of settlement evolution. *Journal of Geography and Regional Planning,* 1(2), 34-40

Musekiwa, A. (1993), "Low-income Housing Development in Harare: An Historical Perspective". In: Zinyama, L. M., Tevera, D. S and Cumming, S. D. (Eds.). (1993). *Harare: The Growth and Problems of the City.* Harare: University of Zimbabwe Publications.

Mutizwa-Mangiza, N. D. (1986). Urban centres in Zimbabwe: Inter-censal changes, 1962-1982. *Geography*, 71(2), 148-150.

Mutondoro, F., Chiweshe M., Mlilo M., Ncube M. J and Rehbock, N. (2017). Land governance in the context of the New Urban

Agenda: Experiences from Harare (Zimbabwe) and Johannesburg (South Africa). Paper prepared for the 2017 World Bank Land and Poverty Conference Transparency International Zimbabwe Corruption Watch South Africa. Available online: https://www.conftool.com/landandpoverty2017/index.php/07 -09- Mutondoro783_paper.pdf?page=downloadPaperandfilename=0 7-09- Mutondoro783_paper.pdfandform_id=783andform_version=fi nal [Accessed on 03 March 2019]

Muzondi, L. (2014). Urbanisation and service delivery planning: Analysis of water and sanitation management systems in the city of Harare, Zimbabwe. *Mediterranean Journal of Social Sciences*, 5(20), 1-11.

Patel, D. (1988). Housing the urban poor in the socialist transformation of Zimbabwe. *The political economy of Zimbabwe*, 182-96.

Rambanapasi, C. O. (1988). Sector versus Territory: Critical perspectives on the integration of economic and physical planning in Zimbabwe. Rural and Urban Planning Occasional Paper No. 12, Harare: Department of Rural and Urban Planning University of Zimbabwe.

Republic of Zimbabwe. (1976). Regional, Town and Country Planning Act (1976) Government Printer, Harare

Wekwete, K. (1989). Planning Laws for Urban and Regional Planning in Zimbabwe - A Review, RUP Occasional Paper 20. Harare: Department of Rural and Urban Planning University of Zimbabwe.

Yoshikuni, T. (2007). *Urban Experiences in Colonial Zimbabwe: A Social History of Harare*, Harare: Weaver Press.

Zimbabwe. (1982). Transitional National Development Plan 1982/83 - 1984/85, Vol 1, Government Printer, Harare.

Zimbabwe. (1983). Annual Review of Manpower, Ministry of Labour, Manpower Planning and Social Welfare, Harare.

Zimbabwe. (1985). Population Factors and Development, Central Statistical Office, Harare.

Zimbabwe. (1986). Population Projections of Zimbabwe 1982 to 2032, Central Statistical Office, Harare.

Zimbabwe. (1986a). First Five-Year National Development Plan 1986-1990, Vol 1, Government Printer, Harare.

Zimbabwe. (1986b). Report on Housing and Urban Development in Zimbabwe: Public and Private Sector Partnership, MPNCH, Harare.

Zimbabwe. (1986c). Socio-economic Review 1980-1985 Zimbabwe, Ministry of Finance, Economic Planning and Development, Harare.

Zinyama, L., Tevera, D and Cumming, S. (Eds.). (1993). Harare: The Growth and Problems of the City, Harare: University of Zimbabwe.

Chapter 3

Zimbabwean real estate finance since 1980

Geraldine Usingarawe and Zebediah Muneta

Introduction

Whereas the growth in urbanisation throughout in many cities and towns in Zimbabwe can be harnessed as a great potential for the real estate sector, the economic challenges in the country have tended to hinder progress and development. This chapter provides a descriptive analysis of the real estate finance in Zimbabwe since 1980. It describes the challenges facing real estate financing in the country. It also explains the state of the economy as well as the existing sources of finance for the real estate. The chapter further reviews the existing opportunities in the sector as well as practices and options. Various sources of finance for the real estate sector are explored and analysed. Many of the challenge which are hindering the development of the real estate sector are centred upon the issue of finance. From the study, it is observed that finance is a pivotal factor in the success and viability of any development in the real estate sector and as such, it needs to be made easily available easily.

Finance has been seen as one factor which is at the core of any viability of a development project. Its importance is seen from the initial stages up to the completion stages of a project. For the real estate development, finance determines the viability of the project. It is a major factor of consideration in any decision-making towards development projects and their execution. The chapter is based on desktop study that reviews literature as the basis of capturing the heart of the argument advanced in the chapter. Unemployment in many of the country's cities is a major hindrance to the growth in the real estate finance as the study has indicated some of the failures by the public who may be willing to develop but would not have the requirements such as valuable assets to use as collateral security or reliable and regular salaries. Overall, the study indicates that there is need to revive the real estate finance in the country and that the government needs to make sure the financial institutions and lending banks lax their stringent demands when giving out real estate funds. The study therefore recommends the assistance of the financial sector in making sure that funds for development in the real estate sector are made available. It also pushes forward the idea that the interest rates for the financial institutions be stabilised and that the availability of funds be ensured. This would ensure the easy accessibility of funds by many potential developers and thus promote infrastructure development in the country at large.

The overall purpose of this chapter is to provide an understanding of the real estate finance in the context of Zimbabwe. It prepares the readers to understand the challenges and opportunities associated with the financing of real estate in the country. The opportunities and challenges related to the real estate financing are set out in the chapter. Some of these include the unemployment rate bedevilling the Zimbabwean economy and the world's financial markets at large has had impacts as well on the real estate market. This is because of high risk experienced by the investors, lenders and many others who take part in the real estate market (Brueggeman and Fisher, 2011). The property investment market of the country cannot be regarded in isolation from other markets and investment sectors. It is of importance note that the property and real estate market faces some competition from other sectors and that it is vital to improve efficiency in the sector. When property developers take the initiative to develop in a particular area, they need first to compare their returns and security. Property and finance are therefore important in any economy's development. This is evidenced by the way property is regarded. It is regarded as a factor of production, as a corporate asset and as well as an investment by many of the financial institutions in which pensioners tends to benefit as well (Isaac, 1994).

It is imperative that much evaluation of the real estate financial market be done in order to proffer possible solutions that would revive the market in the country. This requires therefore, an understanding of the financing in Zimbabwe which the chapter will provide as well. Taking part in the real estate market requires very high capital outlay and this is obtained from various sources which will as well be explored in the chapter. It is a difficult thing in the real estate market to finance large scale investments which would be solely funded by personal savings. Therefore, there is high need for financing from other sources (Brueggeman and Fisher, 2011). There are many and various sources of finance for the real estate sector. Some of them will be explored in the chapter. They include the borrowing from banks, self-savings, the merchant banks and many other sources.

Theoretical framework

When used by property owners, real estate finance may help in optimizing their balance sheets in order to help them acquire more property. Usually, a smaller percentage of the total price from the purchase of the real estate comes from the total savings of the buyer. However, there are other various sources of finance for the real estate which include primary sources, the financial middlemen, the secondary mortgage market and many others. The primary sources of finance include borrowing from the commercial banks, savings and loan associations, life insurance companies and from the mutual savings bank (Brueggeman and Fisher, 2011).

Of the many things to consider when one wants to carry out a real estate development, the major one is that of finance. Without enough financial backup for any project, it becomes unviable. In order to make the development realizable, huge amounts of funds need to be made available and this is due to the complexity of the projects which are naturally very capital intensive and as such demand adequate and proper funding. The availability and smooth accessibility of the real estate finance mainly in sufficient amounts would even determine the trend and the extent of the estate operation. Real estate finance is mandatory in that it is concerned as well with the production of finance which is needed for the building of houses, office complexes and many other large developments. Finance has a powerful influence upon every development in any sector. The cost of borrowing or attaining the finance as well as its availability has an impact on the provision of new developments and investments on real estate. It is of importance that there be some enlightenment of the public on the existence of the various real estate financial options and sources (Ezimuo *et al.* 2014).

Literature review

Financing in the real estate market is a very crucial component for any investment to take place. In a bid to try and acquire funds, many investors tend to pledge their personal property or estate in order that they may be able to get loans from banks. Of the many sources of finance in the real estate market, land contract is the widely used and the most popular one. Land contract encompasses various aliases which together include the real estate contract, the instalment sales contract, the agreement of convey and as well as the contract for the deed, (Brueggeman and Fisher, 2011). A lot of property market investors prefer the land contract apart from the many other sources of finance because of its advantage in that once the transactions are made, the sellers still retain the title in their own names. This is because the deed of transaction will still be showing that the sellers are still the full owners of the property. Apart from the many sources of finance, the land contract is used as a substitute for a purchase-money mortgage and is normally preferred when the latter is available. Real estate finance can be defined as the fund that is required in order carrying out real estate developments and any other related operations, (Ogedengbe and Adesope, 2003). The financing is very important in the carrying out of the real estate developments and other large-scale investments which are enabled to take place without any substantial credit.

It is notable that the housing finance system in many of the country's cities and towns are not that viable and this has the effect of making the housing development in the country very difficult. It is an important thing that the developer gets to understand that finance is a very crucial aspect in the success of any project. Finance is centrifugal in any real estate development. It is the ability of any developer to mobilize enough funds that can make any project a success. In whatever project and especially those pertaining to the real estate sector, it is crucial to note that finance is a *sine qua non*, an all-important factor no matter the nature of the projects. Real estate finance can be best explained as the fulcrum in which the development projects lever is sustained and the overall performance of the real estate financial system would be dependent largely on the proportion of funds circulating in the economy towards the housing sector. Another simple definition for the real estate finance is that it is the acquiring of money so as to carry out the real estate developments (Ogedengbe and Adesope, 2003).

At the attainment of independence in 1980, Zimbabwe experienced a high growth rate in the economy. Many factors contributed to the growth in the economy and some of these include the removal of sanctions on the country as well as the relaxation of regulations on the exchange control. There was also high in flow of aid in the economy from the international community which aided in the reconstruction of the economy (Ndlovu, 1994). However, in recent periods, the country is classified among the poorest nations in the African continent. It still ranks among the least developed nations. Many of the contributing factors include high inflationary periods that the nation has been encountering among many other contributing factors. Hanke and Kwok (2009), reiterate that the nation has since been struggling from high inflationary periods with that of the years 2007 to 2009 topping among the rest. Since then, the country has adopted the multi-currency system in order to meet and curb the financial crisis that had damaged the economy.

In recent years, liquidity problems have been rampant and this has seen the country move towards a cashless society. Overall, this has had negative impact on the real estate financial market and many of those who survive were those who had invested in real estate properties. The foreign countries and donors' initiatives in the country and economy is a sign that the economy still needs to be fully established. Inasmuch as there is no country that is totally independent from other nations, the real estate and property management and finance still need support (Tichaona, 2013). There has been de-industrialisation in the Zimbabwean economy from around 1999 after an economic contraction. From since then, there has been negative economic growth in the country which hovered around 11.9 per cent in 2011 and the growth has declined up to around 3.29 per cent in the year 2015. The deflationary periods that have been experienced in the country have also affected the accessibility of funds for development in the nation at large. In moving along with the nation's general economic conditions, many developers have turned towards the development of stands and clients incrementally construct their own housing (CAHF, 2016). An analysis of how the other nations are faring in the real estate sector would help the nation in upgrading its real estate sector as well.

Sources of real estate finance in Zimbabwe

Various sources have been, and are still being used by the people of Zimbabwe in mobilizing finance for real estate properties and development in the country. Firms and agencies act as help centres in real estate surveying and valuation. For the Zimbabwean economy specifically, many investors tend to borrow from the banks, life insurance companies and other institutional lenders (Senyondo, 2015). These firms or organisations play a very crucial role in providing capital for real estate development. Some of the sources of real estate funds for the country include:

- Equity capital which is the money that comes from one's personal savings as well as the family savings. Of the many sources of finance, the equity capital is usually very low in the country due to that fact that many of the developers would be having low per capita income (Senyondo, 2015). With the high unemployment rate, there has been a decline in the equity capital as many people would find it difficult to save. This has seen the increase in the number of tenants rather than property owners in the country.

- The commercial banks are also providers of real estate finance. The commercial banks are lenders for a variety of loans. They also provide finance for residential purchases which sometimes may be of a permanent nature. They offer direct loans which are other sources of real estate finance. These are the loans which come from various lenders which include the banks and many other financial institutions over a given period. Direct loans include the short-term loans, the medium-term loans and as well as the long-term loans (Senyondo, 2015). However, these financial sources require tangible collateral security which the majority of the people may fail to provide due to unemployment and lack of valuable assets.

- Pension funds are a reliable source of finance for the real estate. In the country, a good example is that of the National Social Security Association (NSSA). Much of the developments in real estate have been facilitated by the funds from the pension funds, besides providing the mortgage loans, the pension funds also own real estate (Senyondo, 2015).

- Real Estate Investment Trusts (REITS), also contribute to the real estate finance. These are pool of funds where many of the investors put in as mutual funds for the purpose of their developments as they are tax-advantaged. REITs include the equity trust where investors put in their money in order to acquire ownership in the real estate. Their income usually comes from the rentals on the property (Senyondo, 2015). A good example is that of the Old Mutual Company.

- Individual investors are an important figure in the real estate finance. Many large investors in the country and even from the international community tend to lend their money towards real estate. These include investment companies which would be willing to have wider portfolios and some individuals with available funds as well as groups of investors which seek mortgage ownership. Many of the investors as indicated, seek to take equity position in real estate. Therefore, it is very imperative that equity capital be raised through the syndication instead of solely depending on the mortgage funds (Senyondo, 2015).

There are major sectors that need immediate improvement towards the resuscitating of the real estate finance. The processes for monetary circulation need to be improved in a proportionate manner make it easier for the last holder of the money to benefit. High dependence on foreign aid to finance much of the developments in the country, has led to increased relaxation by government to correct their fiscal deficits and as such, liquidity challenges continue to be rampant (Coomer and Gstraunthaler, 2011). Due to the fact that the money lending policies in the country are prepared and implemented by the lending institutions, it leaves the housing, development and urban policy-makers in a powerless state over the real estate and development finance. Financial institutions base their policies on their organisational strategy without the recognition of the external stakeholders who are the borrowers and the developers. It is therefore important that developers and policy-makers have a positive influence upon the funding strategies for developments and thus improve on the overall development of real estate in the country (Rowley *et al.* 2014). The multicurrency system in Zimbabwe has reduced the capacity for the country's economy to support domestic projects development initiatives. There is now more risk in putting confidence in the financial sector, particularly the Central Bank as well as the government itself. Therefore, liquidity challenges continue to prevail, thus deterring the real estate projects from becoming functional and viable (CAHF, 2016). Many are the sources of finance for the real estate sector in the country. These need more support and should to be revived. For the easy access of the funding for real estate projects, there is need first to revive the economy which would generally have the multiple effects of improving the real estate markets as well.

Methodology

In exploring the real estate finance in Zimbabwe, secondary data sources were consulted through a desktop research. This study reviews the existing information in the real estate finance of the economy and the way in which funds are mobilized towards real estate developments in the nation. In order to get this information, the literature on real estate finance has been visited so as to validate the arguments that are proffered in the chapter. To garner data, various textbooks, research articles and journals have been visited. The information is useful in the analysis of the present state of the real estate finance in the country. The chapter traces the state of the economy from the attaining of independence in 1980. It further explores the various sources of finance in the country for the real estate market and sector. Accordingly, various factors are deterring the growth of the real estate financial system and these include high unemployment and the lack of collateral security. The chapter further discusses the challenges, opportunities and the possible solutions for the real estate finance in the country. Way forward solutions are given in the chapter in making the real estate finance for the economy of Zimbabwe more viable.

Discussion and synthesis

The issue of real estate finance requires one to understand various rights to real property. This is very imperative in the understanding of real estate finance as these rights that are bought, sold as well as mortgaged. In making every real estate financial decision, it is worthy and very notable to analyse property rights. It is of legal benefit that the risk of making and receiving financial benefits be reduced through the analysis first of the property rights of an individual. It is important for individuals to be in possession of marketable titles as any probable defects pertaining to the title may lead to losses of the potential benefits due to the owner (Brueggeman and Fisher, 2011). Some of the challenges that are experienced in the real estate financial sector are that the money lenders in the market tend to charge very high interest rates and this lessens the real estate development potential in the country. Some other sources of finance apart from those mentioned earlier on may include the government bonds.

However, resorting to such is no longer a reliable option for the developers. The developers in real estate are also encountering challenges which include the bureaucratic bottlenecks in many of the financial institutions which impede in their quest for funds. The bureaucracy encountered make it very difficult for the funds required to reach the developers on time and as such lead to significant delays in the intended developments. The demand for collateral security and the certificates of occupancy by many of the financial institutions is another deterring factor for the developers in their quest to get real estate finance (Brueggeman and Fisher, 2011). With the current cash crisis in the economy, it is difficult to get cash from thee banks for development and as such giving bottlenecks on the developers' intended projects. There is lack of sufficient information pertaining to the amount of funding that can be expected during preparatory budget procedures due to uncertainty of prices. This emanates from the fact that there is no room for making transactions in physical meeting first as there is no focal point for meeting place for that. This results from the nature of the market as it is an integration of separate, uncoordinated and unrelated financial transactions and as well as its complex and diverse characteristics. The combined challenge scenarios are the failure of getting real estate finance (Brueggeman and Fisher, 2011).

Generally, there always tends to be the non-availability of funds put towards real estate developments. This may be ascribed partly to the dwindling economic conditions as well as the huge amounts of capital required for the developments. Repayment of loans tends to be difficult as a result of the high costs that are required for servicing them by the developers. Poor economic conditions and the cash crisis in the country also contribute to the unavailability of loanable funds which may be put towards the real estate developments (Brueggeman and Fisher, 2011). Therefore, due to the delayed and the long periods of gestation for the real estate developments, many investors tend to be discouraged. It is very imperative that after realization of some of the many challenges towards the reals estate financial system, many policies meant to improve the sector be brought up, implemented and as a resulting be effected, revive the real estate market and financial system.

The mortgage banks need to make sure or rather to ensure that their beneficiaries of the loans that they lend out are channelled towards the intended purposes. This is because, despite the existing financial challenges facing the real estate sector, the beneficiaries of the loans may misuse the funds they obtain and then detract the potential developments for real estate. Therefore, for the development sin the given case scenarios, there is need for inspections of the projects in all their development stages in order to check and ensure full implementation of the projects. Profitable returns on the mortgage loans can only be brought about when there is timely imbursement of the funds and the ensuring of site monitoring as well as the proper appraisal of any proposal for development. Stable interest rates for the financial sector, proper and adequate funding by the government as well as the consistency in policy-making are some of the factors that can possibly revive the real estate sector. The issue of public participation in the real estate sector is still of a notable worth. In order that the financial institutions improve their services, the public will have to become aware and be sensitized of the necessity and importance of mortgage banking as well as the importance of repaying the loans that would have been granted to them (Ezimuo, 2014).

Conclusion, policy options and practical recommendations

In summary, the chapter has indicated that real estate finance is a very important aspect and catalyst for development to take place and as such, must not be an isolated economic and development phenomenon. Rather, its availability or shortage has an impact on the general viability of any development and real estate project. There is need for proper financing of the real estate sector in order to have successful developments and real estate investments. Providing a variety of sources and agencies of finance in the real estate environment would be a very important action. Development especially in the real estate and construction sectors is very fundamental and needs to be supported as it has impact on the national economy as a whole. Every loan let out towards the development in the real estate has to be carefully tailored in a way that it fits into every determined scheme and satisfies the stages of the particular project.

Property development projects require huge amounts of funds by their nature and as such, among many other important inputs, finance is at the apex of the prerequisites. It must be available in order to make any project viable and successful. In general, the cost and the availability of funds towards real estate tend to influence the success or failure of a project. For the real estate sector, there is therefore need for a central agency that controls the development funding and that also coordinates the business in the property funding. It is a recommended that there be a record of past transactions that archive lending and borrowing of finance towards the real estate developments and this would assist the prospective developers in future transactions. Many challenges that are clouding the real estate finance in the country are solved simultaneously with the fixing of the economic problems as many of these challenges tend to result from the economic downturn. There is need for government intervention in the financing of the real estate developments through making sure that the financial institutions slack and ease their stringent demands and rules in the lending of money to borrowers (Ogedengbe and Adesope, 2003). There is need for the perfection of the service delivery by the financial institutions in order that they may be able to respond without problem to the demand for development funds from the individuals, developers and various stakeholders. This would, ensure repeat borrowings and improved as well as increased volume of operations for the financial institutions. As such, there is need to move towards diversification of the funding source be it from donor funded sources to the locally funded ones.

When donor funding is initiated and made available, it can, during the times when there are liquidity challenges, be applied as a complement to local funding in the period in which there would be liquidity challenges in the banking system. This ensures a smooth flow of finance and improves overall development in the real estate sector. In order to initiate development for the real estate sector, it is important as well that the developer accesses funding from outside or from the international financial world. This seems to be cheaper as compared to domestic funding. It also ensures the proper use of personal funds without meeting hiccups and shortages as with the local ban king system (Mutambanadza *et al.* 2013). From the analysis in the chapter, it can be concluded that the major issue in real estate development is finance. Therefore, there is need to handle with levity the issue of finance by both the government and the financial institutions (Ogedengbe and Adesope, 2003).

Various solutions can be proffered towards the reviving of the real estate finance in order to improve property development in Zimbabwe. There is need to reduce the time spent in the disbursement of the loans by the banks and this would enable the borrowers and the potential developers to get funds on time. This would minimise the chances of default and at the same time improve on development in the economy. There is need for the stabilising of interest rates and ensuring that the funds are available to all for development to be viable and to take place in an affordable manner.

There is an imperative to protect the depositors' funds through the creation of deposit insurance programs. There is need to subsidize even the inputs that are included in the execution of any project (Ezimuo, 2014).

References

Brueggeman W. B and Fisher, J. D. (2011). Real Estate Finance and Investment. 14th edition. McGraw Hill Irwin.

Centre for Affordable Housing Finance in Africa (CAHF). (2016). Understanding Zimbabwe's Housing Financial Market. CAHF

Coomer, J and Gstraunthaler, T. (2011). The Hyperinflation in Zimbabwe. The Quarterly *Journal of Austrian Economics,* 14(3), 1-36.

Ezimuo, P. N., Onyejiaka, C. J and Emoh, F. I. (2014). Sources of real estate finance and their impact on property development in Nigeria: A case study of mortgage institutions in Lagos metropolis. *British Journal of Environmental Research,* 2(2), 35-58.

Hanke, S. H and Kwok, A. K. (2009). On the measurement of Zimbabwe's hyperinflation. *Cato J.,* 29(1), 1-12.

Isaac, D. (1994). Property Finance. Macmillan Press Ltd, London.

Mutambanadzo, T., Bhiri, T and Makunike, S. (2013). An Analysis of the Challenges Faced by Zimbabwe Micro Finance Institutions in Providing Financial Services to the Poor and Informal Sector in the Dollarized Regime. *Global institute for Research and Education* Vol 2 (3), Global Institute for Research and Education Publishing.

Ndlovu, L. B. (1994). The System of Protection and Industrial Development in Zimbabwe. Avebury, England.

Ogedengbe, P. S and Adesopo, A. A. (2003). Problems of financing real estate development in Nigeria. *Journal of Human Ecology,* 14(6), 425-431.

Rowley. S., Phibbs. P and Costello, G. (2014). The Financing of the Residential Development in Australia. Ahuri Final Report. *Research Gate Publishing,* Curtin University.

Senyondo, V. (2015). Real Estate Financing Techniques and
    Sources. Makerere University of Engineering.

Tichaona, T. (2013). Real Estate and Property Management
    Challenges in the City of Beira, Mozambique. Zimbabwe Open
    University, Harare.

Chapter 4

Understanding rental housing markets in selected African countries

Ruvimbo Makurira and Mike Juru

Introduction

In light of addressing the rental housing sector issues, this chapter focuses on the rental housing market in Africa post 2000 specifically South Africa, Ethiopia, Nigeria and Luanda, a subject on which authors have researched and written extensively. The chapter begins with addressing the fact that the housing deficit in Africa has to be approached with various solutions and Rental Housing is one of them. This is because rented housing appears to be unavoidable while households raise the capital to buy or build their own home, or while searching for land and saving for the building of a self-build home (Cain, 2017). It is not entirely new, as North America, Asia and Europe have homes that are leased with the option to buy through tenant purchase schemes. According to Maass (2012) the study of the rental housing market commenced after several court cases on disputes between private landlords and low-income tenants over house rentals. In each case, the tenants' constitutional right of access to adequate housing was raised as a defence against the private landowner's claim for eviction on termination of the lease, because the effect of the eviction order would in each case have been to render the unlawful tenant homeless since there was no affordable alternative accommodation available, including in the private rental market.

To address the issue a scheme of the same design can be done here in Africa which follows a country's specific trends such as market trends. This is because studies dealing with housing markets in Africa is even greater when one considers that these markets revolve around the role of the various governments in the housing markets, resulting in rent controls, direct provision of housing and infrastructures and poor planning, Thus the nature of housing markets in Africa suggests difficulties with applying results based on the developed countries to Africa (Okpala, 1987). However, there is a cultural limitation when approaching the issue of Rental Housing; automatically as Africans are conditioned to think that this is an inferior option as they have grown up with the notion that owning a house is the ultimate accomplishment and measure of success and while that may be, the study acknowledges that a large majority of Africans live in rental houses as unfortunately financing for home ownership is not nearly universal and where it does exist, it is not affordable (Maass, 2012) also, there is no defined legal framework, meaning that there are no tenancy laws that detail the agreements between lessor and lessee and recourse or redress for aggrieved lessee's who more often than not are subject to arbitrary increases in their rent prices. The key question therefore is 'why are policymakers reluctant to explore the rental housing option?" (Mugwera, 2014).

This chapter organises the study in such a way that options are provided for after identifying the benefits and challenges that African countries are facing in rental housing markets. To start with, there is brief introduction which enlightens on what rental housing market is about and reviewing some of the recent theoretical underpinnings concerning the basis of the study and the global trends of rental housing, that is how other countries in other continents, excluding Africa are managing their population growth through the implementation of rental controls to strike a balanced in the rental housing market. The method used to collect relevant data on this study is also included in this chapter. Finally, results on case studies on rental housing in Nigeria, Luanda, Ethiopia and South Africa are analysed and facts are given and there by concluding on policy options.

Theoretical framework

To support the study of the rental housing market, there are various models which include the demand and supply theory, rent control and rent reviews. In line with this study, this brief confirms the view that rental price changes are significantly affected by excess supply or demand in the rental market. The price-adjustment mechanism and the rental housing market can be viewed as if they are similar. If assumed that, as is usual, that a standardised unit of housing stock yields a unit of housing services during each period of time, then the rent is the price of the flow of services from one standard dwelling unit and the demand and supply of housing services can be considered as the demand and supply of units of housing stock. Although the size of the standardised rental housing stock in any period is increased by newly completed or converted rental dwellings and diminished by removals, demolitions and depreciation, the annual change in the stock is relatively small and hence the stock may be considered as fixed in the short run. The demand for rental stock is usually assumed to depend upon a variety of variables including demographic variables (such as the number of families and age composition of the population), permanent real disposable income, the price of rental accommodation, the user cost of owner-occupied housing, the price of alternative goods and services, the cost and availability of mortgage credit and consumer preferences and the supply of rental stock is affected by availability of building materials, capital and land as land is infinite. These demand and supply functions interact to determine the level of rents and the stock of vacant rental units. However, since numerous frictions and imperfections cause the market to adjust slowly, the rent level determined through this process may not completely clear the market in the sense that actual vacancies equal the normal or optimal vacancies. The natural or optimal vacancy rate, analogous to the natural unemployment rate, is defined by market factors such as the cost of holding inventory, search costs, the variability of demand and the costs of contracting. If rents are such that the housing stock demanded exceeds the available supply less the normal level of vacancies, then vacancies will be less than normal and upward pressure will be exerted on rents (Rosen, 1983).

At times governments impose price ceilings on rental properties and the main purpose of the rent control policy is to help the poor by making housing more affordable. It also aims to critically show the legal construction of rent control and regulation, as both a security of tenure and a rent restriction measure. However, they create shortages of rental housing as landlords would not want to lease their houses at a low rent. Also, it creates backdoor arrangements, ranging from requirements that tenants rent items that they do not want to outright bribes, resulting in rents which are higher than those that would exist in the absence of the maximum rent policy.

Literature review

On this part of the chapter, global experiences and trends from Asia, Europe, Australia and America explaining the rental housing market are critically explained. This is because the rental housing market started in other countries outside Africa and most developed countries are doing exceptionally well in this sector. According to Xinhua (2018), recently China announced its plan to allow the issuance of securities backed by residential rental properties to enable the growth of rental housing through encouraging companies to conduct rental housing asset-backed securitisation and strengthening the supervision of such securities to contain risks, according to a document jointly issued by the Ministry of Housing and Urban-rural Development and China Securities Regulatory Commission (CSRC). This is because the rental housing market is one of the long-term strategies to ensure sustainable and steady development of the real estate market, alongside various home purchase restriction policies and the Chinese Authorities have reaffirmed their commitment to ensure a stable housing market and secure supplies of housing through multiple channels to meet residents' demand.

Over the past few years, Australia increasingly has relied upon the private rental sector to meet the housing needs of low-income households. Funding for public housing has declined in real terms and present funding levels cannot cope with the backlog of maintenance required for the existing public stock (Hall and Berry, 2004). An affordable social housing sector is emerging but, by 2004, this sector had delivered fewer than 1500 dwellings (Milligan *et al.* 2004). Affordability problems affecting low-income households are increasingly addressed through Commonwealth government rent assistance provided to eligible private tenants. Private rental housing is provided almost solely by small-scale landlords and investment in rental accommodation is affected by a range of incentives that, in the main, are not targeted specifically to the affordable end of the rental market. Despite the existence of rent assistance, numerous studies have documented the significant affordability problems faced by many in the private rental market in Australia (Australian Bureau of Statistics [ABS], 2002). In the main, these studies have focused on the burden that housing costs place on low to moderate income renter households. They do not, however, address two critical supply questions: first is the stock of affordable rental dwellings sufficient to meet the needs of lower income households and, second, is the stock that exists occupied by low-income households?

After many years of decline, the private rental sector in England has significantly increased over the past three decades, especially since the turn of the century. The proportion of households renting from private landlords rose from 9 per cent in 1991 to 16 per cent in 2009/10 and the number of private tenants increased by over 80 per cent. Over the same period, the share of renting households who live in the private rental sector increased from 29 per cent to 48 per cent, while the proportion in social housing declined from 71 per cent to 52 per cent. A range of supply and demand side factors were also important, including rising real incomes, innovations in mortgage finance and low interest rates in the decade prior to the credit crunch in 2007 (Crook, 2011). The boom in 'buy to let' housing since the late-1990s has been accompanied by a generally more positive attitude to private renting than was the case in the 1970s and 1980s (Kemp, 2004). Meanwhile, the social housing sector in England has declined in both absolute and relative terms over the past three decades (Hills, 2007). The proportion of households renting from a social landlord, for example, declined from 32 per cent in 1981 to 23 per cent in 1991 and only 17 per cent in 2009/10. This decline seems likely to continue for the foreseeable future. On the one hand, sales to sitting tenants under the right to buy, although well below the levels reached in the 1980s and 1990s, will continue. On the other hand, new construction within the sector is likely to remain at low levels. The scope to build subsidized housing will be constrained by the new era of fiscal austerity in the wake of the Great Recession of

2008/09. Moreover, the Conservative-dominated Coalition Government that was elected in 2010 has an ideological distaste for social housing and the welfare state more generally.

Reversing the long uptrend in homeownership, American households have increasingly turned to the rental market for their housing. From 31 per cent in 2004, the renter share of all US households climbed to 35 per cent in 2012, bringing the total number to 43 million by early 2013. A confluence of factors drove this increase. The enormous wave of foreclosures that swept the nation after 2008 certainly played a role, displacing millions of homeowners. The economic upheaval of the Great Recession also contributed, with high rates of sustained unemployment straining household budgets and preventing would-be buyers from purchasing homes. Meanwhile, the experience of the last few years highlighted the many risks of homeownership, including the potential loss of wealth from falling home values, the high costs of relocating and the financial and personal havoc caused by foreclosure. All in all, recent conditions have brought renewed appreciation for the benefits of renting, including the greater ease of moving, the ability to choose housing that better fits the family budget and the freedom from responsibility for home maintenance. Households of all but the oldest age groups have joined in the shift toward renting. The largest increase in share is among households in their 30s, up by at least 9 percentage points over an eight-year span. However, shares of households across all five-year age groups between 25 and 54 also rose by at least 6 percentage points. In fact, the jump in rental rates for most age groups was well above the 4.0 per cent overall rise, reflecting how the movement of the population into older age groups (when owning is more prevalent) stemmed some of the drop in homeownership. With these widespread increases in the shares opting to rent, the 2000s marked the strongest decade of growth in renter households over the past half-century. After a modest rise early in the decade, the number of renter households soared after 2005, boosting average annual growth to more (Alexander, 2013).

The housing system of the Netherlands has acquired an international reputation because of its special nature and the way it has evolved. In this contribution, it explains how the Dutch social rented sector came to have this specific character. We establish that the position of the social rented sector is strongly influenced by developments in society at large. In particular, its specific position may be explained with reference to the emergence and transformation of the Dutch welfare state. In the Netherlands, the development of the social rented sector coincided with the vigorous build-up of the welfare state. That sector continued to grow in the Netherlands for a longer period than in most other west European countries. Ultimately, the share of the Dutch social rented sector reached its highest point41 per cent of the stock at the beginning of the 1990s. The current position of the social rented sector in the Netherlands is determined not only by the structure of the Dutch welfare state and the country's distinct housing policy. It is also the result of the shifting balance of supply and demand in the national housing market. Compared with other countries, the particular historical development of the Dutch social rented sector makes the adjustment of the housing system to a more market-orientated policy in which more attention is devoted to the freedom of choice of the housing consumer an unprecedented activity to say the least. This process will require the present housing associations to show a large measure of creativity and flexibility (Boelhouwer, 2002).

Housing in the Toronto area consists of three basic types: home ownership, private rental and public rental. Ownership housing accounts for about sixty per cent of the total stock. The average cost of an ownership house in Toronto in 2002 was about $275,000, a 20 per cent increase from 1999. This is a considerable change from the 1960s and 1970s when the relative cost of ownership for European migrants entering Toronto was much lower. Indeed, these immigrants have generally achieved a higher rate of home ownership than the population as a whole, partially because of relatively lower house prices at the time they arrived but also due to the high intrinsic value they place on home ownership. The recent increase in house prices results from higher demand, which was stimulated by the relatively low cost of mortgage finance and the developers perceived advantages of housing as a form of investment rather than the stock market. For lower income newcomers, housing opportunities were restricted to the private rental market. Toronto's rental stock varies widely in structural form, ownership and price. About half of the houses in the rental stock include units in apartment buildings that were built specifically by private landlords for rental occupancy. The rest consists of the informal or secondary private rental market (rented houses, apartments in houses, rented condominium units). Since the mid-1990s, virtually no new rental housing has been built in Toronto.

Vacancy rates in the private rental market have been very low for more than two decades. They were less than one per cent through most of the 1980s, increased to two per cent in the early 1990s and then fell back again to less than one per cent. Vacancy rates are also lowest for the largest units, the kind of accommodation that is most in demand by relatively large immigrant households. The result of the very low vacancy rate has been a 'bidding war' for apartments resulting in higher rents. In late 2002, following the questionnaire survey reported on in this chapter, rental vacancy rates rose to 2.5 per cent, primarily because some tenants with sufficient capital for a down payment were able to take advantage of the low cost of mortgage finance and purchase a house. Regardless, this is still less than the 3 per cent vacancy rate that Canada Mortgage and Housing Corporation (CMHC) considers as the minimum necessary for a normal turnover in rental housing (Firang, 2018).

Trends in property markets are shown to reflect broader political changes and their economic impacts; the pursuit of their interests by various social groups; land, planning and rent-control policies; and programs for the provision of serviced plots and housing finance. Explanations for trends in property development and prices, including the boom and slump which occurred around the turn of the decade are sought (Rakodi, 2001).

Methodology

This study was undertaken using reports from Knight Frank Africa, United Nations and World Bank and articles of authors who are practicing in the related field from Google scholar, b-ok.org, publications and E-resources. The data used in these publications was for assessing the performance and trends of rental housing markets. It also comprises of case studies of other continents including Africa. When analysing the drawbacks and benefits of rental housing markets, case studies were drawn from Nigeria, Angola, Ethiopia and South Africa. Information was gathered using Geographical information system as well as visiting areas of interest relating to this study.

Results

According to the lessons derived from the case studies of African countries (Ethiopia, South Africa, Angola and Nigeria discussed below: some of the key challenges that are being faced in these countries are corruption, political instability, population growth and rapid urbanisation. The major cause of these problems is that there is cultural limitation when approaching the issue of Rental Housing; automatically as Africans are conditioned to think that this is an inferior option as they have grown up with the notion that owning a house is the ultimate accomplishment and measure of success and while that may be, the study acknowledges that a large majority of Africans live in rental houses as unfortunately financing for home ownership is not nearly universal and where it does exist, it is not affordable.

South Africa

Although the public sector provided rental housing for most of the urban black and coloured population for many years, little has been recorded about the functioning of that sector. Even less is known about private rental housing. A limited amount of work has been conducted in inner-city areas, particularly in Johannesburg and recent surveys have also shed some light on the rental and shared housing scene in Cape Town but nothing else has been produced. Even the statistics are rather vague on the number of families renting accommodation. The figures presented in the census are unreliable and too few surveys have asked questions about housing tenure. What is clear, however, is that large numbers of South African families are renting shelter, particularly in the urban areas. One estimate is that across the country more than one-third of people are living in some form of non-ownership shelter and that in urban and metropolitan areas the proportion rise to more than two-fifths (Kemp, 2009). If the black urban population is considered alone, almost one-half are living in some kind of non-ownership housing. When the South African government ceased to build formal houses in the late 1960s and early 1970s (in an attempt to contain urbanisation), the growing urban black population was increasingly accommodated informally as tenants. Initially, they lodged in rooms within the formal houses and doubled up in hostels but as numbers rose many moved into backyard shacks. The construction of such shacks was opposed by the authorities but official efforts at prevention were abandoned in most townships in the late 1980s. Since then, their growth has been slowed only by the tendency of tenants to move out of the backyards into free-standing shack settlements. Nevertheless, backyard shacks and outbuildings still appear to be the principal form of renting in black areas. In 1994, irrespective of tenure, some 38 per cent of urban blacks and 6 per cent of coloureds were living in shacks and outbuildings. Clearly, we need to know far more about the circumstances of these families. Why are they there, how much they are paying, what is the nature of their living environment and what are their future housing prospects? Without better information on such a substantial portion of the urban population, any attempt to formulate an adequate housing policy is bound to be flawed (Alexander, 2013).

Ethiopia
Demographic conditions and housing demand in Addis Ababa Housing demand is determined primarily by demographic conditions (population growth, average family size of households and new household formation). According to the 1994 population and housing census, Addis Ababa's population stood at 2,084,588, accounting for 23.1 per cent of the urban population. Between 1994 and 2002, the population of Addis Ababa rose by 26.93 per cent (an average growth rate of 3.36 per cent per year) and by 2002, the city's population stood at 2,646,000, accounting for 25.7 per cent of the urban population. In absolute terms, Addis Ababa added 561,412 persons during this period, which is an annual increase of over 70,000

64

persons. The factors that related to this phenomenon are the high rates of fertility and high rural-to-urban migration flows. Land is an important component of housing development (Kemp, 2009).

The current land supply system is, to a large extent, characterised by lease holding through auction and negotiation. Following the Urban Land Lease Holding Regulation, the Addis Ababa administration established the lease office and began implementation of the lease system early in 1995 (Hall, and Berry, 2004). The land delivery system in Addis Ababa is underdeveloped. Information obtained from the Addis Ababa City Administration (1994) cooperative organisation office and the city's administration Housing Agency showed that between 1994 and 2003, about 4,147 plots of residential land have been delivered to individuals forming cooperatives. Housing production is impeded primarily by a severe shortage of serviced residential plots. The low supply of residential land in relation to demand has pushed prices beyond the reach of the large majority of the city dwellers. The price of acquiring use rights to residential plots has risen much faster than the inflation rate in recent years as a result of stagnant production and low availability (Tesfaye, 2007).

Nigeria
Housing is a priority for the attainment of living standards and it is important to both rural and urban areas. As urbanisation increases rapidly, the gap between housing need and supply becomes widened due to factors such as preferences, values, social status, taste, financial resources and family demography influence home physical characteristics. In Nigeria, poor housing delivery has been attributed to inadequate mechanisms and systems for land allocation, funding, mortgage institutions and infrastructure (Aluko, 2006). Despite the significance of housing, adequate supply has remained a challenge in Nigeria. The situation is very particular to most developing countries where population grows at an exponential rate and discrepancy in housing need is high. Various authorities have proffered solutions to solving housing delivery problems in Nigeria. While Fasakin (1998) suggested the cooperative housing model, Danmole (2004) advocated for simple land allocation system and Omole (2001)

suggested affordable housing model. The proportion of the Nigerian population living in urban centres has increased phenomenally over the years. While only 7% of Nigerians lived in urban centres in the 1930s and 10% in 1950s, by 1970, 1980 and 1990, 20%, 27% and 35% lived in the cities respectively (Okupe, 2002). Over 40% of Nigerians now live in urban centres of varying sizes.

The problem of population growth has created severe housing problems, resulting in overcrowding, inadequate dwellings and a situation which 60% of Nigerians can be said to be homeless persons (FGN, 2004). The scenario is perceived manifesting in the thickly populated areas of northern Nigeria. The necessity of housing and low potential power to out rightly acquire properties necessitates the idea of rental housing for every citizen. Residential rental properties can be of various classes. Lawal (2000), classified residential houses based on flats, rooming apartments, etc. The demand for each category is determined by the ability to pay the chargeable rent. According to the United Nations Global report on Human Settlements, capital cost of a complete rental dwelling could be 2.5 to 6 times the average annual salary (Okpala *et al.* 2006). Housing affordability uniquely establishes the relationship between people and housing in monetary terms and at a deeper level expresses the link between social and economic systems and the quest for satisfaction of basic human needs that is not merely monetary (Stone, 1993). Private rental housing in Nigeria appears to be failing in aspect of rent, quality, quantity and thus the need for government intervention for improvement. Against this backdrop, this study examines the pace and issues in rental housing in Kaduna, Nigeria. Therefore, landlords are exploiting tenants as they are charging high sums of rent.

Angola
According to the Angolan Ministry of Urban Development and Housing (2016), in 2013 the Angolan government launched a purchase scheme through Delta Imobiliaria, to acquire state-built apartments and housing units. The take-up was weak so these state-financed units as it received a further discount on their unit price by as much as 70%, in order to bring access to the apartments within

the reach of middle-level civil servants (that is, those with monthly incomes over US$ 1,500). On 11 August 2014 a presidential decree was published setting out the rules for renters in Kilamba City to acquire their apartments through a rent-to-purchase scheme. It was explained that "rents" specified in the original contracts could be transformed into payments against purchase of the flats that were provided at the subsidised interest rate of 3% per annum. Rent-to-purchase was to be paid over a 20-year period (or 15 years for those aged over 40) at which time ownership would pass to the resident. Lending rates at commercial and State banks averaged at 12% per annum at this time.

Not well understood by Angolan families who, according to a recent Development Workshop study of residents in Kilamba City, demonstrated that because the transfer of ownership would not be made until the end of the twenty-year payment period almost everyone considered themselves still renters rather than owners of their apartments. The rent-to-purchase scheme gave middle and senior civil-servants access to housing at significantly subsidised rents. The base-line calculation for housing values was reduced by 30 to 40% in 2012 when the first offering of housing in the Kilamba Cent alidade was not taken up by the public. The apartment complex was left almost empty during its first year on the market. The calculation of rents to apply to the Kilamba apartments was calculated at a mere 3% annual interest rate over the already subsidised value of the unit. This interest rate is 15 to 20% below the commercial bank lending rate meaning that the additional rent subsidy was committed by the state to be applied over the full twenty-year period of rental payments until ownership rights were to be granted. It became difficult for the government to continue to provide rental subsidies for housing in the same form as before. Although arguments were raised and people failing to pay the Angolan government is still implementing rental housing market policy (Kemp, 2009).

Discussion

The importance of analysing the housing markets performance and trends is to articulate issues that affect both landlords and tenants. Most of the problems that result in steep housing rental charges in African countries are being caused by lack of adequate sources of finance to fund the different housing projects. Since in different countries there is high demand of houses for accommodation due to increase in population numbers. It is important for the government to intervene in the housing markets so as to avoid the exploitation of tenants by landlords as people earn different amounts of income in a nation (Hall, and Berry, 2004). The government intervenes through polices such as frequent rent reviews to protect landlord's income from inflation and other economic problems, rent control polices to prevent tenants from unfair rent charges from the landlords and also to take part in providing housing schemes for the low-income earners.

Conclusion and policy options

In summary, the long-term view regarding rental housing markets is still a positive one, as jurisdictions that are most likely to interrupt its functionality are those that focus on removal of the common barriers and on the research front, there is strong evidence of the myriad of benefits that tenants and landlords derive from the presence of vibrant rental housing market. In terms of policy direction, the attractiveness of markets to investors would be improved by increasing transparency and minimising sources of friction associated with entering markets and repatriating capital; identifying and testing policy goals for central governments, including their participation in financial structures and risk underwriting; developing scope for inter-country co-operation in critical areas, notably real estate investment; mechanisms for sharing learning and best practice from different forms of policy intervention and market reforms.(CBRE, 2017) This is because developing countries, have emphasised public housing schemes, but with little success. This coincides with global paradigm shift from direct public provision of housing to the enablement of private shelter initiatives and housing production. The chapter discusses private housing development features and dynamics and the factors affecting the sector in the country. It argues for the creation of an enabling environment, including support of housing initiatives and investments by householders, small-scale providers and entrepreneurial private firms. The chapter identifies the implications of enabling strategy for housing finance, access to land, residential infrastructure, institutional regulations and building materials and related industry particularly in the light of the need for the private sector to play greater roles in housing. It draws from aspects of empirical study by the authors and some review of housing policy-related issues (Ogu, 2001)

References

Addis Ababa City Administration. (1994). Urban Land Lease Holding Regulation No. 3/1994

Afolabi, A. (2008). Housing Policy Formulation in Developing Countries: Evidence of Programme Implementation from Akure, Ondo State, Nigeria, *Journal of Human Ecology*, 23(2), 125-1

Alexander, B. (2013). America's Rental Housing Evolving Markets and Needs was prepared by the Harvard Joint Centre for Housing Studies.

Aluko, B. T and Amidu, A. R. (2006, March). Urban low-income settlements, land deregulation and sustainable development in Nigeria. In *5th FIG Regional Conference*.

Angolan Ministry of Urban Development and Housing. (2016). National Report for Habitat III: 73. Presented to the UN Habitat III Conference in Quito, Ecuador, Available online: http://habitat3.org/wp-content/uploads/Habitat-III-New-Urban-Agenda-10-September-2016.pdf [Accessed on 17 October 2016]

Boelhouwer, P. (2002). Trends in Dutch housing policy and the shifting position of the social rented sector. *Urban Studies*, 39(2), 219-235.

CBRE. (2017). Real estate investment in Africa, Available online: https://www.dlapiper.com/~/media/files/insights/publications/2017/06/dla-piper-cbre--real-estate-in-africa--july-2017.pdf. [Accessed on 15 June 2018]

Crook, T., and Kemp, P. A. (2011). *Transforming private landlords: Housing, markets and public policy* (Vol. 43). John Wiley and Sons.

Federal Government of Nigeria (FGN). (2004), *National Housing Policy*, Draft, Abuja.

Firang, D. (2018). Exploring housing careers among Ghanaians in Toronto, Canada. *Housing Studies* 0:0, pages 1-24.

Hall, J and Berry, M. (2004). Operating Deficits and Public Housing: *Policy Options for Reversing the Trend*, Australian Housing and Urban Research Institute Final Report.

Hills, J. (2007). Ends and Means: The Future Roles of Social Housing in England. CASE Report 34, London: London School of Economics and Political Science

HMilligan, V., Phibbs, P., Fagan, K., and Gurran, N. (2004). A Practical Framework for Expanding Affordable Housing Services in Australia: *Learning from Experience,* Australian Housing and Urban Research Institute Final Report, June. ttp://www.ahuri.edu.au/global/ docs/doc593.pdf. [Accessed on 25 June 2018]

Inoki, T., and Suruga, T. (1981). Migration, age, and education: a cross-sectional analysis of geographic labour mobility in Japan. *Journal of regional science*, 21(4), 507-517.

Schwartz, A. (1976). Migration, age and education, *Journal of Political Economy* 8(4), 701-7 19.

Kemp, P. A. (2009). "The transformation of private renting". In Housing, Markets and Policy, Edited by: Malpass: and Rowlands, R. London: Routledge. [Google Scholar]). Wiley-Blackwell.

Lawal, M. I. (2000*). Estate development practice in Nigeria*, Lagos: ILCO Books and Publishers.

Maass, S. (2012). Rent control: a comparative analysis. *Potchefstroom Electronic Law Journal/Potchefstroomse Elektroniese Regsblad*, 15(4), 40-100.

Ogu, V. I., and Ogbuozobe, J. E. (2001). Housing policy in Nigeria: towards enablement of private housing development. *Habitat International*, 25(4), 473-492.

Okpala, D. C. (1987). Received concepts and theories in African urbanisation studies and urban management strategies: A critique. *Urban Studies*, 24(2), 137-150.

Okpala, D., Mutizwa-Mangiza, N and Moiseev. I. (2006). "Financing Urban Housing: United Nations Global Report on Housing Settlements", *Global Urban Development*, 2(1), 1-29.

Okupe, L. (2002). "Private Sector Initiative in Housing Development in Nigeria – How Feasible?" *Housing Today*, 1(6), 21 – 26.

Omole, F. K. (2001). *Basic issues in housing development*, Ondo, Nigeria: Femo Bless Publication.

Rakodi, C. (2001). From a Settler History to an African Present: Housing Markets in Harare, Zimbabwe

Rosen, T. K and Smith, L. B. (1893). *The American Economic Review*, 73(4), 779-786.

Stone, M. E. (1993), Shelter Poverty: *New Ideas on Housing Affordability*, Philadelphia: Temple University Press.

Tesfaye, A. (2007). "Problems and prospects of housing development in Ethiopia", *Property Management*, 25(1), 27-53

Xinhua. (2018). China unveils plans to boost rental housing market, Available online China daily.

Chapter 5

Construction and property development under austerity in Zimbabwe

Emma Maphosa, Ruvimbo Makurira and Mike Juru

Introduction

This chapter examines the construction and development industry under conditions of austerity using the case of Zimbabwe. The construction industry plays a critical role in the growth of the economy. Despite its significance in the economy, the sector continues to reel under critical funding contracts as banks impose stringent borrowing conditions against the backdrop of liquidity challenges. With a focus on Zimbabwe, this study shows how the construction and development industries are functioning. There are plenty of opportunities in the construction and development sector as land should be serviced, sewer provided as well as water infrastructure. The industries are operating below full capacity as they suffer from economic decline. The economy of Zimbabwe has not been performing well despite that there are a lot of projects (Ofori, 1984). The biggest challenge is that there is no funding such that most of the projects that have been done well have got external funding. The problem with external funders is that they come up with terms and conditions that sometimes do not favour locals. For instance, the foreigners might come with their own consultancy team, import materials, as well as, manpower such that it does not have benefit to the citizens of Zimbabwe. However, the industry has been struggling to contain foreigners, especially the Chinese, into the country due to the absence of a legal framework to regulate the industry (Nyoni, 2018).

This chapter is organised in such a way that options are provided for after identifying the challenges that the construction and development industries are facing in the property sector. To start with, there is brief introduction which enlightens on what construction and development is about and reviewing some of the recent theoretical underpinnings concerning the basis of the study and the global trends of the property sector, which is how other countries, excluding Zimbabwe are managing their property industries. The method used to collect relevant data on this study is also included in this chapter. Finally, results on case studies on the construction and development of property under conditions of austerity are analysed, facts are given and conclusions are made on policy options.

Theoretical framework

Technology holds the key; not only to address some of the challenges in the construction and development industry, but also a scheme through which the property sector can react to the changing market conditions more efficiently and effectively. This is because the real estate in Zimbabwe entails property sales, leasing, valuations, management, investment and development. Therefore, the introduction of online technology, increased automation and enhanced accessibility to information will make potential clients well informed since they will be able to harness the power of the internet and marketing of properties as well with online search engines. As the use of internet spreads, people become more aware of its potential from a range of non-property applications and then demand the same level of service from the construction and developments industries. Property investors and developers need to come up with alternative uses for excess space and the conversion of existing city centre buildings into mixed use buildings with a lot of challenges on the infrastructure (Chinjekure, 2017).

The Mirror (6 June, 2018) observes that the main products consumed by the construction industry include cement, bricks, quarry stones and doors. The days of design-bid-build (DBB) domination might be winding down, as experts expect collaborative approaches to become more common for projects. There is a trend towards project team collaboration which will result in more clean resource mobilisation and project implementations. The concept of joint ventures and consortia has proved to be a game changer in improving capacity as construction firms are cautiously optimistic for a future infrastructure spending boost. The advent of international financiers like Geiger International coming into play on the Beitbridge-Harare road will open the gate for more firms which were sceptical on investing in Zimbabwe. On the other hand, Zimbabwe has already shown the appetite to improve the industry by embarking on other projects which include the Hwange Power Station expansion and the plans underway to construct the new parliament building in Mount Hampden. Local banks have also responded to the growth of the industry as seen by banks like Infrastructure Development Bank of Zimbabwe (IDBZ), National Building Society (NBS), First Banking Corporation (FBC) and other property developers taking housing projects in a bid to ease the ballooning housing back log in the country.

According to Mangundhla (2016) the situation in Zimbabwe has changed drastically after a wave of low-income housing cooperatives coupled with increased allocation of land to first time home owners in cities and towns under government and private schemes. As the liquidity crunch and a general macroeconomic slump that costs thousands of citizens' formal employment and steady income streams continue to bite, Zimbabweans seek for affordable residential space as part of an adaption strategy. The central business district (CBD) areas have actually experienced the biggest voids recently as companies are either scaling down or closing due to a myriad of economic challenges. Apart from that, tenants with residential land around the capital also opted to build makeshift temporary structures on their stands in order to start development.

Construction has received the attention of international development finance agencies. There were ambitious goals set for housing expansion in the 1980s including 'Housing for all' by 2000. Amongst some of the principal lenders for urban housing were the World Bank and USAID. The World Bank supported the Urban I programme with a loan of US$50 million in 1980. At its completion in 1994, Urban I had made available 18 000 residential plots and community facilities in four cities (Ramsamy, 2006). Urban II was a relatively large project, totalling US$580 million, to which the World Bank contributed US$80 million. It was implemented country-wide, covering 21 cities and towns. The Bank's report on Urban 11 stated that 30 000 stands for low- and middle-income housing were built by the time the project was completed in 1999 (Ramsamy, 2006). USAID was also involved as one of the funding agencies of urban housing programme. Its scheme for 25 000 beneficiaries in 24 urban local authorities drew from a ZW$760 million local scheme for servicing stands and developing low-cost housing infrastructure. Another critic maintains that Urban 1 and Urban 11 did not reach the poorest segments of the urban population (Ramsamy, 2006). Most of the urban poor have been unable to meet the eligibility criteria for building society loans.

It is argued that while the World Bank's programmes might have increased access for a few low-income residents, they only had a marginal effect on the overall housing shortage (Ramsamy, 2006). The shortage was primarily due to insufficient availability of finance for housing development. Finally, it has been observed that the housing crisis was on only compounded by the development finance agencies' policies of fiscal management and austerity, but also by imprudent choices of the domestic elite in Zimbabwe (Ramsamy, 2006). There was corruption in the administration of the VIP Housing Scheme and the Low-cost Government Housing Scheme (Sunday Mail, 6 December 1998). Meanwhile the housing shortage crisis has grown. The important role of investment in infrastructure in terms of promoting economic linkages and trade is well documented. It is acknowledged that poor infrastructure is a critical barrier to accelerating growth and poverty reduction, especially in Africa. Hence, studies have shown that increasing the stock of infrastructure by 1% can raise GDP by the same margin. Infrastructure typically reduces the cost of doing business, facilitates access to markets and is therefore a key enabler of economic activity, growth and development. The state of Zimbabwe's basic infrastructure for the power, transport, water and sanitation and information and communications technology sectors is detailed in the report by the African Development Bank (AfDB, 2011).

Notwithstanding that the coverage and quality of Zimbabwe's basic infrastructure was among the best in Southern Africa in the early 1990s, it underwent substantial deterioration in quality such that it is roughly in line with that of other countries in the region. The sustained deterioration is related to the inadequate levels of public expenditures for routine and periodic maintenance of the infrastructure networks, especially in power, water, sanitation and transport. In sectors dominated by parastatals such as power, rail transport and fixed line communications, low service prices deterioration, resulting in unsustainable operating losses. This deterioration in the physical infrastructure is exacerbated by failure to build institutional capacities for management and regulation of the basic network services. The problems reflect and are caused by the disjointed approach to regulation and oversight among the various ministries involved. This has been worsened by the loss of technical skills in the sector through brain drain. Furthermore, the institutional and regulatory inadequacies undermined investment by the private sector in basic infrastructure. Given the role of basic infrastructure as an enabler of economic activity, its deterioration impacted negatively on productive sectors of the economy and lowered the level and quality of services. Therefore, AfDB (2011) estimated that at constant 2009 prices, US$14.2 billion is required to rehabilitate the infrastructure between 2011 and 2020.

Literature review

In the case of Greece, housing was not closely related to the causes of the financial breakdown, as was the case in other countries, such as the United States (Gotham, 2009; Immergluck, 2011) or Spain (Lopez and Rodriguez, 2011). Rather, housing problems have emerged as a consequence of the severe austerity measures implemented and the spiral of recession and economic collapse provoked by these measures. The beginning of the crisis in Greece was marked by the introduction of the European Mechanism of Support (ESM) in 2010, the implementation of structural economic adjustment programs and measures as part of consecutive agreement memoranda. As in most places, the promoted measures and reforms primarily aim to protect the financial sector and global investors while consolidating new labour-capital relations (Hadjimichalis, 2011). What started as a public debt crisis since 2010 has evolved into a wider social, political and humanitarian crisis resulting in unprecedented unemployment levels, precarious employment, poverty, massive income losses, the depletion of the social structures and provisions left in an already residual welfare state? In economic terms, austerity measures have led Greece to economic decline and a vicious circle of recession and escalating indebtedness, rendering the public debt socially and economically unsustainable. Within this context, Greece is facing a severe and escalating housing crisis today, which affects broad sections of the population, thereby multiplying housing precariousness, inadequacy and exclusion. Households are increasingly overburdened by housing costs, bad housing conditions, energy poverty, overcrowding, seizures, evictions and homelessness. Today's housing problems must be acknowledged primarily as an income and labour problem, rather than a result of the housing market (Giannitsis and Zografakis, 2015).

Recent developments in the housing market in England saw a shift in tenure structure. Demand for owner-occupied housing is currently extremely low because of the lack of mortgage funding and the lack of confidence. This is driven by high house prices and the restrictive lending environment which have both created the need for prohibitively high deposits. Those struggling to buy their first home have been badly affected by recent changes in the housing market. The average age of a first-time buyer without extra financial support could soon rise to 43. Furthermore, private rents continue to rise, reflecting the growing demand for rented accommodation prompted by a shortage of social housing and the inability of growing numbers of people to afford buying. A research carried out in England by the Chartered Institute of Housing in June 2011 showed that 31% of people renting privately felt they were spending more on housing costs than they could afford.

According to RICS, the recession was relatively moderate in France when compared to other European countries showing that the financial system weathered the crisis well. Previously, high rates of house building were clipped by the onset of the recession but they have partly recovered. Furthermore, the stimulus measures offered in the housing market during the recession were substantial and made considerable impact (Mhlanga, 2017). They include a major social home building programme between 2009 and 2010. A major issue with regard to housing in France nowadays is that of affordability and risk of housing exclusion. Average housing expenditures currently represent about a quarter of households' budget (against 18% in 1984) and this amount is higher for tenants. The foundation Abbe Pierre estimates that currently 3.6 million people in France are inadequately housed and the housing crisis is also increasingly affecting middle-income people.

Compared to the rest of Europe, the financial crisis had the most immediate and strongest impact on the housing market in Ireland (together with Spain), causing the bursting of the 'housing bubble'. Ireland stands out as the country in Europe with the most sustained house price falls, after many years of dramatic increases during its earlier property boom (a reduction of 38% since their peak at the end of 2006). According to RICS, the late 2010 bailout of the country, the continuing economic problems and the substantial overhang of newly built properties mean that the end of the downturn in housing markets is unlikely to be in sight soon. Currently there are a number of unsold properties, ranging from around 35 000 to 170 000 dwellers in the upper end. There is also an issue with 'Ghost Estates' or unfinished housing developments, which brings along problems in anti-social behaviour as well as health and safety concerns. Furthermore, considerable attention has been drawn to the issue of arrears and negative equity. In the first quarter of 2010 about 32 300 mortgages were in arrears for over 91 days (an estimated 4% of all mortgages). Approximately, 116 000 borrowers were in negative equity at the end of 2009, rising to 196 000 by end of 2010.

The impact of the credit crunch on the market was more related to the macroeconomic performance of the country than to any "housing bubble". This impact has translated less in falling prices than in a fall on the transactions side. The numbers of purchases and sales have been facing a decline since 2007 all over Italy. Demand is being constrained by soaring unemployment, especially among younger people, as well as recent budget cuts affecting low-income homebuyers. The median income of the population is decreasing. While in 2008 it was calculated that households spent 32.2% of their disposable income on housing, by 2009 the percentage increased to

33.5%. The most vulnerable part of the population such as the unemployed, recent immigrants and the elderly continue to suffer the problems of living in uncomfortable and inconvenient built-up zones. There is also an issue with homebuyers who can no longer afford to pay their mortgage. Together with a restriction of mortgage credit by banks, this phenomenon is likely to lead to an increase in the demand for social housing (CECODHAS, 2011).

The housing market downturn which started in the aftermath of the financial crisis continued during 2010, despite some evidence that the decline could be slowing. As the wider economy and financial markets still face substantial problems, it is by no means certain that the end of the housing market downturn has actually been reached yet. House building peaked at extraordinarily high levels in the final years of the boom. Since then, output has fallen sharply and starts were expected to be below 80,000 by year end 2010. This may not yet be the bottom. There has been a 15% price fall from the peak for existing housing and somewhat less for new. The scale of the price changes that have occurred and the risks of further downward adjustments vary across the country and by market segment. Taking account of general price inflation, this suggests a roughly 22% real decline in values for existing homes, which is one of the largest in Europe to date. Furthermore, there is substantial vacancy overhang (an estimate 750 000 to one million dwellings). Between 2008 and 2011 about 150 000 families have lost their homes and are left with high debts. It is estimated that overall 510 000 households might have lost their home by 2015 as a consequence of the economic crisis. To tackle this situation, the government negotiated with banks to agree on recommendations - including a code of good banking practices - and legal measures to limit evictions. Proposals include, among others, lowering of the interest rates on mortgage payment arrears and delaying eviction for two years in the case of families whose members are all unemployed and who have declared their inability to pay (FEANTSA, 2011).

By participating in the European Union building process, Portugal had an opportunity to become a developed country for the first time in centuries. It was in the process of doing so, but the EU-IMF austerity policies are setting the country back extremely quickly and, in many instances, irreversibly. The ramifications of these policies extend far beyond Portugal's borders. The EU cannot survive on the current policy course, which will set Europe back for decades. Creating the euro was a difficult, complex endeavour. It was not humanly possible to anticipate all contingencies that would later materialise (Mlambo, 2000).

The architects of the euro, policy-makers in EU institutions and member states, who designed the third phase of the EMU and/or managed it up to its present state of affairs. These are people like Otmar Issing, Jean Claude Trichet, Klaus Regling, Marco Buti, Mario Draghi, Jürgen Stark, Durão Barroso, Vitor Constâncio, Vitor Gaspar and many others who have been widely praised, earning and have the admiration and respect of their peers in academia, government, business and politics. They acted according to their beliefs of what was best for the euro area and for the EU. However, their ideas and decisions have driven the European Union to be on the brink of failure. The policies they helped put in place or managed have led the euro area to be the largest peacetime balance of payments and external debt crisis the world has ever seen. Their remedial policy known as "stay the course" policy10 – is actually aggravating the crisis, not solving it. Widespread hardship, despair, hunger and suicides are not unavoidable random events but predictable outcome of their weak policies. Unless a major policy change is quickly adopted, their names will forever be linked to the hubris, the blind ideology and the wilful ignorance that doomed the euro and the European Union (Monastiriotis, 2012).

Methodology

Secondary data were used in undertaking the study. Relevant information was identified from existing literature on the construction and development of property. Some data were collected from stakeholders in the property sector which included articles from Google Scholar and unpublished papers presented in the past on some of the key themes about development and construction.

Results

Property development is the most lucrative between that gives the highest returns when investing in the Zimbabwe's property sector as investors buy huge tracts of vacant land and subdivide it into smaller residential and commercial stands. What makes property development lucrative is that the market for serviced stands in Zimbabwe is readily available. The prevailing economic situation in Zimbabwe has created customers that can only afford to buy serviced residential stand and build the house over a more flexible period of time instead of purchasing an already built house. So huge is the demand that buyers are even paying for stands before they are serviced, as long as they are satisfied by the progress of the projects. Madokero Estate in Tynwald is one such project whose stands were sold off plan. The liquidity crisis in Zimbabwe since 2008 has starved many property development projects from investment and left various opportunities in this sector untapped. There are many players in the development sector that are not adequately funded, a situation that creates opportunity for new well-funded investors (Chase Contractors, 2017).

The construction sub sectors in Zimbabwe can be split into commercial residential development. Infrastructure development is a priority to Zimbabwe at this moment because the resuscitation of the economy is anchored on the refurbishment of worn out infrastructure. The quality and quantity of a nation's infrastructure have important bearing on long- and medium-term economic growth. Our recovering economy needs to resuscitate the dilapidated infrastructure and carry out new capital projects. Economic growth cannot be achieved without appropriate economic and social infrastructure services. On the contrary, commercial development in Zimbabwe is quite lucrative because well-funded players have very little competition and exhibit great bargaining power when negotiating contracts (Ela Africa, 2017).

According to Mapakame (2018), demand for mortgage loans in the country has increased as Zimbabweans turn to real estate as a store of value. The market has been stagnant on the back of pricing statement spurred by currency risk and uncertainty. Sellers are not willing to reduce prices to meet buyers' needs whilst buyers cannot go beyond what they have offered. Resultantly, development has mainly been skewed towards residential properties as new settlements continue to increase in urban centres. On the commercial side, the sector is battling high voids, resulting in low occupancy levels that reflect negatively on rental incomes. Therefore, the challenges that are being faced could be a mirror image of the economy, where voids and defaults are a common feature. Beyond that, agility in adapting to the demands of the market is subsequently in mismatch. However, there is hope as development is expected to boom in the next few years due to high demand for residential and institutional infrastructure. A number of property development projects are on the pipeline whilst others have already been launched. To achieve growth, government and other stakeholders need to take a leading role in creating a conducive environment by adopting policies that promote the growth of the property sector to attract investment.

A case study that demonstrates how the construction industry operates under conditions of austerity is that of ZIMRE Property Investments' (ZPI) $13million mall. ZPI considered investing in the mammoth structure to optimise its portfolio mix. The project is anchored by one of the major retail chains, understood to be Pick n Pay. It provides approximately 5000 square metres of retail space, comprising of 23 shops of various sizes including banks, concept stores, food courts, a restaurant, coffee shops, jewellery and curio shops, a gym and a fuel service station (Chinjekure, 2017). ZPI expects the construction of the mall to be completed early in 2020. Masimba workers are busy working on the project and reasonable ground has so far been covered with a number of pillars having been raised. The bulk of the funds of the Sawanga Shopping Mall will be generated from the sale of ZIMRE Centre in Harare. ZIMRE Centre was sold for $10.3 million as the property firm sought to restructure its portfolio mix as part of restricting its portfolio mix. ZPI also intends to convert Nicoz house in Bulawayo to student accommodation. The refurbishment of the Nicoz house is estimated to cost $1, 8 million and renovations started in January 2018 and are expected to be complete in August 2018. Last year, ZPI's rental performance was 11 percent performance lower than the prior year.

According to the listed firm's annual report for 2017, the decline was attributed generally by the performance of the economy (Chinjekure, 2017).

Settler colonial rule from 1890 to 1979 was characterised by racial land dispossession as well as political and economic discrimination (Mlambo, 2000; Moyana, 2002), which defined Zimbabwe's land question and mass nationalism. The settler colonial state sought to turn most of the peasantry into full-time industrial workers disconnected from the land (Yeros, 2002). The development strategy was structurally imbalanced and discriminatory, seeking to secure mainly the domestic markets of the white minority and exports, while providing minimum incomes for the subsistence of the black poor and the reproduction of migrant labour. The uneven allocation of economic infrastructures in rural areas was integral to this strategy, which emphasised import substitution industrialisation. Under these conditions, nationalist struggles mobilised extensive militancy in the rural areas.

The United States and Britain facilitated a negotiated settlement towards 'majority rule' in 1979, (Lancaster House Agreement and Constitution 1979). This provided critical parameters to protect property rights, proscribing land reform within a market oriented liberal democratic governance framework and bringing unequal parliamentary power sharing with the white minority. At independence, the key development policy challenge was to promote re-distributive strategies to reduce racial inequality, poverty and promote broad-based economic growth, focusing on the domestic needs, particularly of the poor (GoZ, 1982). Land and agrarian reform policy vested on development strategy focused on import-substitution industrialisation within a heterodox macroeconomic policy framework. The expansion of agricultural production envisioned land reform, leading rural development and poverty reduction. The development strategy activities of Zimbabwean civil society organisations (CSO) during the 1980's focused on welfare projects, with little emphasis on land reform (see Moyo, 2001). From the mid-1990, their focus tilted towards demands for accelerated democratisation and limited interrogation of the failure of neoliberal economic policies to deliver development. Proactive land reform within a more developed mentalist economic strategy was called for by the Zimbabwean Congress of Trade Unions (ZCTU) for some time. The underlying land conflict which limited the productive use of land and access by the poor was underplayed (Mlambo, 2000). Economic policies implemented helped in the development and phasing out of discrimination amongst blacks and whites in Zimbabwe.

Conclusion and policy options

The importance of analysing the construction and development of property industries performance and trends is to articulate issues that affect the citizens of Zimbabwe. Most of the problems that are resulting in the property sector are being caused by inadequate sources of finance to fund the different construction and development projects. As in different countries, there is high demand for construction in terms of commercial, residential and even industrial space due to the increase in population numbers. It is important for the government to intervene through expansionary monetary and fiscal policies such that banks can provide mortgages to developers. The construction and development industries in Zimbabwe have been negatively affected by the prevailing acute liquidity crunch as the country is not using its own currency. This is resulting in monetary authorities being unable to contain and manage the supply and demand side of the currency. Resultantly, property developers are now selling their projects on plan soon after acquiring the permit and necessary paper work due to difficulty in raising initial capital to start the projects. This suggests that, apart from national influences on development and land policies, external influences on development and land policy are critical to explaining domestic state-civil society policy interactions. Understanding how the institutional framework mediates the interests of local capital, workers, peasants, policy elites, CSO elites, as well as international finance is critical. Therefore, high disposable incomes, affordable debt options and healthy banks are very important foundations that will propel the Zimbabwean property market to attractive heights.

References

African Development Bank. (AfDB). (2011). Infrastructure and Growth in Zimbabwe: *An Action Plan for Strengthened Recovery*, 33 (2009), 355–371.

CECODHAS Housing Europe Observatory. (2011). Housing Europe Review 2012 - The nuts and bolts of European social housing systems

Chase contractors. (2017). Investing in Zimbabwe's properties sector; property development. http://www.chase.co.zw/investing-in-zimbabwes-properties-sector-property-development/. [Accessed on 25 April 2018]

Chinjekure, F. (2017). ICT changing face to Zim real estate. *Herald*, Available online: https://www.herald.co.zw/ict-changing-face-of-zim-real-estate/. [Accessed on 25 April 2018]

Ela Africa. (2017). Investing in Zimbabwe's properties sector; commercial development, Available online: http://www.chase.co.zw/investing-in-zimbabwes-properties-sector-property-development/. [Accessed on 25 April 2018]

FEANTSA. (2011). Impact of anti-crisis austerity measures on homeless services across the EU. FEANTSA Policy Paper

Mhlanga, *P. (2017)*. "Construction industry shrinks", *The Financial Gazette February 23, 2017*. Available online: https://www.researchgate.net/publication/316514709_A_Theoretical_Harmonization_of_Critical_Success_Factors_CSFs_in_the_Construction_Sector_in_Zimbabwe_Introducing_the_3P_Model. [Accessed on 25 April 2018]

Giannitsis, T and Zografakis, S. (2015). *Greece: Solidarity and adjustment in times of crisis* (No. 38). IMK Study.

Gotham, K. F. (2009). Creating liquidity out of spatial fixity: The secondary circuit of capital and the subprime mortgage crisis. *International Journal of Urban and Regional Research*, 33(2), 355-371.

Government of Zimbabwe. (1982). Transitional National Development Plan (1982-85) Vol 1. Harare: Government Printers. Government of Zimbabwe. (1999). The Inception Phase Framework Plan of the Second Phase of Land Reform and Resettlement Programme (Harare: Ministry of Land and Agriculture, 1999).

Hadjimichalis, C. (2011). Uneven geographical development and socio-spatial justice and solidarity: European regions after the 2009 financial crisis. *European Urban and Regional Studies*, 18(3), 254-274.

Immergluck, D. (2011). The local wreckage of global capital: The subprime crisis, federal policy and high- foreclosure neighbourhoods in the US. *International Journal of Urban and Regional Research*, 35(1), 130-146.

López, I and Rodríguez, E. (2011). The Spanish model. *New left review*, 69(3), 5-29.

Mangundla, T. (2016). Property market hits a new low. The *independent*

Mantouvalou, M., Mavridou, M., and Vaiou, D. (1995). Processes of social integration and Urban Development in Greece: southern challenges to European unification. *European Planning Studies*, 3(2), 189-204.

Mapakame, E. (2018). Demand for Mortgages on the rise. *Herald* assessed on 31 July 2018, Harare. Available online: https://www.herald.co.zw/category/articles/top-stories/. [Accessed on 25 April 2018]

Ministry of Environment, Heritage and Local Government. (2010). Housing Market Overview 2009, Harare.

Mlambo, A. S. (2000). 'Manufacturing in Zimbabwe, 1980–90', in Zimbabwe: *A History of Manufacturing*, 1890–1995, A. S. Mlambo, E. S., Pangeti and Phimister, I. Harare: University of Zimbabwe Publications.

Monastiriotis, V., Hardiman, N., Regan, A., Goretti, C., Landi, L., Conde-Ruiz, J. I and Cabral, R. (2012). Austerity measures in crisis countries—results and impact on mid-term development. *Intereconomics*, 48(1), 4-32.

Moyana, H. V. (2002). The Political economy of land in Zimbabwe. Mambo Press, Gweru, Zimbabwe.

Moyo, S. (2005). 11 Land policy, poverty reduction and public action in Zimbabwe. *Land, poverty and livelihoods in an era of globalization: perspectives from developing and transition countries*, 344.

Available online:
http://hubrural.org/IMG/pdf/iss_pnud_overview.pdf.
[Accessed on 13 July 2018]

Nyoni, M. (2018). Construction industry reels from funding constraints. Newsday

Ofori, G. (2000). Globalization and construction industry development: research opportunities. *Construction Management and Economics*, 18(3), 257-262.

Ramsamy, E. (2006). 'The World Bank and urban programmes in Zimbabwe: A critical appraisal'. *Review of African Political Economy,* 33(109), 515-523.

Yeros, P. (2002). 'Zimbabwe and the Dilemmas of the Left', *Historical Materialism*, 10, 2, 3–15.

Chapter 6

Facilities' management in Zimbabwe

Zebediah Muneta

Introduction

This chapter examines the meaning and dimensions of facilities management in Zimbabwe. Facility Management (FM) is defined as a profession that encompasses multiple disciplines to ensure functionality of the built environment by integrating people, place, process and technology (IFMA, 2006). Simultaneously, FM is also an integrated approach in monitoring, improving and adapting the buildings and infrastructure of an organisation in order to create an environment that strongly supports the primary objectives of that organisation (Barret and Baldry, 2003; SFMS, 2006). In previous years, FM has been a professional integrated approach to help a lot of business organisations, educational institutions and government departments in managing property facilities effectively and providing a high degree of support services (Gao and Cao, 2015). Due to technology and rapid development of this profession, FM is suffering especially in developing countries like Zimbabwe due to the lack of a unique knowledge base which is causing the identity crisis in the meaning and dimension of facilities management.

In developed countries, the diversification of FM services has severely impeded the recognition of the essence and core value of FM in achieving organisational goals through effective outsourcing of services, management and maintenance of facilities (Marco and Mangano, 2012). In this particular context the FM function has been gaining increasing recognition for the important role it plays to create cost savings and efficiency of the workplace, managing support services to meet the needs of the organisation, its core operations and employees (Marco and Mangano, 2012). In practice, it has not yet reached the status it deserves from the point of view of advantages it offers, especially in the area of management system coordination of the enterprise support processes (Babiaková, 2009; Potkány, 2013). This chapter is structured as follows the first section of this study is the introduction, followed by theoretical underpinnings of this study and literature review of global and regional experiences of facilities management practice. The next section describes the methodology then the results and discussion of key findings. Lastly, conclusions and policy directions shall be proffered for effective facilities management practice in Zimbabwe.

Theoretical underpinnings

Facilities Management is a management discipline that has not been clearly identified in developing countries because of its different meanings since it has its close business management relations in human resources, finance and information technology. The main obstacle is that many processes that are undertaken by the facilities management function are being regarded as business expenses and not seen as contributing to maximising shareholder and business value –unlike human resources, finance and information technology (McEwan and Shiem-Shin Then, 2004) As facilities management is multidisciplinary, its identity can be lost through a specific discipline focus within a business; whether that be architectural, engineering, property management or maintenance. This apparent lack of focus erodes the power of facilities management performance to grow internally through building internal capability. Most FM problems in applied area unit targeting building a holistic atmosphere in providing a secure and economical setting for users that later help the business performance. There are four basic factors that might influence FM delivery which include organisation size, facilities location, facilities possession and management problems. It has been observed that FM serves organisations, otherwise upon its life-cycle stages the disciplines has been affected by stable and unstable periods (Pitt *et al.* 2016).

According to Atkin and Brooks (2004) change management is an important feature of facilities management. Change may be an individual's central demand of businesses result modification. Facilities management is per se aligned the client's business wants and can preponderantly concerned with meeting the dynamic wants of purchasers (Atkin and Brooks (2004). In most cases, facilities management is also regarded as a key branch of property management which is responsible for the operation, control, overseeing and monitoring of the organisation in achieving its key goals. Alternatively, property management is simply the management the whole facility. Organisational goals which are fulfilled by effective facilities management in the real estate industry include increasing tenant satisfaction, reducing operating costs of a building, maximising investment return and increasing operational efficiency (IFMA, 2006). The facilities manager's key role is to minimise operating costs, especially some in property companies and others who manage corporate entities they are always thriving to reduce the operating costs of a building for both occupiers and owners. Operational costs are generally expenses such as municipal charges, electricity and insurance costs. With effective facilities management, operational costs will always be at their minimum possible level, especially to the income generating properties. They will achieve a higher investment return since some of the costs will be turned into revenue.

Based on Atkins' research (2000, p13), facilities management is the application of the total standard techniques to improve quality, add value of a building, reduce the risks involved in occupying a building and delivering reliable support services. Having a facilities management department at an organisation helps to provide and sustain an operational environment to meet its strategic needs. Quality can be ensured since the organisation will focus more on core business processes, hence creating an integrated and supported operational environment which is favourable to the employees as well as customers. Through facilities management, one can produce results that can be tested against user satisfaction with the service such as space management, technology, environment support services and infrastructure (Isa *et al.* 2016). Abd Rahman (2008) suggested that, facilities management is divided into three major categories such as property, equipment and services for which it depends on the respective management to manage and provide the facility to the users. He adds that the scope of facility management includes a number of areas such as maintenance and management of assets, space, projects and renovations, security and cleaning and others. These are broadly categorised into two; hard and soft issues (Isa *et al.* 2016).

On the other hand, Pheng (1996, 21) has noted that FM has four main principles. These include the continuous programme coordination of all effort, namely planning, designing, construction and management of facilities towards enhancing the working environment for the people and the organisation's ability to meet its business objectives. They include total integration of diverse field of business, architecture, behavioural and engineering science under one entity in an organisation in order to oversee all facilities functions which were previously controlled by independent departments; the management of activities proactively rather than reactively; adhering to policies and procedures, guided by organisational goals and objectives as well as available resources ar5e concepts that influence FM (Isa *et al.* 2016).

Finally, to achieve all these four principles, there are three levels of facilities management strategy which should be adopted in managing a facility (Abd Rahman, 2008). The categories include the strategy analysis, completion strategy and implementation of the strategy. The Strategy analysis involves examining all the information and facts collected together targeting the organisation's policies, needs, resources, processes, physical plus conditions, use of house and performance and prices concerned. In the completion strategy, results of information collected little by little, as well as the objectives of the organisation is evaluated and analysed. For the ordinal time a head facility management strategy is established. The stage of implementation consists of event strategy through the belief of associate implementation set up which contains a timetable designing such amount or periods and complete risk management. It includes human and labour and therefore the system, communications, planning and resources acquisition are put into operation (Isa *et al.* 2016).

Literature review

This section reviews literature on global experiences and trends of facilities management practices that have shown signs of rapid growth in America, Europe, Australia and New Zealand in the last two decades.

FM is a multi-disciplinary kind of work that covers a wide range of various activities, responsibilities and knowledge. What is more interesting is that every aspect of an organisation seems to be drawn into FM. If the building is said to be one of the important things in real estate, facilities management is part of the management of the building that needs to be emphasised by the management body (Isa *et al.* 2016). One of the facilities management objectives is to reduce maintenance costs while maintaining high standard or the quality of facilities provided. Facilities management is a delegated service which is provided to the industry which gives proficient counsel and administration of clients' building facilities including residential, commercial, industrial, airports terminals and offices (Isa *et al.* 2016 and Rozilah (2011: 9) has stated that:

> Facilities management is associated with supporting core business activities of the organisation with the main aim of minimising costs and maximising return on investment of the business and also facilities management integrates people, place, process and technology which has a major convectional function between organisational culture, people and physical assets hence the increase in demand of facilities management services and experts

Over the years, researchers and practitioners alike have provided various definitions that specify the objectives and scope of FM. However, these definitions have avoided a common platform that is so crucial for cohesive theoretical development in FM.

Alexander (1999) defines FM as a scope of discipline that covers all aspects of property, space, environmental control, health and safety and support services. Hinks and McNay's (1999) common interpretation of the FM remit: maintenance management; space management and accommodation standards; project management for new-build and alterations; the general premises management of the building stock; and the administration of associated support services. Varcoe (2000) focuses on the management and delivery of business "outputs" real estate and construction industry as well as the productive use of building assets as workplaces. Nutt (2000) the primary function of FM is resource management at strategic and operational levels of support. Generic types of resource management central to the FM function are the management of financial resources, physical resources, human resources and the management of resources of information and knowledge. IFMA (2003) posits that Facilities must be managed as an integrated system. The International Facility Management Association defines facility management as the practices of coordinating the physical workplace with the people and work of the organisation. In addition, Kerdia *et al.* (2011) viewed facilities management as the cost/price/value issue considered above. Facilities management means one thing or another, depending on where in the management process one is located or, in practice, whether one is managing a task, organising and directing the whole range of activities or sponsoring the provision (Kerdia *et al.* 2011).

In many organisations, the aspect of facilities management depends on their organisational culture. For example, wherever the directive management is in-house possibly managing a combination of direct labour and bundled contracts the fire-fighting operates conventionally, leading very little time for thinking and time for developing the intelligent customer aspect which is essential in a very perpetually evolving state of affairs amid dynamic service technology and delivery regimes. The correct allocation of resources to every one of those aspects is totally important in auctioning price effective facilities (Kerdia *et al.* 2011).

Facility management is one of the services provided by facility managers enable the management of the organisation which includes managerial work, maintenance and technical support. In practice, many organisations usually outsource most of its facilities management services such as cleaning, maintenance and security services. The contracted staffs are not necessarily always on site and so workloads have to be planned carefully to make the best use of people through benchmarking, key performance indicators and service level agreements (Yassin and Razali, 2008). Facilities management plays a greater role in enhancing property value in the real estate industry through regular maintenance and outsourcing of services to the competitive service provider to provide the necessary service to the organisation. Facilities management provides property service which mainly includes maintenance works such as lifts, escalators, elevators and air-conditioning. The thrust of the facilities managers is to know the cost of these services and then analyse them attempting to influence them positively and monitor them closely. In addition, the unit costs should be a basis for benchmarking (Atkin and Brooks, 2014). A facility manager should benchmark effectiveness (as perceived by customers) since tenants always look for space to rent in a building that is fully serviced, with facilities that are convenient and accessible. The facilities manager should always ensure that these assets are fully functional for the convenience of the tenants and their clients (Atkin and Brooks, 2014). This will increase property value in the sense that the functionality of the building will improve. It will also increase the leasehold value of the facility if the building is let out to tenants who are capable of paying rentals when they fall due since all the services will be provided.

Since late 1980s, FM has gradually gained a foothold as discipline and profession within the property and construction industry. The establishment of professional FM institutions around the world (e.g. IFMA in the USA, JFMA in Japan, BIFM in UK, FMA in Australia, etc.) testifies to its growing importance (Linda *et al.* 2001). Though popularity of this subject has been on a steady upward trend, nowadays there are still people who do not really appreciate and to certain extent are misguided on the roles and responsibility of FM (Mahamat *et al.* 2014). It is therefore very pertinent for FM practitioners to understand the evolution of FM, which has developed from just looking at hardware such as buildings, furniture, which is reflected by Becker (1990) and equipment to looking at "software" such as people, process, environment, health and safety which is depicted by Alexander (1999). Thomson (1998) stated that it is clear he was referring to what the Americans referred to as facility management. However, in the UK 'facilities' become the preferred term; one adopted by both workplace design specialist and the operational managers of buildings, in particular in the computing and electronics industries (Price, 2001). This clearly indicates the confusion that FM went through once it evolved from the US to the UK (Mahamat *et al.* 2014).

In the United States of America (USA), FM is more process-oriented, as the focus is towards planning and coordinating activities. The advantage seen here is that there are detailed work processes in existence for monitoring and auditing purposes, but the drawback of this approach is that it is not human focused and can be perceived as a non-socially obligated model. It is construed as more profit driven; end result oriented, but without the necessary elements in place to provide a human touch to doing business (Mahamat *et al.* 2014). The American FM style describes the work processes clearly without much room for creativity. As such, consideration for feelings and emotions is not in the forefront of business decision. This is to say that people could just be treated as a soldier in a war game. They are there to do the defined work. If they are not there, another soldier can be deployed to replace them amicably. Alternatively, if the soldier is not effective, replace it with a more effective soldier (Mahamat *et al.* 2014).

While on the other hand the British stress the quality of environment and good support services, which is essentially quite general in the sense; it is more open to one's creative interpretation and at the same time indicates less dependency on predefined work processes (Mahamat *et al.* 2014). This approach can be perceived as meaning that it is effectively up to the practitioner's prerogative to make the process more transparent and systematic. Of course, with this more generic principle it is also possible to be more chaotic. Nonetheless, the human touch part is definitely emphasised in the British system, which essentially means appreciation towards fellow employees is part and parcel of doing business. Hence, corporate social responsibility and obligatory roles in the British FM style does take into consideration the emotions and feelings of people, who are very important in fostering high productivity and efficiency in running the office (Mahamat *et al.* 2014).

The last two decades in Japan have seen the growing recognition of facilities management as a management process that embrace the whole life of an asset. This had the impact of raising awareness to the need to consider the operational period of building assets (Sato *et al.* 2004). There is growing recognition of the need for financial management method that gives proper evaluation to overall cost of facility, including operational and maintenance expenses throughout its life-cycle. Various studies seem to indicate that the standard of the overall life-cycle cost of building facilities in Japan is higher comparing to those in other countries (Sato *et al.* 2004).

In developed markets, FM administrations are firmly incorporated with some different administrations in the real estate sector, for example rent collection and land lease management. However, in developing countries such as Malaysia the idea of FM has not sufficiently developed to give complete property management practices (Isa *et al.* 2016). As mentioned, FM is the provision and management of resources, physical environment and business support services to complement the strategic and operational objectives of an organisation, integrating key functions like processes and technologies with people in a flexible and integrated manner.

What is common for Bulgaria and most Eastern European countries is the fact that facility management (FM) is a new business sector when compared to some West European countries, where it has been a strategic activity for more than 20 years (Tashev *et al.* 2011). Having in mind the wide scope of services encompassed in FM, the companies in Europe and worldwide are trying to consolidate the sector. This is a way to establish and maintain good contact between the companies and FM professionals, in order to share information and expertise between all stakeholders, which leads into the shaping of this sector and increasing quality of the services provided (Tashev *et al.* 2011). The importance of FM for all public and private companies and institutions led to the preparation of the first two norms for FM, made by the European Committee for Standardisation (Tashev *et al.* 2011). This standard gives the definition of facility management, which is also officially adopted by the Bulgarian Facility Management Association. Facility management is defined as "the integration of processes within an organisation to maintain and develop the agreed services which support and improve the effectiveness of its primary activities" (Tashev *et al.* 2011: 19).

Facility management is becoming more and more popular in Bulgaria. After an initiative, from the Bulgarian Facility Management Association (bgfma.bg), facility management was officially recognised as a profession in the Bulgarian National Classification of Professions. Nevertheless, many organisations directly or indirectly connected with facility management are not yet familiar with this term. In Malaysia, FM is described as a second wave market by the FM industry (Moore and Finch, 2004). Their study revealed that the region acknowledged a common FM definition as set by the industry.

It is noted that the research findings could not be generalised and adopted by respective countries in the constituency due to limited sample size used in the study. Moore and Finch (2004) identified that the Malaysians seem confused over FM identity and coined FM as a subset of property management profession. In Malaysia, property assets in the form of building and infrastructure are commonly managed by an in-house, out-source service team or combination of both through co-sourcing approach where subject-matter experts or service providers are combined within the in-house team to undertake the responsibility of delivering the necessary FM services. NAPIC (2009) reported that there are more than 26 million square meters of existing stock of commercial properties (combination of shopping centres and purpose-built offices) in Malaysia. While the values of all properties are still being studied by NAPIC, the above information shall be sufficient to indicate that Malaysia has significant values of assets owned by both public and private sectors (Tashev *et al.* 2011). The term asset management in the financial market is commonly confused with property management in the physical asset development domain. However, with the introduction of Valuers, Appraisers and Estate Agents Act in 1981 (incorporating all amendments up to 1St January 2006), property management means the management and control of any land, building and any interest therein, excluding the management of property-based businesses (Tashev *et al.* 2011). Property-based businesses include; a hotel, motel, hostel, plantation, quarry, marina, port, golf course, cinema, stadium, sports complex and hospital.

Methodology

The study is a desktop inquiry which utilised various secondary data sources from reports, journals, PhD and masters' dissertations books as well as some internet websites. Literature review enabled lessons to be drawn from global and regional experiences while document review was mostly used to explore local cases in Zimbabwe.

Results

Banks in Zimbabwe such as Barclays, CBZ and Standard Chartered outsource facilities management services such as maintenance, cleaning and security so that they concentrate on their core business activities (Chotipanich and Lertariyanun, 2014). They put in place the FM department which take responsibility for all FM work that needs to be done in the organisation. They direct its purposes towards adding or creating value to the Bank's business operations, to achieve the aim of customer and worker satisfaction. FM departments intend to reduce operating costs through implementing energy management plan so as to minimise expenses such as utility costs of the occupied facility. They enhance worker and customer satisfaction through provision of favourable heating, ventilation and air conditioning systems and also ensured that all lifts and escalators are being serviced and maintained.

Real estate companies and facilities management in Zimbabwe

Companies such as Dawn Properties, Zimre Properties and Mashonaland Holdings have adopted FM in most of their commercial properties. The key role of FM in this case is to support the core operations by providing effective working environment. Its main purposes are centred on minimising costs and effective responding to the service providers within the organisation. The key issues that the department is highly concerned about include reputation of the building, the performance of facilities and workplace, the legitimacy of its practices that must strictly meet all regulations and standards, health and safety of building users, energy saving and environmental conservation. FM departments are planning to develop the FM software as a total management tool featuring maintenance, asset and space management to enhance the overall efficiency (Chotipanich and Lertariyanun, 2014).

Corporates such as telecommunication companies, life insurance companies and pension funds invest in buildings. They have adopted FM so as to maintain a pleasant atmosphere, safe and secure workplace. They also aim to increase the business productivity through effective management and minimisation of risk. The companies outsource FM services from service providers to ensure quality service delivery so as to meet organisational requirements (Kamarazaly *et al.* 2013). In this case key priorities are placed on occupation cost, effectiveness of support, project return on investment, organisations' image, value addition to the core business activities, environmental and sustainability issue. In turn, the concept of FM practice is emphasised on balancing between customer orientation and cost-efficiency, sustainable practices and effective adaptability to changing needs and patterns of work. In future, FM is determined to improve performance by implementing technology and improving energy saving performance through replacing building equipment with new technologies and smart systems.

The property managemental divisions mainly take care of project design and construction projects, while General Service division is responsible for security, cleaning, fleet, mailing and office service tasks. The department policy includes providing services with cost consciousness, securing major investment for new branches, implementing actions that improve the corporate identity and having single service contact point for every branch in the country. FM department concentrate on cost reduction, energy saving, health and safety, service quality through standard practice, responsiveness of space, preparation for organisation expansion and workplace design to maintain the corporate image (Chotipanich and Lertariyanun, 2014). FM departments have to oversee the whole process and plan for working more properly, work procedures and quick decisions. Their goals are centred on improving the accuracy of FM database, reducing the energy cost, increasing the customer/user satisfaction in services and effectively supporting the opening of new branches. For the future on FM department sets to establish centralised database operating costs in order to improve its ability to monitor and forecast facility performance. Moreover, they have planned to install FM software to take care of building maintenance work and asset management so as to enhance property value as well as maximising return on investment.

Facilities management is fundamentally a service industry in which people provide services to people. The topic presented in this chapter shows that facilities management is a key aspect in asset management since it requires arrangement of experts. The facilities managers in Zimbabwe face numerous challenges from both internal and external factors that prevent the accomplishment of vital objectives and outcomes due to lack of knowledge and skills in this particular profession (Isa *et al.* 2016). The study results are expected to be of advantage to any institutional facilities manager in Zimbabwe, particularly in planning and coordinating proper reaction to recognised problems in managing their assets. Represented in the table below are key areas which facilities managers have to take note of in order to manage their assets properly.

Table 6.1 Areas where Facilities Management is Practiced (IFMA, 2006)

Aspect	Description
Space management	To create adaptive working spaces, well serviced for the effective utilisation of the space in the building.
Environment	To create healthy and sustainable working environments to the workers as well as tenants.
Information technology	To support effective communications in all departments in the organisation through implementing local network area, intranet and extranet.
Support services	To provide quality services to satisfy users, for example outsourcing non-core business services such as cleaning, security to the better competitive service providers so as to satisfy tenants as well as workers.
Infrastructure	To provide appropriate capability and reliability infrastructure through effective design briefing, facilities management briefing.

From existing literature, only a few studies have considered funding elements or other issues in the implementation of FM in specific developing countries such as in Zimbabwe. A study done by Kamarazaly *et al.* (2013: 18) showed that

> the critical challenges currently facing the UFMs (Australasian university facilities managers) comprised issues relating to the following (in diminishing order of significance): inadequate funding, emergency management and business continuity planning, statutory compliance, sustainability and environmental stewardship, keeping up with rapid changes in technology, operational efficiency, identifying and meeting stakeholder needs, maintenance and manpower. Preparing for and responding to disaster/emergency was perceived as the most critical challenge of the future, perhaps, due to the recent natural disasters.

In many managerial levels in the Zimbabwean context, FM functional components are not document due lack of soft and hard skills which a facilities manager should have. Kamarazaly *et al.* (2013) also argue that;

> Facilities managers would benefit from the prioritisation mainly due to the fact that it would enable them to leverage the limited resources at their disposal to address those factors that have a higher impact on the FM functional areas.

Some property companies in Zimbabwe and corporate occupiers such as banks view Facilities management as the process by which an organisation ensures that its buildings, systems and services support core operations and processes as well as contribute to achieving its strategic objectives in changing conditions (Alexander, 2003). They focus their resources on meeting user needs to support the key role of people in organisations and strive to continuously improve quality, reduce risks and ensure value for money. It is clearly an important management function and business service. Major organisations world-wide are using it as part of their strategy for restructuring to provide a competitive edge. It can also ensure that buildings and support services improve customer responsiveness and contribute to business objectives (Alexander, 2003).

Although FM practice is lagging behind in Zimbabwe, the scope of the discipline covers all aspects of property, space, environmental control, health and safety and support services. It requires that appropriate control points are established in the organisation. The facilities department will set out these policies and identify corporate guidelines and standards. It will describe the organisation, its structure, procedures and responsibilities. Facilities management policies lay out an organisation's response to vital issues such as space allocation, environmental control and protection, direct and contract employment. The policies will set a direction for the organisation and establish the values of and attitudes towards the facilities users, the corporation, its operating units, customers, individual employees and the public. Facilities management is relevant to organisations in all sectors and in developed and developing countries. However, differences in culture and management style must be recognised when delivering the operating environment and services needed for business effectiveness in a particular context (Alexander, 2003).

Discussion and synthesis

The way to successful facilities management relies on bringing to the operation of the organisation an appropriate balance of business and technical skills. Although facility management is in our conditions progressing, it is still in the phase of searching its substance and complexity of use. In practice, it still has not reached such a status that from the point of view of advantages, it can offer such a system of company support processes as it deserves (Potkány and Babiaková, 2013). Outsourcing, with its principle of outside process utilisation; creates an environment for facility management frequent application within small and middle companies' management systems. Outsourcing of support services will result in loss of confidential information to other competitors and the issue of lack or limited control of the services as compared to offering them within the company (Potkány and Babiaková, 2013).

Despite the current practice models identified locally; FM operations being practice in the United States and United Kingdom (in particular). However, this discipline does not mean that the opportunity is limited. As mentioned before, FM ought to be advantageous for diminishing the general expense of upkeep and expanding the life of the asset or building (Isa *et al.* 2016). Factors such as absence of accessibility of technical and non-technical manpower, expanded lead times in assembling resources/staff after a project has been effectively contracted because of labour lack, an expansion in swelling and labour cost and inadequate procurement of services at low rates by chaotic industry members were among the reason why in-house facilities practiced nowadays are lagging behind (Isa *et al.* 2016). In comparison, not only in the mentioned agencies, but other such as libraries, railway stations and airports do uses anticipate the intensification of opportunities in the FM market (Isa *et al.* 2016).

On the other hand, Brackertz and Kenley (2002) argue that facilities management is becoming more widely recognised as a component in the business value chain. Ultimately, in the performance indicators that relate directly to the core business drives are keys to success of the organisation performance. Most services that are provided through facilities should relate to the main business indicators for the primary tasks such as customer satisfaction. Facilities management is the enabling function by which an organisation delivers and sustains a quality working environment for its human and physical resources so that managers can meet core business objectives (Alexander, 1999). Property in particular, as one component of an organisation's facilities, is seen as a depreciating physical cost burden rather than as an asset that, when properly managed, can add strategic value to an organisation (Berr, 1988; Tucker *et al.* 2012). One reason for this negative perception is that the connection between buildings and organisational performance is not fully appreciated (Loosemore *et al.* 2002).

However, facilities management is not limited to simply reducing operational costs or expenses of the built facility; it should focus on enhancing efficiency of physical assets as well. Effective facilities management encompasses multiple acts under various disciplines combining resources and is vital to the success of any organisation (Barret and Baldry, 2003). In order for facilities management to be effective, both the hard issues such as financial regulation and the soft issues such as managing people have to be considered. To gauge the effectiveness of facilities management, it is necessary to reach an understanding of the current conditions of the facility and to postulate changes in the facility management practices. Facility managers need to achieve the desired performance goals despite facing challenges such as non-existent pre-construction facility management provisions, financial constraints, lack of government support and late implementation of facilities management decisions. These hinder regular and efficient management of dwellings other hindrances include use of non-professional facility managers and poor administration of service charge account. They deter effective facilities management (Chotipanich and Lertariyanun, 2014).

Conclusion and policy direction

All in all, the evolution of FM in Zimbabwe starts from property management and maintenance practices. For future development of asset and facility management, programmes must integrate key activities within property and maintenance domains as part of the overall asset management plan of the physical built environment. There are many functions between property management and maintenance as well as facility and asset management that should be clearly implemented so as to have a successful FM practice in the country. There is need for a clear distinction on which services should be provided in-house (core business services) and the ones to be outsourced from service providers so as to achieve best service delivery standards in the country. In short, some scholars mentioned that the future interest for FM is very enthusiastic. As the saying goes, 'As long as buildings exist, there will be a demand for facility management'. On the other hand, the challenge is to educate building owners about the benefits of FM. The ultimate advantage of FM, such as value appreciation of the property, image and long-term cost, must be completely understood and increased by building owners for the industry to develop. In other words, building owners ought to have the capacity to see the long-term gain (Isa *et al.* 2016).

As for future recommendations regarding to facilities management practice in Zimbabwe, there is need to establish a body to regulate the profession. That has to be spearheaded as a degree program in universities and colleges to promote good FM practices. A professional development institution to support research and training requirement and a centre of FM excellence is needed in order to provide valuable information sharing. The platform must be critically considered in the future development of FM master plan. The Zimbabwean FM market is still lacking significantly on awareness and recognition of this profession in the industry. Enforcement, consolidation of acts/regulations/guidelines, government incentives and asset ratings need to be considered for future programmes that will promote good FM practices in the Zimbabwean business environment.

References

Aishah Kamarazaly, M., Mbachu, J and Phipps, R., (2013). Challenges faced by facilities managers in the Australasian universities. *Journal of facilities management*, 11(2), pp.136-151.

Alexander, K. (2003). *Facilities Management Theory and Practice*, London: Taylor and Francis e-Library.

Alexander, K., (1994). A strategy for facilities management. *Facilities*, 12(11), 6-10.

Alexander, K. (1999). *Editorial in Euro FM practice: Facilities Management*. Nieuwegein, ARKO Publishers.

Atkin, B and Brooks, A. (2014). *Total Facility Management*. John Wiley and Sons.

Barrett, P. P and Baldry, D. (2003). *Facilities Management: Towards Best Practice* (2nd Ed.). Oxford: Blackwell Publishing Ltd

Berry, R. L. (1988). Can the market create what the city wants? Boston's midtown cultural district (Doctoral dissertation, Massachusetts Institute of Technology).

Brackertz, N and Kenley, R. (2002). A service delivery approach to measuring facility performance in local government. *Facilities*, 20(3/4), pp.127-135.

Chotipanich, S and Lertariyanun, V. (2011). A study of Facility Management Strategy: the case of Commercial Banks in Thailand. *Journal of Facilities Management*, 9(4), 282-299.

Cigolini, R., Fedele, L., Garetti, M and Macchi, M. (2008). Recent Advances in maintenance and facility management. *Production Planning and Control, 19*(4), pp.279-286.

Crawley, D. B., Hand, J. W., Kummert, M., and Griffith, B. T. (2008). Contrasting the Capabilities of Building Energy Performance Simulation Programs. *Building and environment*, 43(4), pp.661-673.

Gao, X and Cao, J. (2011). The Research of Facility Management Based on Organisation Strategy Perspective. In: Zhou M. (Eds.). *Advances in Education and Management. ISAEBD 2011. Communications in Computer and Information Science*, 211. Springer, Berlin, Heidelberg

Hassanien, A and Losekoot, E. (2002). The application of facilities management expertise to the Hotel Renovation Process. *Facilities*, 20(7/8), 230-238.

International Facilities Management Association (IFMA). (2006). Empowering Facility Professionals Worldwide. Available online: http://www.ifma.org. [Accessed on 17/07/2018]

Isa, N. M., Kamaruzzaman, S. N., Mohamed, O., Jaapar, A and Asbollah, A. Z. (2016). Facilities Management Practices in Malaysia: A Literature Review. In *MATEC Web of Conferences* (Vol. 66, p.: 00054). EDP Sciences.

Kasim, R., (2011). *Community-based facilities management theory and practice.* Penerbit UTHM.

Kurdia, M. K., Abdul-Tharim, A. H., Jaffar, N., Azli, M. S., Shuib, M. N., and Ab-Wahid, A.M., (2011). Outsourcing in facilities management-A Literature Review. *Procedia Engineering, 20*, pp.445-457.

Lepkova, N and Žūkaitė-Jefimovienė, G., (2012). Study on customer satisfaction with facilities management services in Lithuania. *Slovak Journal of Civil Engineering*, 20(4), pp.1-16.

Loosemore, M., McGeorge, D., Reilly, C and McCormick, J., (2002). A customer-focused risk and opportunity management system for facilities management. In *Proceedings of the CIB W* (Vol. 70, p.: 2002).

Mat Yasin, M. F. (2013). The contributions of knowledge mapping in facilities performance evaluation practice in Malaysia (Doctoral dissertation, University of Salford).

Mohamat Nor, N. A., Mohammed, A. H., and Alias, B. (2014). Facility Management History and Evolution. *International Journal of Facility Management*, 5(1), 1-21.

Moore, M and Finch, E. (2004). Facilities management in South East Asia. *Facilities*, 22(9/10), 259-270.

NAPIC. (2009). Malaysia Commercial Property Stock Report Q3 2009 Malaysia Property Stock Report. Putrajaya, National Property Information Centre.

Noor, A. R. M., (2004). *Pengurusan hartanah komersil dan awam*. Leeds Publications.

Noor, M and Pitt, M. (2010). Defining Facilities Management (FM) in the Malaysian Perspective. In: *ERES 17th Annual Conference* (pp. 23-26).

Nutt, B. (2000). Four competing futures for facility management. *Facilities*, 18(3/4), 124-132.

Okoro, C. S and Musonda, I. (2016). Effective Facilities Management of Residential Properties: a literature review. Available online: ujcontent.uj.ac.za.

Pitt, M., Chotipanich, S., Issarasak, S., Mulholland, K and Panupattanapong, P. P. (2016). An examination of Facility Management, Customer Satisfaction and service Relationship in the Bangkok healthcare system. *Indoor and Built Environment*, 25(3), 442-458.

Potkány, M and Babiaková, M. (2013). Areas and Forms of Facility Management from the Standpoint of Slovak Enterprises. Available online: https://depot.ceon.pl/bitstream/handle/123456789/3357/D%2002%20-%20POTKANY_BABIAKOVA_areas.pdf?sequence=1andand isAllowed=y. [Accessed on 25 June 2018]

Price, I. (2002). The Complex Adaptive Workplace: A Theoretical Link between Office Design and Productivity? Available online:

https://core.ac.uk/download/pdf/294052.pdf [Accessed on 25 June 2018]

Sato. T., Sugita. H., Murakawa. S and Fujikami. T. (2004). The use of life-cycle costs data in facilities management – some comparative analysis of costs in Japan and USA. Available online: http://www.irbnet.de/daten/iconda/CIB33.pdf [Accessed on 25 June 2018]

Sui Pheng, L. (1996). Total Quality Facilities Management: a framework for Implementation. *Facilities*, 14(5/6), 5-13.

Tashev P., Dimitrov Y and Georgiev A. (2011). National survey - Facility and property management services market in Bulgaria. Available online: https://www.publics.bg/en/publications/58/National_survey_"Facility_and_property_management_services_market_in_Bulg aria".html [Accessed on 25 June 2018]

Tay, L and Ooi, J. T. (2001). Facilities management: a "Jack of all trades"? *Facilities*, 19(10), 357-363.

Then, S. S. D and McEwan, A. (2004). Capturing knowledge from facilities management practice-issues and possibilities. Available online: http://158.132.160.122/bitstream/10397/5874/1/Then_captu ring_knowledge_from.pdf [Accessed on 25 June 2018]

Thomson, T., (1990). The essence of facilities management. *Facilities*, 8(8), pp.8-12.

Tucker, M., Masuri, M. R. A and Noor, M. N. M. (2012). September. Optimising the Role of Facilities Management (Fm) in the Development Process (Dp): The Development of Fm-Dp Integration Framework for Sustainable Property Development. In *Proceedings of 28th Annual ARCOM Conference* (pp. 1355-1365).

Yu, K., Froese, T and Grobler, F. (2000). A development framework for data models for computer-integrated facilities management. *Automation in construction*, 9(2), 145-167.

Chapter 7

The institution and practice of property valuation in Zimbabwe

Wendy Tsoriyo and Geraldine Usingarawe

Introduction

Space for housing, manufacturing, leisure, business and institutional uses is supplied by the real estate industry and it has become a major driver of the national economies in most parts of the world (Europe Real Estate Yearbook, 2008) including Africa. Real estate assets change hands through transactions between different parties which include sellers, investors, buyers and renters. The exchange occurs in an imperfect property market that has problems of externalities, illiquidity, heterogeneity and indivisibility (DiPasquale and Wheaton, 1992; Barass, 1993) following negotiations between the parties or their agents. The price or rent for the transactions is reached upon through valuation. Millington (2014) defines valuation as 'the art, or science, of estimating the value for a specific purpose of a particular interest in property at a particular moment in time, taking into account all the features of the property and also considering all the underlying economic factors of the market, including the range of alternative investments.'

The definition has shown that valuation can be done for different interests in property such as freehold, leasehold and assignments among others. It also noted that valuation is time dependent because the factors that determine value, demand and supply of the requisite property market, can change with time (Mooya, 2009). Valuers tend to use five different methods when undertaking a market valuation which are comparison, investment, cost, residual and profits method. The valuer should deliver a written valuation report, which shows the market value of the property and how the assessment was done in order to reach the amount provided which is to be accepted by both parties involved in a transaction. Valuers should refer to the legislation which is applicable in their particular country, thus the relevant code of ethics, practice guidelines and show the highest level of professionalism when carrying out a valuation, regardless of the nature of the task. For a person to become a valuer, he should possess an accredited degree in Property valuation or an equivalent qualification from a recognized tertiary institution or university and the law requires the valuers to be registered with a national valuers' association in that particular country, in this case Valuers Council in Zimbabwe.

Theoretical Underpinnings

Analysing the property market from an institutional perspective, it is seen as a network of rules, conventions and relationships which collectively represent the system through which property is used and traded. The institution of property, for example, encompasses the attribution of ownership of a discrete object by a legal person, attached with certain rights and obligations (Ostrom 1990, 2010; Searle 2010). Such ownership is documented by well accepted authoritative agents and with due care on the procedures, it is subject to accountability and means of conflict resolution. The formal statement of ownership creates the institution, the norms of which the owner and others should observe. The trade for real estate is highly regularised globally. This is so because real estate has well defined property rights and are strictly controlled by different law bodies, for example zoning laws. Also, real estate market value is not simply negotiated between the parties involved in a transaction, but it is based on an assessment performed by a professional valuer. Institutional characteristics have key influence on the performance of the property sector in a particular nation and these features vary from one national property market to another and from different time-periods. These differences are important to the analysis of market behaviour and their outcomes. Institutions also reflect the interests of different groups and the judgement on efficiency will vary between them.

The global and local environment of Real Estate Industry is characterised by unprecedented changes such as volatility and uncertainty. Market information that valuers depend on to carry out their professional assignments successfully without compromising on quality derive their legitimacy from unbiased sources. For example, valuers using the comparison method usually adopt the comparative market analysis (CMA) approach and it relies on dependable market data obtained from comparable properties that are either currently or have been on the market to establish market value (McComb, 2008). Therefore, learning where correct information may be found is essential to a valuer's success. Problems associated with the valuation practice include the realisation that valuers cannot estimate correct market value that are accurate or precise (Aluko, 2007; Havard, 2001; Crosby, 2000). Even the reputable or most experienced valuers who are given the same property to value many come up with different market prices (Mooya, 2009). There is no explanation which is convincing about the inaccuracy of valuation rather than accepting that valuation is not an exact science (Havard, 2001). The problems identified include anchoring; which is a practice whereby valuers rely on the first piece of information which they find during their research to make final judgement of the market value. Client influence is also referred as a problem by which valuers allow themselves to be controlled by their client's opinion instead of relying on their own judgement.

Efforts have been made to try to resolve these problems of valuation practice. Regulations have been set for the profession and the practice is subject to the principles, guiding norms of good practice and valuation methods codified in international standards (IVSC, 2013) and regional standards. Although there are different valuations methods that are recommended nationally, the results should be comparable (Schnaidt and Sebastian, 2012). Hence, a valuer should not to be seen merely as a professional expert but rather an actor operating in an environment which is regulated (Ramsey 2004). The UK courts set forth a permissible bracket around a correct value which is between 10%-20% (Crosby 2000). Failure of valuers to exercise due diligence may end up compromising their decisions with owners of the property leading to overvaluation of the property for the purpose of selling it at a higher price or in the case of a mortgage, it may end up with a foreclosure when the mortgagor defaults in repayment of the loan. Therefore, the actors of the property market, including buyers and renters, can receive professional advices which are of high quality from qualified valuers and ensure that valuers' public reputation is protected from framing and distorted presentation of real estate market information.

Literature review

What led the evolution of institutionalist thinking in more recent years was the lack of institutional content in the core of neoclassical theory. It became an issue at theoretical level, because of new concepts and analytical tools being developed that were contrary to practical level on the comparison of market outcomes with regulatory alternatives. Concern on unregulated markets and on overregulation of markets partly motivated the revival of institution interest. However, the established formal theory was thought to be missing important elements of reality in both cases. Institutions and institutional change have been generally analysed as ways of reducing transactions costs, reducing uncertainty, internalising externalities and producing collective benefits from coordinated or cooperative behaviour. Institutions tend to provide efficient solutions to economic problems, working to select the most efficient organisational form, or set of rules, or routines.

This new institutional economics has been identified as an attempt to extend the range of neoclassical theory by explaining institutional factors, like property rights and governance structures unlike the old institutionalism, not as an attempt to replace the standard theory (Eggertsson, 1990; Furubotn and Richter, 1991, 1997). New institutional economics consist in large part of transactions cost analysis of property rights, contracts and organisations. Institutionalists' movements made positive contributions within the practice of property valuation. Bonbright's (1937) also dealt with the difference between commercial and social valuation, although emphasising on issues of the valuation of public utilities. Bonbright (1937), Hale (1921) and Glaeser (1927) all had concern on issues of public utility regulation, with Hale probably having great impact on the direction of court decisions on the "fair value" concept as a basis for rate regulation (Bonbright, 1961: 164). The courts are changing interpretation of the doctrine of "affectation with public interest," which was used to justify regulatory intervention and the "public" character of much supposedly "private" business (Tugwell, 1922; Clark, 1926; Hamilton, 1930; Fried, 1998).

The formation of market economy in 1990s resulted in the necessity to develop assessment of urban lands. The establishment of the price of urban lands was viewed not only in theory but also in practice. Moscow and St. Petersburg mostly developed the practice of establishing price of urban lands. The formation of the cadastral price for taxation encouraged the improvement of land assessment process and also the division of the cities' land to functional zones to create General plans. Market price was introduced by the federal law on appraisal activity in Russian Federation. However, in the framework of assessment of urban land cadastral price was computed in this time, there was the formation of the state cadastral land appraisal system to establish the land price. In the same time the notion "cadastral price" was not fixed in valuation legislature. Practically the land market did not exist, but only some bargains were struck.

The method of distinguishing on the basis of market information about the transactions of buying-selling and lease of dwelling and commercial real estate property determined the price. Serious distortions were obtained from the results because of mass estimation of the land cost to apply approximate price of buildings and constructions on the land. The focus on mass assessment was shifted to individual assessment during the first decade of the twenty-first century. The specialists of appraisal contributed a lot in improving current methods and approaches to assessment of urban lands. Cadastral price, according to the 65th article of the Land Code of Russian Federation, is established for taxation purposes and can be applied to determine rent for a plot of land in a state or municipal property. The cadastral price of the plot was sometimes established equal to its market price to determine the market prices of the plot of land. The urban lands market price is mostly important to show the index of investment attractiveness of the city. Market price variables of the land within the city area, shows the functional-planning structure of the city, the presence of business centres of attraction, ecological characteristics of different areas and even social-psychological characteristics, such as prestige of various city districts.

Valuation of real property is done using two major systems that are Traditional Valuation Applications (manual) and Automated Valuation Models (computerised) globally (Calhoun, n.d.; IAAO, 2003). The use of these systems requires a strong back up of a property transactions data. Automated valuation models help to store a large amount of data which they have collected for several years. It is however important to note that, "with the coming of computer technology and computerised databases, the United States regional authorities were first to implement computer assisted valuation methods" (Calhoun, n.d: 15). Automated Valuation Models (AVMs) supported by quality data has the advantage of producing objective and efficient estimates of property values. The use of property databases is now common in countries with stable and big economies in Africa, for example South Africa. It has two popular residential property data collectors which are, the Deeds Office- which is responsible for registering fixed property ownership and changes in ownership and Absa residential property market (ARPM) database – which has the duty of collecting data from financial applications in the market (Luus, 2003; Els and Von Fintel, 2008). The ARPM data are captured by property valuers onto the mainframe database before data warehouse tables are populated (Luus, 2003).

In UK, there were two main property crushes in the 1970s and 1990s respectively and result in an increase in the litigation by banks against valuers due to negligence in valuation. Therefore, the UK's valuers' professional institution, particularly the Royal Institution of Chartered Surveyors (RICS), started research into the methods of valuation and they developed guidance notes concerning the practices in the form of the Red Book and procedures in the valuation process (RICS, 1976). The Red Book continued to be expanded and developed and provided further guidance for different valuation purposes. It was suggested that the value to be tolerated would be generally ten per cent either side of the figure which should be said to be right.

Regionally, in Africa the most critical issue of property assessment in southern Africa is the lack of capacity with many of the valuation rolls being out of date in many countries except South Africa. It is also a serious problem in Kenya (Konyimbih, 1996; Olima, 2000) and Tanzania (Masunu, 2000; Masunu, 2001). Currently Nairobi, Kenya (see *IPTI Observer*, 2001) and Cape Town, South Africa (Marten, 1999) are examples of the problems of undertaking revaluations irregularly. There is a serious problem due to the capacity to assess properties properly especially for property tax purposes. The number of registered valuers is very low except in South Africa, Kenya and Tanzania and the shortage of skilled valuers and technical staff requires urgent attention. These result from the lack of proper training facilities in countries like Malawi, Botswana and Lesotho presently and in Kenya, Tanzania and Zimbabwe - to certain extent - offering appropriate academic programmes at tertiary level. Regional training facilities) should be seen as a way forward, suggesting that the national professional institutions ought to also work toward closer co-operation. International professional institutions e.g. RICS can also play a vital role in building capacity by providing appropriate practical training programmes and set sustainable goals. In Nigeria, valuers operate in an environment in which indiscipline and corruption are widespread, thus affecting their devotion to ethical codes and causing difficult challenges in the society. Furthermore, valuation market of Nigeria is characterised by a large number of small firms and a small number of large firms. There are also relatively more young valuers than old ones; the reason being that the profession is relatively new and its growth had been limited as a result of small number of institutions offering such programmes. However, there is no specialization or limitation to any specific valuation areas or property class, such as concentrating on mortgage valuations or commercial valuations. Therefore, the firms are better classified as general valuers.

Methodology

The information in this study is based on qualitative methodology and utilise mostly secondary data. Secondary data were gathered from existing literature in the form of books, reports and newspapers among others. Also, case studies from global, regional and local were used to show comparable results between the practices in those areas in which some practices maybe applied in the particular country of study. The study is analysing the practice of property valuation in Zimbabwe and some challenges have been revealed which are being faced by practitioners or valuers in this country.

Results and interpretation

Africa is a diverse continent with divergent challenges. It is a product of a history that encompasses the slave trade, colonialism, the First and Second World Wars, the Cold War and its concomitant situation, internal tribal conflicts and a myriad of post-independence challenges. The colonialists replaced Africa's pre-colonial socio-political systems with coercive laws that were enforced brutally. Particularly in areas like Zimbabwe where "settler" communities existed, development was aimed not at the whole society but only settler segments and the rest of the population lived in dire poverty. Colonialism focused on the exploitation of the large reserves of mineral, land alienation from native populations, plantation economies establishment and, more significantly, the establishment of what Wekwete (1994) terms "settler colonies." Zimbabwe being a British colony from 1890 to the year of its independence in 1980, political economy, distorted by racial, economic, political and social segregation, produced gross regional inequalities. Zimbabwe's liberal political economy after independence was built into the institutions that the independent African government inherited from their colonialist. The publication of the new policy framework of the new order was done in a document entitled "Growth-With-Equity: A Policy Statement" (Government of Zimbabwe, 1981).

During the Colonial Era (1890–1980), concession hunters were given rights by African chiefs to search for minerals in their territories. In 1890, the BSAC dispatched the Pioneer column, a mixture of soldiers and settlers, to occupy Mashonaland and thereby begin colonisation in earnest. The company raised the British flag on September 13, 1890 in Mashonaland and built a fort on the site and named it Fort Salisbury, in honour of the then–British Prime Minister Lord Salisbury. Their political framework for planning and development was racist and the urban areas were managed for the benefit of the European population. It was merely part of the colonisation process. In this regard, Rakodi maintains:

> The colonial state was a peculiar extension of the metropolitan capitalist state, intervening in the processes both of accumulation and reproduction by ensuring a labour supply, controlling labour, maintaining law and order, devising means of controlling land allocation, raising revenue to finance the colonial administration and investing in infrastructure… Urban policy required the creation of an urban population which was available on wages below the full costs of reproduction and which could pose no threat to colonial administrative control (1986: 212).

Town planning was largely a technical activity to create a built environment. An urban area was regarded as any centre with a population of more than 25 non-Africans and all urban areas were said to be on European land, according to the land tenure system established by the land commission of 1894. This was developed into the various land apportionment acts which alienated land from Africans (Moyana, 1984).

Various regulations were put in place to control the residence, labour and mobility of the indigenous populations. There was the Land Apportionment Act, No. 30 of 1930, which provided for different land rights that segregated the native Africans and prohibited them from owning any urban land and were forced into native reserves, mostly in marginal and low potential areas of the country, where they were to exist under a system of customary tenure (Moyo, 1996). The Land Apportionment Act was amended in 1961, culminating in the Land Apportionment Act Nos. 37 and 66. Regularisation of a number of anomalies in the legislation was the first amendment and secondly, provision for home-ownership schemes in the municipal townships" (Alban Musekiwa in Zinyama, *et al.* 1995: 52). The Act was later updated and amended, resulting in the Land Tenure Act No. 55 of 1969, which stressed the need for municipalities to establish decent African townships.

The Town Planning Act of 1933, moulded by the 1932 British Act, gave powers to local authorities to guide and control land-use development, thus giving the municipalities of Bulawayo, Gweru, Masvingo, Kadoma, Harare and Mutare powers to prepare urban planning schemes (Wekwete, 1987). With the coming of the automobile, it was also necessary for this act to be a control mechanism for peri-urban sprawl. The Act was later consolidated in 1945, further elaborating the role of urban planning schemes. According to Wekwete, this act resulted in the appointment of town planning officers for Harare and Bulawayo and the establishment of a town planning court that would arbitrate the conflicts between the public and private interests in urban schemes. There was also the Native (Urban Areas) Accommodation and Registration Act No. 6 of 1946, which allowed the police and municipal authorities to carry out inspections regularly in African townships and it also provided for strict control of squatters and any unlawful urban development (Wekwete, 1987). Employers were also required to provide free housing for their employees or to rent and pay for their accommodation in the townships.1973 Urban Councils Act, amended in 1980, like all the other statutes adopted from the colonial era, it is based on delegated authority. Local authorities have powers relating to development control and provision of infrastructure. Councils can raise their revenue, but only from fees and taxes on land and basic services such as water, electricity supplies, sewerage and drainage, fire services and entertainment, rather than from the operation of industrial and commercial projects (Rambanapasi, 1991).

The balance of power shifted from the white minority to the black majority after the independence in 1980 and immediately the key objective, was to change government structures and institutions in order to maximise potential benefits to the majority Zimbabweans who were formerly discriminated against. Institutionally, there was a lack of a clear mandate through which the various urban development stakeholders can operate. Planning remained a technical activity that was poorly integrated at municipal levels. After independence the most fundamental change was the democratisation of the political system and the removal of racial overtones, which removed the system of institutionalized racial discrimination whilst even the public servants also lacked professionalism in the way they conducted business and their attitude towards the public because it was a product of colonial administration.

Lacking is a participatory planning system in peri-urban areas which can effectively link people with local governments and other stakeholders, therefore service provision is weak. The Harare case confirms that state institutions continue to suffer from the lack of financial and manpower resources thus constraining the formulation of economic and social policy. Due to colonisation, the Zimbabwean urban development system in is still hierarchically structured and top-down in approach and therefore fails to mobilize community participation. Planning is failing to respond to the changing socio-economic needs of society and also lacks innovation, because planners face political pressures that tend to have short-term political gains.

The study reveals that regularisation of land started during the colonial period but it was done to benefit only the settlers, not the indigenous population. After independence policies were reviewed by the new government to allow for the benefit of the land rights to everyone. Efforts were made for house provision to those who were in urban areas because people had moved from rural areas to urban areas in search of employment to earn a living because their productive land had been taken by the settlers. Therefore, for the municipalities to raise revenue to improve service delivery, they have to set a charge for the services. Property valuation for the purpose of rating has to be done for the authorities to come up with a value to charge on the services. Valuation for rating is a statutory valuation which is required by law to be done after a certain period and in the case of Zimbabwe it is after 10 years.

Traditional Valuation - which is a manual process is the main valuation system used in Zimbabwe and property transactions data are very difficult to obtain. According to Marongwe *et al.* (2011:7) "... there is no public information on the details of urban land market transactions in Zimbabwe". He also argued that information available online from the Deeds Office is very difficult to access and is dogged with its own limitations. For example, property transactions information for registered properties is the only available one (properties with title deeds) while there are a lot of transactions of unregistered properties (properties without title deeds) in the market. This means that valuable data of unregistered properties is not captured. On the other hand, the captured selling prices of registered properties at the Deeds Office have been found to be in some cases understated for the purposes of evading payment of high transfer fees and tax such Capital Gains Tax (Marongwe *et al,* 2011). Therefore, an updated database is expected to improve both the valuation and the valuation processes by making comparables readily available and support the introduction of AVMs in the property market in Zimbabwe to produce high quality property values.

It emerged from the study that the realtors in Harare have adopted different strategies in order to surmount the scarcity of property transactions data in Harare. The two major strategies are, to rely on their own databases and experience and reliance on professional networks for comparable evidence. Realtors that have been in the industry for more than 10 years have built their own property transactions databases based on sales and rental transactions. However, these datasets do not have 'recent past transactions' that are useful when a formal valuation or a quick appraisal is needed and the databases also do not record property attributes and monetary value attached to each thus compromising their usefulness. Therefore, when undertaking a quick property valuation, the practice in Harare entails contacting four or more close professional contacts in the industry to look for valuable comparables (Mphambela, 2012). After given comparables the realtor is now supposed to visit all the suitable comparable properties and collect data which is to be used when comparing them to the subject property.

Discrepancies have been a major worry for Real Estate Institute of Zimbabwe (REIZ) as the situation raises questions about ethics and professionalism in the sector. The REIZ president, Mike Juru, raised concern on the members of the board saying they were not adhering to the valuation standards (*Financial Gazette,* February, 18, 2018). Zimbabwe on its own it does not have its own valuation standards but stated in the Valuers Act is that the profession is to be guided by the international valuation standards. With acceptable bracket set internationally which is 5%-10%, in Zimbabwe the difference can be seven-fold which raised question on the skills of the valuers, their professionalism and ethics. In different valuation purposes, there are chances were some people may try to either inflate or deflate the value of the property depending on their interests. Other valuation reports tend to worsen the disputes because of huge differences they provide. Moreover, a general manager for valuation services at Dawn Properties, raised concern against unavailability of information on recent transaction and of the same locality because the transactions are made privately between the parties involved but rather the information should be made available on websites like in South Africa. A former REIZ president, urged valuers not to be easily influenced by their clients and they should also carry out a programme called Continued Professional Development (CPD) to increase skills, knowledge and personal qualities necessary for the execution of their professional duties (Mphambela, 2012).

Discussion and synthesis

The study shows that regularisation of land started during colonisation by British implementing political systems which were the same with their countries. Some laws suppressed the Zimbabwean population because they were introducing laws which were of benefit to them and had taken all productive land; they saw Africans as a source of labour. The study reviews the efforts which were made by the Zimbabwean government after the independence to make sure that there was equality resources allocation, ensuring that people have access to good living conditions. Some systems remained which had adopted the political practices of the settlers still suppress others. Therefore, the valuation practice in Zimbabwe is done for several different reasons, although it has its own challenges which are being faced by those who practice it.

Emerging from the study are the major challenges which resulted from the lack of national property transactions database and can be summarized as, lack or delay of computerisation of government departments including the Deeds Office in Zimbabwe; dollarization of the economy in 2009; lack of the will power by either public or private organisations to take up the challenge; and economic hardships among others. Property transactions data by nature is voluminous, thus making it difficult for data to be systematically gathered and stored. Some data has been lost due to manual filing system. However, the study revealed that some government departments for example National Registry, are now computerised and plans are underway to progressively computerise all departments.

The study also reviews that the realtors in Harare have adopted diversification in terms of specializations in order to avoid the risk in the real estate business. The majority of them now tend to mix valuation of properties with auctioneering and property management – both commercial and residential no longer focus on one specialisation. Therefore, in most cases, the managing director is both a registered valuer and registered estate agent which mean this person is certified to practice valuations and also undertake agency and auctioneering in Zimbabwe. In any case, it is rare to find a firm that specialises only in the valuation of properties; rather some firms are now specializing in valuations, sales, rentals and even property development. This move towards diversification has helped real estate businesses to stay alive in the prevailing economic hardships. Furthermore, realtors that have been in business for a short period of time have been also affected by scarcity of property transactions data as compared to realtors that have been in business for long. The realtors that are fairly new in the industry are finding it difficult to attract and retain meaningful business. Their major challenge is finding valuable comparable evidence before attaching market value to a property. To survive in the property industry, you need vast experience and to create a name for yourself and interact with your colleagues. This instils confidence in you and even in the clients that you deal with. The experienced realtors pointed out that their experience and wide professional networks have been helpful when undertaking valuations. These challenges can be wiped out easily by an electronic national property database that is easily accessible to both real estate industry actors and the public at large. This will result in the elimination of information asymmetry and put all players of the market at par in terms of knowledge of the market.

Conclusion and policy direction

In conclusion, the valuation practice in Zimbabwe has to be developed day by day as new approaches to it are introduced to make it easier and quicker to arrive at an estimated market value. The government of Zimbabwe has to review some other policies towards the land-use and planning for them not to hinder the practice. As technology is changing day by day, government should also try to implement new ways of doing things in an easy manner like what other countries are doing. Attention ought to be given on improving the property database and make sure that every property has to be registered and the transactions should be publicized. The national valuation association in this case REIZ, under the umbrella of the International Valuation Standards Council (IVSC), should start reviewing and enforcing policies on mandatory continuing professional development (CPD), which should include short courses on the effectiveness of the professional. Annual CPD requirements for practicing valuers are to be reviewed and enforced to incorporate training in framing and information presentation in property marketing and advertising property. Els and Von Fintel (2008) argue that it is the responsibility of government to set up a Valuers' Registration Board in every country for the regulation of the affairs of the profession and to prevent inappropriate conduct. In addition, most of the legal system in each country should be strengthened in fighting corruption and money laundering in real estate transactions. National valuers' association and the country's government have a mandatory role in curbing unfair contract terms and corruption through their legal systems.

References

Aluko, B. T. (2007). Examining valuers' judgement in residential property valuations in metropolitan Lagos, Nigeria. *Property Management*, 25(1), 98–107.

Amin, Samir. (1972). "Underdevelopment and Dependence in Black Africa-Origins and Contemporary Forms." *Journal of Modern African Studies* 10(4) 1-10.

Bonbright, J. C. (1937). *The Valuation of Property*. New York: McGraw Hill.

Bonbright, J. C. (1961). *Principles of Public Utility Rates*. New York: Columbia University Press.

Calhoun, C. A. (n.d.). Property Valuation Methods and Data in the United States. Available online: http://www.housingfinance.org/uploads/Publicationsmanager/0112_Pro.pdf [Accessed on 25 June 2018]

Clark, J. M. (1926). *The Social Control of Busi-ness*. Chicago: University of Chicago Press.

Crosby, N. (2000). Valuation accuracy, variation and bias in the context of standards and expectations. *Journal of Property Investment and Finance*, 18(2), 130–161.

Crosby, N., Lavers, A. and Foster, H. (1998). Commercial property loan valuations in the UK: implications of current trends in valuation practice and legal liability. *Journal of Property Research*, 15(3), 183-209.

Dijkman, M. (2008). Europe Real Estate Yearbook. The Hague: Real Estate Publishers BV.

DiPasquale, D and Wheaton, W. C. (1992). The markets for real estate assets and space: A conceptual framework. *Journal of the American Real Estate and Urban Economics Association*, 20 (2), 181–198.

Eggertsson, T. (1990). Economic Behaviour and Institutions. Cambridge: Cambridge University Press.

Els, M and Von Fintel, D. (2008). Residential Property Prices in a Sub-market of South Africa: Separating Real Growth from Attribute Growth. Stellenbosch Economic Working Papers: 14/08. Available online:

https://www.ekon.sun.ac.za/wpapers/2008/wp142008/wp-14-2008.pdf. [Accessed on 25 June 2018]

Enever, N., and Isaac, D. (2002). *The valuation of property investments.* London: Estates Gazette.

Fried, B. H. (1998). The Progressive Assault on Laissez Faire: Robert Hale and the First Law and Economics Movement. Cambridge, Mass: Harvard

Furubota, E. G., and Rudolf R. (1997). Institutions and Economic Theory-The Contribution of the New Institutional Economics. Ann Arbor: University of Michigan Press.

Furubota, E. G., and Richter, R. (1991). "The New Institutional Economics: An Assessment," in Eirik G. Furubotn and Rudolf Richter, (Eds.). The New Institutional Economics. College Station, Tx, Texas A and M Press.

George, H. (1879). Progress and poverty: An enquiry into the cause of industrial depressions and of increase of want with increase of wealth. The Remedy. K. Paul, Trench and Company.

Glaeser, M. G. (1927). *Outlines of Public Utility Economics.* New York: Macmillan.

Hale, R. L. (1921). "The 'Physical Value' Fallacy in Rate Cases." *Yale Law Journal.* 30(1), 710-31.

Hamilton, W. H. (1930). "Affectation with Public Interest." *Yale Law Journal* June, 39(1), 1089-1112.

Havard, T. (2001). Valuation reliability and valuer behaviour. RICS Foundation Research Paper

Interborough Rapid Transit Company. (1904). *New York Subway: Its Construction and Equipment.* Interborough Rapid Transit Company.

Jacob, A. B. (2015). Asset valuation and the role of news in sub-Saharan Africa: Valuers' rationality and the hype dilemma, Pacific Rim; *Property Research Journal,* 21(2), 139-159Luus, C. (2003). The ABSA residential property market database for South Africa- key data trends and implications. BIS Papers Number 21. Proceedings of the IMF/BIS Conference on Real Estate Indicators and Financial Stability, Washington DC, USA. Available online http://www.bis.org/publ/bppdf/bispap21l.pdf. [Accessed on 25 June 2018]

Marongwe, N., Mukoto, S and Chatiza, K. (2011). Scoping Study: Governance of Urban Land Markets in Zimbabwe. Available online: http://www.urbanlandmark.org.za/downloads/scoping_study_gov_ulm_zimbabwe.pdf. [Accessed on 25 June]

Mooya, M. M. (2009). Market value without a market: Perspectives from transaction cost theory. *Urban Studies*, 46(3), 687–701

Moyana, H. (1984). *The Political Economy of Land in Zimbabwe*. Gweru: Mambo Press.

Moyo, S. (1996). *The Land Question in Zimbabwe*. Harare: SAPES Books.

Musekiwa, Alban. (1993). "Low-Income Housing Development in Harare: A Historical Perspective." In *Harare: The Growth and Problems of the City*, (Eds.) Lovemore Zinyama, Daniel Terera and Sioux Cumming. Harare: University

Nwuba, C. C., Egwuatu, U. S., and Salawu, B. M. (2015). Client influence on valuation: Valuers' motives to succumb. *Journal of Property Research*, 32(2), 147-172.

Ogunba, O and Ojo, O. (2007). Resolving reliability, consistency and rationality problems of professionally prepared valuations in Nigerian practice. *The Estate Surveyor and Valuer*, 30(1), 39–48.

Proudhon, P.J., (1876). *What is property? An inquiry into the principle of right and of government* (Vol. 1). BR Tucker.

Rakodi, C. (1986). "Colonial Urban Policy and Planning in Northern Rhodesia and Its Legacy." *Third World Planning Review* 8.

Rambanapasi, C. (1991). "Provincial Development Plans in Zimbabwe: An Analysis of Their Content, Structure and Methodology." Occasional paper 12. Harare: University of Zimbabwe.

Steven J. S., and Toyin F. (2005). African Urban Spaces in Historical Perspective. United States of America. New York: University of Rochester Press.

The Financial Gazette property- (MARCH 8, 2018). 'Valuation discrepancies worry REIZ'. Available online:

https://www.financialgazette.co.zw/valuation-discrepancies-worry-reiz/. [Accessed on 25 June]

The Real Estate Record Association. (1898). A History of Real Estate, Building and Architecture in New York City during the Last Quarter Century. New York: Arno Press,

Tugwell, R. G. (1922). The Economic Basis of Public Interest. New York: Augustus M. Kelley.

Wekwete, K. H. (1994). Urbanisation, urban development and management in Zimbabwe. *Planning Urban Economies in Southern and Eastern Africa. Avebury: Belmont.*

Wekwete, K. (1987). "Growth Centre Policy in Zimbabwe: A Focus on District Centres." Occasional paper no 7. Harare: University of Zimbabwe.

Chapter 8

Statutory valuation in Zimbabwe

Ruvimbo Makurira and Mike Juru

Introduction

Property valuations perform an essential role in property markets. They provide advice on prospective purchases and sales and supply material information to underpin the property lending decision. As with any legislation, the practice is guided by Land Valuation Act and Valuer's Act. The Act sets out the legislative requirements and direction for the activities identified therein and for which the Government has control. In this case, the legislation regulated to the manner in which real property is to be assessed for the purpose, inter alia of establishing site value (in the case of non-rural lands) and unimproved value (in the case of rural lands) upon which certain taxes and land rents will be applied by relevant authorities. This chapter is organised in such a way that options are provided for after identifying the benefits and challenges that valuers are facing when practicing statutory valuation. To start with, there is brief introduction which enlightens on what statutory valuation is about and reviewing some of the recent theoretical underpinnings concerning the basis of the study and the global trends of statutory provisions, that is how other valuers in other countries and continents, excluding Africa are managing their valuations whilst striking a balance with the Valuers Act and International Valuation Standards (IVSC). The method used to collect relevant data on this study is also included in this chapter. Finally, there are results on case studies regarding the challenges that valuers are facing and generally the practice of statutory valuation in Zimbabwe as information is analysed and facts are given as well as concluding with policy options.

Theoretical framework

This study is generally guided by the Sales Comparison Model. Comparison is the most widely used approach and forms the basis of any valuation (Millington, 1988; IAAO, 2003). When using this approach, a valuation is undertaken by directly comparing the property under consideration with similar properties that have been sold, thus finding its value from these past transactions (Millington, 1988; IAAO, 2003). The Hedonic Pricing Model as developed by Kain and Quigley (1970) and further improved by Sirmans, Macpherson and Zeitz (2005) will be the basis for understanding and explaining the different housing attributes that affect the ultimate property sale price in the real property market. Apart from that, the performance of the traditional comparative method of valuation will be assessed in light of the Comparative Approach theory for real estate valuation as explained by Cupal (2014). The initial procedure in the theory gives emphasis on the first stage of creating a reliable property database hence the same will be used to evaluate the reliability and credibility of valuation and appraisal values used in the real estate industry in Zimbabwe and how this has affected the performance of real estate businesses.

ICT is also important in the practice of property valuations. Valuations are undertaken for a wide variety of reasons including sales, development, mortgage financing, collateral purposes and taxation using automated valuation models with data input from current market transactions. Professionals in the field, use their market knowledge and their judgment to process property characteristics or variables using mathematical models such as discounted cash flow, cost-based method and capitalisation techniques. The models range from traditional, to advanced systems. However, the lack of market information which includes GDP and inflation forecasts which are inputs in coming up with rental over the property investment period are a major challenge. ICT can also be applied to basic activities such as property inspection forms and Computerised Maintenance Management System (CMMS). The use of software for valuations is slowly becoming widespread in the profession but there is little evidence of innovative use.

There are a number of studies which have investigated the behaviour between valuers and their clients. Working with US commercial appraisers, Kinnard, Lenk and Worzala (1997) found that two out of five appraisers were willing to revise upwards their valuation estimate at the request of their client, despite having no documentary evidence to support their client's argument for a higher valuation. Client size was found to directly affect the behaviour of the appraisers (the bigger the client, the more likely the appraisers were to revise their estimate). Gallimore and Wolverton (2000), in a survey of mortgage valuers, found that almost a third had reformulated the mortgage valuation goal, believing that this was to validate pending sale price rather than produce an objective opinion of value. Residential valuers, especially those who performed little or no other professional tasks, were particularly prone to this. This tendency, however, appeared not to be linked to experience of feedback from clients following an unsupportive valuation report. In a similar study in the US, Wolverton and Gallimore (1999) also found that residential appraisers were more likely than were commercial appraisers to have reformulated the appraisal goal to validate sale price. However, feedback from clients following an unsupportive report had a bigger impact in this respect on commercial appraisers than on residential appraisers.

Literature review

Valuation practice started in Nigeria by a handful of RICS general practice surveyors and valuers who were trained mainly in the UK in the late 1960s. By 29th August, 1975, Decree No 24 Of 1975 was promulgated to establish the Estate Surveyors and Valuers Registration Board of Nigeria as the official machinery for the regulation of the profession of estate surveying and valuation in the country. In addition, this decree gave official recognition to the Nigerian Institution of Estate Surveyors and Valuers as the national professional organisation to cater for the interest of those in real estate practice. Valuation practice fashioned in line with the UK practice continued without occasion for complaint in the 1960s and 1970s. For example, the definition of open market value as given by the RICS and adopted by the Nigerian Institution of Estate Surveyors and Valuers in her Guidance Notes on Property Valuation (NIESV, 1985) is: the best price which the sale of an interest in property might reasonably be expected to have been completed unconditionally for cash consideration on the date of valuation. Studies conducted by Ogunba (1997), Ogunba and Ajayi (2000) and Ogunba *et al.* (2005) reveal that the Nigerian valuation practitioners believed that the investment method currently provides capital value estimates that are lower than market prices. In order to use this method now, adjustment of constituent variables would be required to produce accurate capital values; and that the depreciated replacement cost method of valuation produces estimates that are closer to market prices. Therefore, it is a more realistic and appropriate method of valuing income producing property in the current economic circumstance. The issue was the inconsistency between valuation figure arrived at using theories derived from UK literature and the actual property values presented by local market evidence. Consequently, valuers manipulated of capitalization coefficient to adjust theoretically computed property value to match the actual market prices (Igboko, 1992).

In discussions with the United Kingdom (UK) valuers, a number of issues emerged relating to the structure and economics of the valuation sector. Interviewees indicated that the delivery of periodic portfolio valuation services has been characterised by economies of scale leading to the dominance of the sector by four or five providers. A commonly cited development reinforcing this concentration was consolidation trends amongst both clients and providers. However, while it was apparent that the boundaries between the two were becoming blurred, firms normally preferred to act as external rather than independent valuers in order to take advantage of possible 'spinoffs' from valuation work. When focusing on valuers, these findings prompted detailed research on the valuation formation process for periodic performance valuations. Two main issues were addressed. Firstly, the process in terms of research, timing and consultation through which valuations were produced was investigated. Secondly, the nature and extent of client influence on the valuations produced was explored. In terms of levels of effort and research, it was clear that varied with time period. In essence, annual valuations received most attention from both clients and valuers – with annual valuations being given the 'full Red Book treatment'. However, in monthly valuations, it was clear that this was not the case. Many respondents expressed scepticism on the utility of monthly valuations, given limited information flows in the property market. It was commonly held that the market was subject to lengthy 'flat' periods (Gallimore, 1997).

Valuation of real property valuation is done using two major systems that are Traditional Valuation Applications (manual) and Automated Valuation Models (computerised) globally (Calhoun, n.d.; IAAO, 2003). The use of these systems requires a strong back up of a property transactions data. Automated valuation models help to store a large amount of data which they have collected for several years. It is however important to note that, "with the coming of computer technology and computerised databases, the United States regional authorities were first to implement computer assisted valuation methods" (Calhoun, n.d: 15). Automated Valuation Models (AVMs) supported by quality data has the advantage of producing objective and efficient estimates of property values. The use of property databases is now common in countries with stable and big economies in Africa for example South Africa. It has two popular residential property data collectors which are, the Deeds Office- which is responsible for registering fixed property ownership and changes in ownership and Absa residential property market (ARPM) database – which has the duty of collecting data from financial applications in the market (Luus, 2003; Els and Von Fintel, 2008). The ARPM data are captured by property valuers onto the mainframe database before data warehouse tables are populated (Luus, 2003).

In the Brazilian context, the valuation process operates in four pillars; the engagement or instructions from the client, valuation bases, valuation methodology used and finally the method of reporting. This type of information referred to includes defining the valuation purpose, identification of the property and its purpose, the rationale and level of precision to be achieved, the report deadline and any associated conditions. There is also further reference to

135

checking documentation, legal restrictions, the typical details that should be reflected when inspecting the property, capturing the characteristics of a wider region, the choice of methodology and a market diagnosis. Further restrictions on the growth of the real estate market in Brazil have been the relative lack of engagement with the English language, commonly accepted as the international medium for business and a general lack of understanding amongst foreign investors of the Brazilian valuation culture, reporting styles and methodologies. Whilst local appraisers are very proud of their standards and the complex mathematical and methodology driven approach to value, this is far removed from international practice. Similarly, the role played by architecture and engineering professions, which is supported through local statutes, has led to a scientific and objective approach to valuation with less importance paced on the skills of the valuer, their judgement or market sentiments. This will necessitate a shift in local standards towards international best practice, a movement that is already being reflected in revisions to the current standards.

In China, there are three distinct tiers of valuation operations. The first tier consists of international firms which have the pool of expertise across a range of real estate services such as agency and management. These firms also have a good understanding of the real estate market which is well supported by their in-house research teams and actively uphold the reputation and the integrity of the profession at global, regional and local levels. The second tier comprises the top, large scale domestic firms with the capital and capability to undertake large appraisal instructions mainly from large corporations, whereas the third tier are mostly smaller appraisal firms that deal with the residential sector and offer some estate agency and property management services. Furthermore, the regulation of appraisal services on China remains fragmented, given the control of three different ministries and clear separation between land and buildings in the valuation process. As local appraisal firms are becoming better trained and more competent with central and regional government backed certification through licensing programs, perceptions of the local appraisal industry is beginning to change. Despite the increase in professionalism, it must be noted that the appraisal industry is still relatively immature; with many appraisers having yet to experience a market downturn and their awareness of market risk and economic indicators is often underdeveloped.

The appraisal approach in the US is underpinned by the mandated standards and excellent market data. The US has a strong and well-established appraisal profession and regulatory environment which includes a reputable professional body, a uniform set of standards and state level regulation of appraisers. In this regard, regulatory environment governing real estate has evolved in response to savings and loans crises of the 1980s and 1990s. Therefore, legal provisions now ensure that real estate appraisers follow a prescriptive and rules-based approach to property appraisal. However, the remit of US standards is wider than real property as they also cover mass appraisal, business valuation and personal property appraisal. There is increasing pressure on the appraiser practice in US from both the financial reporting and accountancy standards, especially in relation to fair value appraisal. Furthermore, the International Valuation Standards (IVS) and RICS Red Book are becoming more prominent in their use especially for international transactions, despite the US standards remaining the only mandatory standard applicable to local appraisers. In this regard, local appraisers are beginning to recognise the importance of being aware of international valuation, accounting and financial standards.

The chartered surveying profession, presided over by the RICS, provides a strong context for valuation regulation and practice in the UK. Broad ethics that govern the UK valuers can be linked directly to the RICS and its royal charter which requires the profession to work for public advantage and therefore display excellence and integrity. Both the RICS and IVSC have been proactive in developing standards or codes of principle relating to ethical behaviour, to ensure that valuers are aware of their wider ethical responsibilities not only to the profession but also the public. The RICS, as the world's oldest, most established and recognised professional body for chartered surveyors has an increasing global membership, all of whom accept the responsibilities and standards to be upheld in representing the profession through RICS membership and compliance with the Red book. The RICS Red Book acts as the main property valuation standard in the UK although recent editions have also reproduced the IVS in its entirety to ensure members are reflecting the international nature of property investment and valuation. This is a somewhat unique position for a local standard to adopt and converge with the complete IVS text, but again demonstrates the increasingly important role played by international property standards. A further unique aspect of the property valuation community in the UK is the open sharing of market information between competitor firms and within in-house agency and valuation departments.

Valuation is regarded as a "matter of opinion subjective to an individual's assessment of different factors" (Isaac, 2002: 7). As a result, valuation standards at national and international levels play important roles in the promotion of ethics, integrity and impartiality in valuers (Hemphill, Lim, Adair, Crosby and McGreal, 2014). Controversy surrounding the field of valuation calls for the critical analysis of valuation theory and the creation of frameworks for members of the valuation profession to adhere to in their normal practices (Australian Property Institute, 2007). Anecdotal evidences found in Fiji highlighted the needs for standardisation to be implemented in the valuation sector (Myers, 2013). Not on par with international practices, the valuation profession in Fiji had been administered by the Valuers Registration Act 1986, which was only responsible for determining the suitability of approved persons for registration as valuers (ACT No. 7 of 1986, 1986). The Act lacked in-depth information on day-to-day valuation practices, code of conduct and standards. Therefore, there had been calls for the implementation of formal valuation practice standards in the country (Myers, 2013). Recent developments in the field have assured adoption of the IVS from 1st January, 2016 and the creation of an Act of Parliament to regulate valuation practices post registration. Yet, the field will still face issues preventing it from fully standardising its practices. This chapter therefore outlines challenges that will remain, categorized into institutional, informational and technical domains.

Methodology

Relevant also are a range of other support documents and procedures to assist in effecting successful outcomes. These include government and departmental regulations and guidelines, valuation principles and information sources, alternative dispute resolution processes and quality control, statistical analysis, reporting arrangements and, where necessary, litigation. Secondary data were gathered from existing literature in the form of books, reports and newspapers among others.

Results

In 1944, auctioneers and estate agents in the then Rhodesia were represented by two separate associations and at a meeting of the Bulawayo Association, held on 5th December, 1944, it was decided to form an Institute embracing all the members of the two associations. The following year on 12 February, 1945 an inaugural meeting of the Southern Rhodesia Institute of Estate Agents and Valuers was held and the first members were duly elected. On 5 May 1947, a constitution, rules and by-laws were adopted, under which the Institute pursued its objectives which resulted in the Estate Agents Act [chapter 220]. The main purpose of the Estate Agents Act [Chapter 220] is to unite in one body all persons concerned with the profession of an auctioneer, estate agent and Valuer. It set to secure advancement and facilitate the acquisition of knowledge which, from time to time, constitutes the professions of Auctioneering, Estate Agency and Valuation and to maintain and promote the usefulness of these professions for the public advantage. The Act aimed to protect and promote the general interest of its members and the professions of Auctioneering, Estate Agency and Valuation.

With evolving developments in the real estate industry, there was need to further separate estate agency from valuation work. This subsequently led to parliament separately enacting the Valuers Act (Chapter 27:18) and the Estate Agents Act (Chapter 27:17). Prior to the formalisation of the real estate profession in Zimbabwe, anyone could freely enter and exit without being accountable as the industry was not regulated. Against such a background, there was need to come up with means of formalising the profession and bring order. This need saw the formalisation of the profession through the enactment of the above-named statutes. The Valuers Act makes it mandatory for all Valuers to be registered with the Valuers Council established by the law. The same applies to Estate Agents who should register as Estate Agents with the Estate Agents Council before practising. This process of registration has made it possible to establish standardised approaches to promoting fair and equitable practice amongst the members through dictating how agents should act towards each other and the general members of public as enshrined under Professional Conduct Rules.

The Real Estate Institute of Zimbabwe has called for more professionalism among players in the real estate industry in order to gain public confidence. The public has over the past years been slowly losing confidence in some of the estate agents because of lack of professionalism in the discharge of their duties. In the bid to make sure that professionalism and transparency continues to prevail in the industry, the institute has introduced the Continued Professional Development Policy (CPD). CPD is a commitment by members of the Real Estate Institute of Zimbabwe to continually update their skills, knowledge and capabilities in order to remain professionally competent, relevant and achieve their optimized potential. Embodied in it is an appeal and requirements for all members of the Institute to seek education and practical skills continuously so as to enhance their practice and improve public confidence in their service.

Undertaking CPD is an individual responsibility. In identifying needs, individual members should be focused, plan consistently and review regularly their progress. Employers in the process should also support the process of identifying the learning needs and satisfying them. Individuals are expected to explore all avenues of relevant skills enhancement. Speaking during the REIZ Valuation Seminar held on the 27th of March 2015, Mr. Mike Juru made great emphasis on the need to keep an eye on corporate governance issues that also have a greater inclination with the concept of professionalism. In his cited definition of corporate governance is "the process by which corporations are made responsive to the rights and wishes of stakeholders" (Demb and Neubauer, 1992) the tone has been set clearly that modalities should be put in place on a professional background to make sure all stakeholders in the real estate industry are satisfied by the service they get. Mr. Juru emphasised the key elements of corporate governance which he pronounced as compliance, ethical, transparency, professionalism, honesty and integrity. He indicated that the role of the Board is to ensure corporate governance and professionalism. It involves strategy formulation, behaviour and performance monitoring of executives and the organisation, policy formulation, compliance with the laws, statutes and regulations and to ensure effective procedures for auditing. Taking a cue from his presentation, there is greater need to develop, enhance and maintain professionalism for the greater success and integrity of the real estate industry.

The real estate sector has become one of the safe havens for investors seeking meaningful returns (Baker, 2001). However, this sector thrives on property transactions data collection and manipulation especially when undertaking valuation and appraisal of properties (Calhoun, n.d.; International Association of Assessing Officers [IAAO], 2003; Luus, 2003; Cupal, 2014). In Zimbabwe, public access to property transactions data are not only difficult, but close to impossible (Marongwe, Mukoto and Chatiza, 2011). The absence of national property transactions database has not only hindered the introduction of automated valuation systems but has also hampered the quality and credibility of property values produced by valuation and appraisal processes. Information asymmetry has been exacerbated by lack of commitment from agents, whether public or private, to take the initiative and responsibility of collecting and constantly updating an electronic national property transactions data for the purposes of aiding future valuation and appraisal processes. According to Marongwe *et al.* (2011) the Deeds Office has a small database that is not only difficult to access but is also limited to registered properties disregarding unregistered properties that have flooded the real property market.

Therefore, it has become important to investigate the impact of information asymmetry caused by the non-existence of a national transaction database that captures both registered and unregistered properties in Zimbabwe. This chapter explores the implications of data deficiency that exists in the real estate industry in Zimbabwe to realtors. The major questions inquired in this chapter are; why is it difficult to create a national property transactions database in Zimbabwe? How are real estate businesses coping in the absence of a national property transactions database? What are the impacts of information asymmetry to different real estate businesses – differentiated along experience and lengthy of time in business?

Various regulations in Zimbabwe were put in place to control the residence, labour and mobility of the indigenous populations. There was the Land Apportionment Act, No. 30 of 1930, which provided for different land rights that segregated the native Africans and prohibit them from owning any urban land and were forced into native reserves, mostly in marginal- and low-potential areas of the country, where they were to exist under a system of customary tenure (Moyo, 1996). The Land Apportionment Act was amended in 1961, culminating in the Land Apportionment Act Nos. 37 and 66. Regularisation of a number of anomalies in the legislation was the first amendment and secondly, provision for home-ownership schemes in the municipal townships" (Alban Musekiwa in Zinyama, et al. 1995: 52). Financial constraints, however, meant that Africans could not afford the full cost of a house and land, the development of infrastructure services. The Land Apportionment Act was later updated and amended, resulting in the Land Tenure Act No. 55 of 1969, which stressed the need for municipalities to establish decent African townships.

Traditional Valuation, which is manual, is the main valuation system used in Zimbabwe and property transactions data are very difficult to obtain. According to Marongwe et al. (2011:7) "...there is no public information on the details of urban land market transactions in Zimbabwe". He also argued that information available online shows that the Deeds Office is very difficult to access and is affected by its own limitations, for example, property transactions information for registered properties is only available (properties with title deeds) while there are a lot of transactions of unregistered properties (properties without title deeds) in the market. This means that valuable data of unregistered properties is not captured. On the other hand, the captured selling prices of registered properties at the Deeds Office have been found to be in some cases understated for the purposes of evading payment of high transfer fees and tax such as Capital Gains Tax (Marongwe *et al.*). Therefore, an updated database is expected to improve both the valuation and the valuation processes by making comparable information readily available and support the introduction of AVMs in the property market in Zimbabwe to produce high quality property values.

Discussion and synthesis

In line with the major aim of this research, it may be said that the practice of statutory valuation has raised a number of further questions concerning the use and impacts of valuations and the process by which prices were formed during the practice. The initial research highlighted the practice of valuers in Zimbabwe. As a result, detailed research was carried out into the process by which periodic valuations were produced and for this purpose how they reached performance measurement organisations in their final form. The examination of the evidence revealed a number of strands to the research which are the market structure of valuation providers; the role of valuations in the acquisition and disposal process; the effect of valuations on trading; the valuation 'production process'; client influence on valuations; the issue of the status of different valuations; and the accuracy of and lag in valuations. The research suggested that valuers and market participants are having challenges as they are using different methodologies to estimate price. This is because the fund manager/owners are carrying out explicit cash flows to determine bids whilst the conventional comparison-based approaches are still being used by valuers to determine market value.

Conclusion

This study has revealed the inadequacy of a standard valuation practice being used by the Zimbabwean real estate appraisers and hence confirmed the need for valuers to employ techniques that will enhance the quality of valuation services rendered to their clients.

Despite the scarcity of property transactions data in the real property market in Harare, the realtors are managing especially those who are experience and have been operating for long. The experience they have gained over time and wide professional networks have been helpful in their valuation and property appraisal endeavours. However, an electronic national property transactions database is lacking and will greatly improve operations in the real property market. This can lead to the development of automated valuation models that in turn improve efficiency in the valuation process and the quality of property values produced. Consequently, this will advance the business operations of the actors in the real estate industry and also improve the performance of new entries in the real estate business.

The study further revealed that, in spite of the obvious need for the standard valuation practice, there is a low level of awareness, understanding and usage of these Acts by valuers. The inability of the majority of these appraisers to understand the theoretical basis underlying these valuation techniques could be linked to the nature and content of their practice. This need for Estate Surveyors and Valuers to provide qualitative service to their clients calls for changes in academic programs and universities offering courses in estate management as well as the post qualification professional training provided by the Valuers Institute of Zimbabwe and the Real estate Institute of Zimbabwe. In this regard, the Valuers Institute of Zimbabwe and the Real estate Institute of Zimbabwe is urged to formulate policies that will promote the promulgation and discussion of ideas, opinions and issues related to these areas.

References

Act No. 7 of 1986. (1986, March 21). Valuers Registration Act, 1986. Fiji: Parliament of Fiji.

Australian Property Institute. (2007). Valuation Principles and Practice (2nd Ed.). ACT: Australian Property Institute, Australia.

Baker, B. (2001, January). Residential rental real estate: An investment in need of a theory. Proceedings of the Pacific Rim Real Estate Society Conference, Christchurch, New Zealand. Available online: http://www.prres.net/papers/baker_residential_rental_real_estate_an_investment.pdf. [Accessed May 22, 2018].

Calhoun, C. A. (n.d.). Property Valuation Methods and Data in the United States. Available online: http://www.housingfinance.org/uploads/Publicationsmanager/0112_Pro.pdf [Accessed May 22, 2018].

Cupal, M. (2014). The Comparative Approach theory for real estate valuation. Procedia- *Social and Behavioural Sciences*, 109(2014), 19-23Gallimore, P and Wolverton, M. L. (1997). Price knowledge induced bias: a cross – cultural comparison. *Journal of Property Valuation and Investment*, 15(3), 261-73.

Gallimore, P., and Wolverton, M. L. (2000). The objective in valuation: a study of the influence of client feedback. *Journal of Property Research*. 17(1) 47-58

Hemphill, L., Lim, J. L., Adair, A., Crosby, N and McGreal, S. (2014). The Role of International and Local Valuation Standards in Influencing Valuation Practice in Emerging and Established Markets. London: Royal Institute of Chartered Surveyors.

Igboko, N. P. (1992). Research project on Valuation Methods in Nigeria with special reference to Years Purchase. Research report for the Nigeria Institution of Estate Surveyors and Valuers, 1 – 43.

Kain, J. F and Quigley, J. M. (1970). Measuring the value of house quality. Journal of the American Statistical Association, 65(330), 532-548. Available online: http://urbanpolicy.berkeley.edu/pdf/KQ_JASA70.pdf [Accessed May 22, 2018].

Kinnard, W. N., Lenk, M. M and Worzala, E.M. (1997). Client pressure in the commercial appraisal industry: how prevalent is it? *Journal of Property Valuation and Investment*, 15 (3), 233-44.

Luus, C. (2003, October). The ABSA residential property market database for South Africa- key data trends and implications. BIS

Papers Number 21. Proceedings of the IMF/BIS Conference on Real Estate Indicators and Financial Stability, Washington DC, USA. Available online http://www.bis.org/publ/bppdf/bispap21l.pdf [Accessed May 22, 2018].

Marongwe, N., Mukoto, S and Chatiza, K. (2011). Scoping Study: Governance of Urban Land Markets in Zimbabwe, Harare. Available online: http://www.urbanlandmark.org.za/downloads/scoping_study_gov_ulm_zimbabwe.pdf. [Accessed May 22, 2018].

Millington, A. F. (1988). *An introduction to property valuation* (3rd Ed.). London: The Estates Gazette Limited.

Moyo, Sam. 1996, *The Land Question in Zimbabwe.* Harare: SAPES Books Press.

Musekiwa, A. (1993). "Low-Income Housing Development in Harare: A Historical Perspective." In *Harare: The Growth and Problems of the City*, (Ed.). Lovemore Zinyama, Daniel Terera and Sioux Cumming. Harare: University

Myers, M. (2013). International Valuation Standards: Coming Soon to Fiji. Fiji Institute of Valuation and Estate Management Annual Conference 2013. Nadi: Fiji Institute of Valuation and Estate Management.

Ogunba, O. A. (1997). A study of Valuation and Pricing Practices in the Residential Property Market in Lagos Metropolis. MSc Thesis submitted to The Department of Estate Management, Obafemi Awolowo University and Ile-Ife.

Ogunba, O. A., and Ajayi, C. A. (2000). A Critique of the Conduct of Valuation in Lagos Metropolis; Contemporary issues in Real Estate. *Journal of the Department of Estate Management University of Lagos,* 2(4), *1-18.*

Royal Institution of Chartered Surveyors. (1994). The Mallinson Report: report of the Presidents" Working Party on Commercial Property Valuations. London: RICS.

Sirmans, S., Macpherson, D. A and Zeitz E. N. (2005). The composition of hedonic pricing models. *Journal of Real Estate literature*, 13(1), 3-43

The Herald. (2017). ICT changing face of Zim real estate, Zimpapers Herald, Harare, Zimbabwe.

Wolverton, M. L., and Gallimore, P. (1999). Client Feedback and the Role of the Appraiser. *Journal of Real Estate Research.* 18(3), 415-432.

Chapter 9

Real estate, green urbanism and environmental sustainability

Zebediah Muneta and Wendy Tsoriyo

Introduction

In this chapter the future of sustainable green urbanism, real estate and technology are discussed. In current times, there is a great need of green urbanism, sustainable environments and recognition in the Zimbabwean real estate industry that all these three aspects are being demanded in order to attain high levels of investment opportunities and improves the national output. Firstly, cities in Zimbabwe are lagging behind in terms of growth of the real estate sector. Urban areas are not being developed in a sustainable way which favours green environments to reduce pollution levels and this has direct impact to climate change. Secondly, urban environments are places where most of economic activities occur and have encountered generation of renewable energy as well as other sustainability transitions. The other key aspect which is also recognised in this chapter is the importance of the real estate industry to achieve high levels of sustainability in the country since there is increased exposure of urban populations to a spectrum of uncertain developments and climate impacts. Sustainability has long been a part of urbanism, however, in completely different ways in different periods in history. When learning from the past, the analysis of sustainable urbanism brings about several aspects, which show that sustainable urbanism has evolved. Key characteristics of each period may and can still be used to design sustainable cities (Roggema, 2016). Based on these characteristics two strategies and a potential third one, have been identified to fix the future, to indulge the future and to create anti-fragile urban environments. Where fixing the future implies the reparation of environmental qualities and closing environmental flows within the urban boundaries, indulging the future focuses on the creation of sufficient space to accommodate the possible spatial impacts of unprecedented events and change. Anti-fragility supports the city in raising its resilience under threat of uncertain impacts (Roggema, 2016).

Theoretical framework

In this section of the chapter, we proffer a discussion of the meanings of new urbanism, green urbanism, real estate and sustainability from various scholars. New urbanism is an urban design movement, which arose in the USA in the early 1980s, promoting walkable, mixed-use neighbourhoods and transit-oriented development, seeking to end suburban sprawl and promote community (Lehmann, 2010). Its characteristics include narrow streets, wide sidewalks and higher densities; qualities which we can all find in the European cities where more of mixed land-uses are being practiced due to scarcity of land. Green urbanism is a conceptual model for zero-emission and zero-waste urban design, which arose in the 1990s to promote compact energy-efficient urban development, transform and re-engineer existing city districts and regenerate the post-industrial city centre (Lehmann, 2010). Furthermore, in the case of environmental sustainability, some green urban spaces such as parks, forests, green roofs, streams, and community gardens, provide critical ecosystem services (Wolcha, Byrne and Newell, 2014). They promote physical activity, psychological well-being and the general public health of urban residents.

This chapter reviews the Anglo-American literature on urban green space, especially parks and compares efforts to green US and Chinese cities. Most studies reveal that the distribution of such space often disproportionately benefits predominantly white and more affluent communities (Wolcha, Byrne and Newell, 2014). Many US cities have implemented strategies to increase urban green space, especially in park-poor neighbourhoods. Strategies include greening of remnant urban land, reuse of obsolete utiliser and revamping underutilised transportation infrastructure. Similar strategies are being employed in Chinese cities where there is more state control of land supply despite similar market incentives for urban greening. In the Zimbabwean context, some of the green spaces in the cities are lacking effective maintenance since the responsible authorities do not have adequate knowledge of the green effect. Greening such spaces, will reduce pollution and improve the land value through proper and effective management of natural resources. However, urban green space strategies may be paradoxical. While the creation of new green space to address environmental justice problems can make neighbourhoods healthier and more aesthetically attractive, it also can also increase housing costs and property values (Wolcha, Byrne and Newell, 2014). Ultimately, this can lead to gentrification and a displacement of the very residents the green space strategies were designed to benefit. Urban planners, designers and ecologists, therefore, need to focus on urban green space strategies that are 'just green enough' and that explicitly protect social as well as ecological sustainability.

Literature review

Looking back in time at the evolution of sustainable urbanism, environmental sustainability has always been a central theme in green urbanism and real estate. It brings out the famous image of the architectural designs on the landscape hence improving natural values on land for developing cities in a sustainable way. In this case, many cities should be recognised as ecosystems, green lands and others with urban designs, such as the garden city movement (Howard, 1902) and the modern city of Le Corbusier (Cohen and Benton, 2008) and Frank Lloyd Wright's Broadacre city (Wise, 2013). All these aspects are there to incorporate roles of citizens and the local scale, giving attention to health, greening the city, renewable energy and recycling. Roggema, (2016) define urban sustainability as a multi-layered concept in which aesthetics is equally as important as economic viability and ecological value. On the other hand, sustainability is not similar to environmental quality as a high environmental quality only does not guarantee high sustainability. Similarly, an urban environment with a high environmental quality or a high economic value, but without beauty is also not sustainable (Roggema, 2016).

Firstly, for cities to be considered sustainable they must have efficient transport and good public space that are compact. They should be poly-centric cities good public space networks and efficient low impact public transport system for post fossil fuel mobility. How can we get people out of their cars, to walk, cycle and use public transport? Good access to basic transport services is crucial, as it helps to reduce automobile dependency and it does reduce the need to travel. We need to see integrated non-motorised transport, such as cycling or walking and, consequently, bicycle pedestrian friendly environments, with safe bicycle ways, free rental bike schemes and pleasant public spaces. It is important to identify the optimal transport mix that offers inter-connections for public transport and the integration of private and public transport systems. Some ideas here include: eco-mobility concepts and smart infrastructure (electric vehicles); integrated transport systems (bus transit, light railway, bike stations); improved public space networks and connectivity and a focus on transport-oriented development (`green TODs'). It is a fact that more and wider roads result in increased car and truck traffic, more carbon dioxide emissions and allows for sprawling development and suburbs that increase electricity-demand and provide less green space. The transport sector is responsible for causing significant greenhouse-gas emissions ranging above 20 percent. To combat this effect, we need to change our lifestyles by, for example, taking public transport, avoiding driving cars or pooling them. Alternatively, we can ride a bike or walk, if the city district has been designed for it. Personal arrangements have the potential to reduce commuting and to boost community spirit. We want a city district which is well-connected for pedestrians, has streetscapes that encourage a healthy, active lifestyle where residents travel less and less by car. `Green TODs' are the future, as these developments can create a range of medium-density housing typologies and provide a variety of transportation choices, achieving a balance of residences and employment.

For a country to attain effective green urbanism, it has to have local and sustainable materials with less embodied energy to be used during construction of its infrastructure, City construction should utilise regional, local materials with less embodied energy. What kind of materials are locally available and appear in the region? The various aspects of this principle of green urbanism includes advanced material technologies, using opportunities for shorter supply chains, where all urban designs focus on local materials and technological know-how, such as regional timber in common use (Lehmann, 2010). Affordable housing can be achieved through modular prefabrication. Prefabrication has come and gone several times in modern architecture, but this time, with closer collaboration with manufacturers of construction systems and building components in the design phase, the focus will be on sustainability. There is need to support innovation and be aware of sustainable production and consumption, the embodied energy of materials and the flow of energy in closing life-cycles as well as the importance to emphasise green manufacturing. It is vital to establish an economy of means, such as process-integrated technologies that lead to waste reduction (Lehmann, 2010). It is more environmentally friendly to adopt lightweight structures, enclosures and local materials with less embodied energy requiring minimal transport. We need improved material and system specifications, supported by research in new materials and technological innovation; reduced material diversity in multi-component products to help facilitate the design for resource recovery, disassembly, value retention and the possibility of reusing entire building components. Success in this area will increase the long-term durability of buildings, reduce waste and minimise packaging.

On the aspect of sustainability strategies for cities in developing countries, designers should harmonise the impacts of rapid urbanisation and globalization growth. What are the specific strategies and measurements we need to apply for basic low-cost solutions appropriate to cities in the developing world? Developing and emerging countries have their own needs and require particular strategies, appropriate technology transfers and funding mechanisms (Lehmann, 2010). Cities in the developing world cannot have the same strategies and debates as cities in the developed world. Similarly, particular strategies for emerging economies and fast-growing cities are required, as is the problem of informal settlements, urban slums and slum upgrading programs. Low-cost building and mass housing typologies for rapid urbanisation are required in cooperation with poverty reduction programs. It is essential that we train local people to empower communities, creating new jobs and diversifying job structures so as not to focus on only one segment of the economy (e.g. tourism). Achieving more sustainable growth for Asian metropolitan cities is a necessity. Combating climate change, which was mainly caused through the emissions by industrialised nations and which is having its worst effect in poorer countries in Africa, Asia and Latin America, with a focus on Small Island States, is a priority (Lehmann, 2010).

Many new urbanisms have to consider their alliance with the environmental movement. Without the specific design principles provided by New Urbanism, efforts to achieve compact development, open-space preservation and transportation alternatives fail. People will resist living in higher-density environments unless professional design an array of benefits (walkable streets, well-designed town centres, access to transit and high-quality urban design). In this view, New Urbanism defines planning strategy from the region down to neighbourhoods and individual building on the principles of sustainability and smart growth. Written policies are not enough. Planning professionals must provide detailed templates for new sustainable urban growth. Newly implemented models for sustainable development should comply with modern urbanisation and development goals. It therefore prioritises conversation and protection, enhancing the natural recovery-oriented approach. Furthermore, the models strive to establish ecological concepts, improve the ecosystem, maintain ecological safety and optimise the environment. In addition, it preserves resources, protects the environmental formation of spatial patterns, and promotes industrial structure, mode of production and lifestyle (Chaochao *et al.* 2015). To fully understand the current critical environmental situation in order to protect the principle of priority, adhere to the conservation of resources and change the development mode.

The first plan of action is to stick with the existing urban and rural areas in order to improve public ownership of land, strengthen the regulation of urban and rural planning as well as laying tracks for orderly urbanisation. China has 7% of the total global arable land to support 21% of the world's urban population, which means that it is explaining the period of rapid development of urbanisation. We have paid great attention to the protection and conservation of arable land, the establishment of arable land's red line, to protect arable land and meet agricultural production needs. Authorities should value science and good urban planning, improving land-use efficiency, utilising land of Hollowed villages and prohibit overextension. Secondly, they should transform industrial development, vigorously develop green GDP, develop low carbon economy as a new driving force of urbanisation, optimize the structure in the eastern region, improve efficiency, reduce consumption, protecting the environment, expand advanced manufacturing equipment, support strategic emerging industries and modern services as well as promote the development of marine economy. In order to foster development of new urban agglomerations, cities in the western region should designate "ecological red-line" based on strict protection of the ecological environment. City designers would guide the market through cost-effective transfer of labour-intensive industries that prioritise the mid-west. This would absorb returnees and foster transfer of nearly of eastern migrant workers, speed up industrial cluster development and population concentration (Chaochao *et al.* 2015).

Third, in order to build an ecological civilisation as a guide, to promote the construction of beautiful countryside, combining Urban and Rural Land Circulation, planners should vigorously develop modern agriculture, improve its technological content maximise the efficient use of arable land, achieve economies of scale and intensive pollution reduction. Moreover, there is need to promote the coordinated development of urban and rural differences, so as to maintain a reasonable rate of urbanisation and sustainable development. In addition, it is vital to effectively strengthen the rural areas, by strengthening basic position of the development of agriculture and farmers. Development of resource-saving and promotion of the environment-friendly agriculture, preserve and carry forward the fine traditional culture, the natural ecology of rural farming patterns, clean water and soil, food production capacity. This helps to maintain the beautiful natural landscapes, resources and development of specialised tourism (Chaochao *et al.* 2015).

Fourth, there should be commitment to basic state policy of conserving resources and protecting the environment. The unit GDP energy consumption, resource consumption included in local government assessment should focus on improving the resources, energy efficiency and protection of mineral resources, the origin of the environment from damage. We should reduce pollutant emissions per unit of GDP, in the development process of urbanisation give attention to the construction of infrastructure; eliminate "Treatment after Pollution". There should be efforts to improve the protection and management of water resources, banning all that affects the water security of the project launched (Chaochao *et al.* 2015).

Fifth, give priority to the development of public transport and promote green travel, scientific planning road network as well as the development of intelligent transportation. Start from a rational allocation of urban space resources; strengthen transportation demand management, promotion of urbanisation and motorisation harmonious development. All plans should be people-oriented, to protect the rights of citizens to travel, provide multi-ways to solve the travel problems and strictly control the number of cars and motor vehicle lanes of the area. There is need to protect the right of way for the city's non-motorised vehicles, improve environmental standards of the car, promote the development of new energy vehicles, reduce usage of private small automobiles (Chaochao *et al.* 2015).

Methodology

The study is a desk review which utilised various secondary data sources from reports, journals, PhD and masters' dissertations books as well as some internet websites. Literature review enabled lessons to be drawn from global and regional experiences while document review was mostly used to explore local cases in Zimbabwe.

Results

The increase of urbanisation in the whole world during the 20th century has brought about designs, innovations and practices for sustainable green environments. It shows that, both Western capitalist and communist countries adopted urban development in their countries. Urban liberalism and privatisation were sometimes reluctantly implemented by most communist countries. Countries like China and Russia, which resented economic non-interventionist policies, however, adopted a liberal approach to urban development in the 20th century (Nyandoro and Muzorewa, 2017). Ding and Lichtenberg (2009:1) note that the expansion of Chinese cities has been catalysed by the creation of a secondary market, which gave the private sector long-term leasing rights to urban land. The private sector's intervention in property development and policies have accounted for the rapid expansion of cities like Shanghai, Guangdong and Guangzhou in China (Ding and Lichtenberg 2009:1). Similarly, private urban land developers in Zimbabwe consisted of land developing companies, unit trusts, building societies and life insurance companies that are taking part in the construction of sustainable structures which are environmentally friendly. According to Marongwe *et al.* (2011:36), private institutional investors were responsible for about 85% of all property and land development in Zimbabwe's urban areas. The activities of building societies can be traced back to the enactment of the Building Societies Act in 1951.

A city with special concern for affordable housing, mixed-use programs and healthy community reflects a sustainable and conducive environment for habitation. How does urban design recognize the particular need for affordable housing, to ensure a vibrant mix of society and multi-functional mixed-use programs? Land-use development patterns are the key to sustainability. A mixed-use (and mixed-income) city delivers more social sustainability and social inclusion and helps to repopulate the city centre. Demographic changes, such as age, are a major issue for urban design. It is advantageous for any project to maximise the diversity of its users. Different sectors in the city can take on different roles over a 24 hours cycle. For example, the Central Business District is

157

used for more than just office work. In general, needs are connected and compact communities built for a liveable city, applying mixed-use concepts and strategies for housing affordability whilst simultaneously offering different typologies for different housing needs.

To this end, we need affordable and liveable housing together with new flexible typologies for inner-city living. These mixed-use neighbourhoods (of housing types, prices and ownership forms) have to avoid gentrification and provide affordable housing with districts inclusive for the poor and the rich, young and old and workers of all walks of life. It should also provide secure tenure (ensuring 'aging in place'). Housing typologies need to deal with demographic changes. We have to understand migration and diversity as both an opportunity and a challenge. Mixed land-uses are particularly important as it helps reduces traffic. Master plans should require all private developments to contain 40 to 50 per cent of public (social) housing and have it integrated with private housing. Higher densities should centre on green TODs. Essentially, these changes will aim to introduce more sustainable lifestyle choices, with jobs, retail, housing and a city campus being close by with IT and tele-working from home significantly helping to reduce the amount of travel (motto: 'Don't commute to compute'). By integrating a diverse range of economic and cultural activities, we avoid mono-functional projects, which generate a higher demand for mobility. Green businesses would be supported through the use of ethical investments to generate funding. The question is: how specific or adaptable should buildings be to their use?

There is a general consensus among planners and scholars that mixed land-use has an important role in achieving sustainable urban form. Mixed-use or heterogeneous zoning allows compatible land-uses to be located in close proximity to one another and thereby decrease the travel distances between activities. Mixed land-use indicates the diversity of functional land-uses such as residential, commercial, industrial, and institutional as well as those related to transportation. Reducing the need for travel is on the agenda of achieving sustainable urban form and mixed land-use has a prominent role in achieving it. Mixed land-use reduces the probability of using a car for commuting, shopping and leisure trips, since jobs, shops and leisure facilities are located nearby (Alberti 2000; Van and Senior 2000). Mixing uses ensures that many services are within a reasonable distance, thus encouraging cycling or walking (Thorne and Filmer-Sankey, 2003). In addition, mixed use of space can renew life in many parts of the city and in turn enhance security in public spaces for disadvantaged groups.

For the past several decades, urban planning has been "unmixing" cities by the use of rigid zoning that separates single land-uses into differently collared parts of the city plan. The result is a city with less diversity in local areas and more traffic, as well as reduced safety and diminished attractiveness of local streets (Newman 1997). For a sustainable urban form, mixed uses should be encouraged in cities and zoning discouraged (Breheny 1992b, 22).

A rapidly expanding literature continues to investigate the potential for causal links between urban design and travel behaviour, yet there remain many gaps and considerable disagreement (Crane 1999). The motivating question is how to design built environments to reduce automobile use. The aim is to reduce air pollution and traffic congestion, as well as to stimulate the interaction of residents, by increasing pedestrian traffic and generally improving neighbourhood charm. Numerous studies report that higher densities, mixed land-uses, more open circulation patterns and pedestrian friendly environments are all associated with less car travel. Others argue that these results are difficult either to confirm or to interpret (Daniels, 2009).

China's urbanisation and environmental sustainability cannot continue to rely on high pollution, high energy consumption model of development. It is adopting new models of sustainable development of the environment to promote urbanisation, good rational planning, protection of arable land and development of agricultural modernisation. China is adopting more efficient use of resources, the development of green GDP and promoting green urbanism (Chaochao, Xiangqin, Xiuqin and Zhou, 2015).

In America, environmental planning has evolved substantially in response to social, political and environmental circumstances (Daniels, 2009). Since the 1909 national planning conference, the nation's population has more than tripled, the economy has multiplied many times, government and corporate sectors have mushroomed and threats to the environment have become more wide spread and often cross political boundaries (Daniels, 2009). In response, environmental planning has grown from a handful of thinkers and practitioners who emphasised physical planning and urban design to an institutional policy and legal framework that includes government, business and non-profit groups, as well as individuals. The problems that originally prompted environmental planning still exist: the need for parks and play grounds, inadequate urban infrastructure for clean water and disposal of waste, the need for safe and healthy places to live and the desire to balance wise use of natural resources with the preservation of wilderness (Daniels, 2009). However, modern environmental planning aims to go beyond protecting regional ecosystems and cleaning up local pollution to embrace national and international sustainability. Government and private sector capacity to plan for the environment has increased enormously over the past 100 years. The willingness to plan has wavered recently, particularly on the part of the federal government (Daniels, 2009). Strategies have changed over the period from physical design, to command and control regulation, to financial incentives for pollution control, regional ecological protection, urban greening and global cooperation.

Such changes in American culture and values will involve difficult investment choices, trade-offs and political decisions. For example, better mass transit will be essential for the conservation of energy and reducing air pollution and greenhouse gas emissions in U.S. metropolitan areas (Yaro and Carbonell, 2007). However, investing in mass transit will cost hundreds of billions of dollars and will compete with high way projects. The goal should be for the United States, the world's wealthiest country, to set an example for the world in environmental planning and environmental quality: act locally, think globally. Environmental planning must involve more international cooperation to manage the global biosphere (Daniels, 2009).

Portland is Oregon's largest metropolitan area that has an international reputation as a leader in battle against urban sprawl through sustainable urban development. In 1991, Metro, Portland's regional government, began work on the 2040 plan. Following the principles of new urbanism, the goals of the plan includes the transformation of the metropolitan area into a multinucleated urban form, the development of a multi-modal transportation system and the designation of mixed use regional and town centres such as Metro, Katz and Calthorpe (Song and Knaap, 2003). The Plan was approved in 1997 along with its implementation vehicle, the Urban Growth Functional Plan, which specified binding targets and performance measures for each of the subordinate cities and counties. Under Metro's Charter, cities and counties are required to change their comprehensive plans and subdivision regulations to assure that local plans comply with the Functional Plan. Armed with this charter, a State mandate to manage Portland's urban growth boundary and a close association with Tri Met, the regional transit district, Metro has substantial capacity to implement its new urbanism plan (Song and Knaap, 2003).

In Zimbabwe's post-independence era, building societies such as National Building Society and the Central African Building Society (CABS) were not involved in developing land for urban purposes. Rather, they just financed European housing development schemes. In the independence era, building societies became the major private sector companies involved in land development since property development is lagging behind in the country. Building societies such as CABS, the Commercial Bank of Zimbabwe Building Society and ZB Building Society were directly involved in the servicing of land, development of offsite infrastructure (water and sewer) and the construction of public amenities like schools, hospitals and recreational facilities in the urban areas (Nyandoro and Muzorewa, 2017).

Conclusions, recommendations and future suggested polices

In Zimbabwe all improvements on land are guided by land development permits issued to the developers under the provisions of the Regional Town and Country Act of 1976. These development controls play a critical role in infrastructural development and facilitation of public amenities such as roads, sewerage and water systems, educational institutions, electricity and health facilities. They also improve land values through allocation of different land-uses as guided by the Regional Town and Country Act. In many cities around the country, real estate developers and the local authorities are the most appropriate vehicles for urban development. Government controls all the improvements on the land so that land value, environmental sustainability and green urbanism is achieved through allocating open spaces, parks and recreational places for the benefit of its citizens.

For future recommendations in the case of Zimbabwe, there is need of creating more investment opportunities in the real estate industry through formulation of favourable polices which attract local or foreign investors in the country so that the industry will be widely recognised on the globe. Government should work in conjunction with communities of citizens and workers. This could mean different things from a valorisation of alternative eco-developments, to support for local initiatives and interests, to investigation of policies and processes which will enable more grassroots innovation, sustainable urban living and resilience. Green urbanism is common sense urbanism. In future, Green Urbanism has to become the norm for all urban developments. Increased material and energy consumption worldwide, coupled with an inadequate and unsustainable waste management system and a lack of resource recovery, has forced governments, industry and individuals to explore how to rapidly put into practice new measures to achieve responsible, closed loop solutions in waste management and resource recovery (Lehmann, 2010).

There is need of achieving sustainable materials flow in cities and 'zero waste' remains difficult and requires continued and combined efforts by industry, government bodies, university researchers and the people and organizations in our community. The real estate industry and the infrastructure construction sector has to catch up with other sectors in better managing its material, construction of environmentally friendly structures such as green buildings to reduce waste and increase the focus on reusing entire building components at the end of a building's life-cycle. This will increase the economic value of recycled commodities such as rare metals in e-waste, metals, paper, glass and plastics as they remain an area for future development and investment (Lehmann, 2010).

This chapter has touched on some of the urgent topics around sustainable urban development. It will be essential to continue to reduce wasteful consumption and to promote the cyclical reuse of materials in the economy by maximising the value of our resources to make resource recovery the common practice (Buckminster Fuller, 2013). The main objective must be to reconcile the scarcity of our natural resources with the almost infinite quantities of waste produced by our cities and industries, which we must unfailingly recover. Some of explained principles of Green Urbanism are practical and holistic, offering an integrated framework, encompassing all the key aspects needed to establish sustainable development and encouraging best practice models. The applicability of models is hereby very important (Buckminster Fuller, 2013).

Finally, it is important to note, that a couple of innovative engineering solutions will not deliver a vibrant city. All the technology in the world cannot achieve sustainability and vitality by itself. The problem of urban design is far more complex (Lehmann, 2010). Designing a city requires holistic, multi-dimensional approaches and each time the adaptation of strategies to a unique context calls for: the integration and combination of qualitative and quantitative knowledge. The only way to solve the looming environmental crises is through ecological imagineering of green urbanism and policy networks forged between entrepreneurial urban regimes (and transnational capital) eager to reinvent themselves with a purported eco-city model (Pow and Neo, 2015).

References

Buckminster-Fuller R. (2013). Earth, Inc. New York: Fuller Research Foundation (later republished in an anthology, also called "Earth, Inc.".

Caprotti, F., (2014). Eco- urbanism and the Eco- city, or, Denying the Right to the City? *Antipode, 46*(5), pp.1285-1303.

Chaochao, H., Xiangqin, S., Xiuqin, B and Zhou, X. (2015). Urbanisation and environmental sustainable development. Advanced Materials Research Vols. 1092-1093 Trans Tech Publications, Switzerlanddoi:10.4028/www.scientific.net/AMR.1092-1093.1629

Daniels, T. L. (2009). A trail across time: American environmental planning from city beautiful to sustainability *Journal of the American Planning Association, 75*(2), 178-192.

Goodling, E., Green J and McClintock, N. (2015). Uneven development of the sustainable city: Shifting capital in Portland, Oregon. *Urban Geography, 36*(4), 504-527.

Jabareen, Y. R. (2006). Sustainable urban forms: Their typologies, models and concepts *Journal of planning education and research, 26*(1), 38-52.

Lehmann, S. (2010). Green urbanism: Formulating a series of holistic principles. *SAPIEN. S. Surveys and Perspectives Integrating Environment and Society*, (3.2). University of South Australia, School of Art, Architecture and Design, City West Campus, Accessed on 01 August 2018 URL: http://journals.openedition.org/sapiens/1057.

McCann, E. J and Ward, K. (2011). Assembling urbanism: mobilizing knowledge and shaping cities in a global age University of Minnesota Press, Minneapolis

Nyandoro, M., and Muzorewa, T. (2017). Transition from growth point policy to liberal urban development in Zimbabwe: The emergence of Ruwa Town, 1980–1991, *The Journal for Trans disciplinary Research in Southern Africa* 13(1), a426. https://doi.org/10.4102/td.v13i1.426

Pow, C. P., and Neo, H. (2015). Modelling green urbanism in China. *Area, 47*(2), pp.132-140.

Roggema, R. (2016). The future of sustainable urbanism: a redefinition. *City Territory and Architecture, 3*(1), 22.

Schilling, J and Logan, J. (2008). Greening the rust belt: A green infrastructure model for right sizing America's shrinking cities. *Journal of the American Planning Association, 74*(4), pp.451-466.

Song, Y and Knaap, G. J. (2003). New urbanism and housing values: a disaggregate assessment. *Journal of Urban Economics*, *54*(2), pp.218-238.

U.S, Census Bureau. (2004). Population estimates and projections. Washington, DC: U.S. Government Printing Office.

Wolcha, J., Byrne, J and Newell, P. (2014). Urban green space, public health and environmental justice: The challenge of making cities 'just green enough', University of California, Berkeley.

Yaro, R. D and Carbonell, A. (2007). Reinventing megalopolis: The north east mega region. In J. Barnett (Ed.), Smart growth in a changing world (pp.77–93). Chicago: APA Planners Press.

Chapter 10

GIS as tool in real estate and urban planning

Knowledge Murenje

Introduction

Many developing countries are still using old the system of data capture, analysis, storage and usage for planning the present and the future. With the fast growth of towns and cities in developing countries of Asia, Latin America and Africa (UN-HABITAT 2013), it has become imperative that urban planners adopt new spatial GIS planning technologies that are not only efficient and effective, but also user friendly in order to solve the divergent spatial urban planning issues. Among the various uses of GIS in urban planning hereby outlined in this chapter, site planning or site selection, settlement upgrading and urban land-use planning and design have been given here as such examples where GIS can be applied within the City of Harare to aid decision-making process. The City of Harare is characterised by unprecedented water and land pollution, slum settlement and a host of other related problems such as traffic and pedestrian congestion. Slum settlement is characteristic of most cities of the developing world (Clapson and Huctchison, 2010), for example, Kibera in Kenya, Soweto in Johannesburg, Manzese in Dare Salaam and Hopley in Harare of Zimbabwe. There is a knowledge gap between theory and empirical evidence indicating the spatial development, trend in growth over time and the general characteristics of slum settlement.

The aim of this chapter is to give a general overview of the use and application of GIS in urban planning within the global context and show how this can be applied in Zimbabwe. The specific objectives of the study are to define GIS and show how the tool can be used to solve spatial planning problems, demonstrate different sources of GIS and their relative importance in spatial problem analysis, indicate by way of examples the various ways in which GIS can be useful in solving spatial problems of towns and cities in both developed and developing countries, illustrate the use and applicability of desktop Quantum GIS software in urban layout planning design with reference to Chinyuka area in Zimbabwe and to examine various GIS methodological stages that can be used in settlement upgrading and suitability assessment with reference to the City of Harare in Zimbabwe.

Theoretical framework

There are a lot of theories that are related to urban development. Earlier theoretical works were linked to Weber's (1909) Industrial location theory, Losch (1943) and Isard (1956). There are the other classical theories that are commonly associated with urban development and these include Cumulative Causation Theory (1957), Von Thunen Theory (1826) and the classical Central Place Theory (1933). Linked to these theoretical models are the Burgess concentric zone model (1925), Hoyts' (1939) sector model, Harris and Ullman's (1945) multiple nuclei model. All these theories try to describe towns and cities as the products of social, economic and market forces interacting with each other. With these theories, urban development was understood as taking place as one move away from the city centre (CBD). Recent developments in town planning however have shown that towns are themselves a system and therefore dynamic. According to Bertalanffy (1968), everything within an urban area operates within a system that consists of various but related elements. These elements are interrelated and linked to the systems environment. The physical environment itself is its own system. According to Gammage (2016) a city is a living organism, with human beings as the most active living species within the urban space. There is flora and fauna within the urban ecosystem which is compelling urban landscape designers today to think about eco-city planning. Cities are themselves products of millions of individual decision-making processes about how people intend to survive and live, recreate and enjoy themselves, work and interact with each other and also with various organisations and the physical environment. There are also elements within the urban area that are interacting with each other through social, economic and spatial dimensions while they also interact with the environment. In essence, urban systems consist of a set of other elements that are called subsystems that are interlinked. In this urban set-up, typical examples are the urban population itself, the urban land market, employment (both formal and informal), services as well as private and public transport amongst others.

Neoclassical theories approach to urban planning was based on the firm belief that urban development is in essence an economic activity that is driven by market forces and the natural forces of space competition. Forces of demand and supply relationships shape and create urban structures, giving rise to homogeneous cities and monocentric city developments. Proponents of these theoretical perspectives include Wingo (1961), Alonso (1964) and Lowry (1964). However, these theories were criticised for their lack of depth and their rigidity. They are therefore taken sometimes as a dead horse which no one has a cart of, because of their limited applicability. Batty (1976) used systems dynamic technique for simulating industrial process in firms, showing the dynamism in cities. The systems approach to urban planning came about especially in the 1980s with the increase in the use of GIS technologies. With the invention of such GIS open source and GRASS software, urban centres were now seen as open systems with multi nuclei centres (polycentric as opposed to monocentric development). Cities are dynamic organisms with complex and open systems that are self-organising (Liu, 2009).

Conceptual framework

GIS is seen as a general –purpose system. Systems are known to consist of three main activities of input (data sources, aerial photos, satellite images, maps, statistics etc.), process (data processes and analysis) and output (results e.g. visual maps). Conceptually GIS is a system such as the Decision Support System as it aids decision-makers in creating solutions. Spatial urban planners need to rely upon spatial information systems which can present objective resolutions to disputes that may arise with respect to the location of a wide

169

variety of spatial problems. The ideal GIS enable a planner to model a process and to create scenarios that aid in finding spatial solutions to competing views (Berry, 1991). A data model is defined as a collection of conceptual tools for describing data semantics and data constraints (Korth and Silberschatz, 1986).

Remote Sensing and GIS have been used to detect the extent of slum settlement and the possible ways of upgrading them. GIS has also been used in the production of development plans that are used as strategic planning documents for present and future planning purposes. It is within this context that Chinyuka satellite map has been geo-referenced and extracted from Google Map to show how GIS can be used in town planning to solve a spatial planning problem-the need for residential housing. The development and origin of GIS is closely related to urban planning. As far back as in the 1960s, transparent overlays were used in the identification of sites that were in harmony with nature (McHarg, 1969). Steinitz (1976) and Hopkins (1977) asserted that map overlay analysis through the use of hands was a basic skill in urban planning. Computerisation of overlay analysis was done by Carl Steinitz of the Department of Landscape Architecture of Harvard University in 1967 and refined by David Sinton (1977) into MGRID in the 1970s.These grid –based packages played a key role in the development of GIS in the 1970s (Chrisman, 2006). They laid a solid foundation for the spatial processing, statistical and analytical functions of modern-day GIS. The Environmental Systems Research Institute (ESRI) was founded by Jack Dangermond in the 1970s together with its vector-based Arc Info package. This type of package is now called ArcGIS and has very strong map overlay and spatial analysis functions. Today this package has become the leading GIS spatial tool in urban planning.

As part of spatial planning process within urban centres in developing countries, policy-makers prepare zoning plans (master plans) that give the general direction of land development and also impact on the property values of planned entities. The siting of schools, hospitals, community halls and libraries which are public facilities constitute some of these policies. The ideal planning concept requires that there must be a balancing act between the provision of economic developmental needs and social services provision. Urban planners now depend upon GIS systems to find best spatial solutions to these spatial problems. GIS as a concept is the necessary tool to aggregate a multiplicity of spatial problems into an integrated format that improves the ability of planners in problem solving. The applicability of GIS in urban planning depends upon the available data.

Sources of GIS data

Data from aerial photographs refers to the data that is extracted from panoramic pictures taken by overhead flights at consistent time intervals. Usually aerial photos are taken at five-year intervals. Mosaics are photographic images indicating a combination of contiguous aerial photos that are linked together. Such data from aerial photographs can be used to show temporal spatial variations of urban growth. Remote-sensed data are the data obtainable from images created from sensors or cameras mounted on aircraft or spacecrafts specifically meant for satellite imagery. The data are obtained from a distance as opposed from direct human eye contact or observation. Landsat satellites from France or America satellites within the orbital space can detect earthly images as small as 0, 5 metres. Such images can be collected together for GIS use and applications (ITC Journal, 1996). Data from existing paper maps are normally sourced from the Surveyor Generals Office where geodetic maps are created. Base maps and all cartographic maps drawn to various scales are usually obtainable from this office for a nominal fee. Data from field survey - This the type of information that is collected from the field, usually by way of questionnaires or field observations. Tabular data are the data that can be extracted from the central statistical offices of any Government. In Zimbabwe such information can be sourced for free. Data from other sources refers to that which are collected from other type of sources such as newspapers, the internet and existing paper files, books, TVs amongst others.

Literature Review

Land- use planning, spatial planning, town and country and physical planning have all been seen to mean the same thing. They refer to the art and science of ordering the use of land character and siting of buildings and communication routes, development control and the physical arrangement of the built environment, with emphasis on the use and location of physical space (Keeble, 1969). This planning is associated with the promotion of public health and an orderly settlement (preamble Regional Town and Country Planning Act (RTCPA) Chapter 29:12 of 1996). History has it that town planning in Europe came about to promote order and create an orderly settlement within the built environment and was at some time carried out by municipal police to enforce public health which was deteriorating at the time. Spatial planning problems within the built environment created this interventionist approach to planning. These spatial planning problems which need intervention range from poor road infrastructure, water and sewerage problems, poor street lighting services, housing, poor sanitation facility and garbage disposal methods, urban land market and management issues to heavily polluted water bodies, poor drainage systems, transport and congestion problems.

The spatial urban planning problems need spatial solutions hence the need to use GIS. The application of modern-day GIS technologies has been found to offer quicker and more effective ways of solving the spatial problems of urban centres in the developing world, than the use of traditional planning systems, that are cumbersome, time consuming and outdated. Urban planning involves many different and interrelated municipal functions done at different scales, sectors and stages. Within these scales and sectors, there are different stages of planning that involve planning objectives, analysis of the prevailing situation, modelling and projection, selection of planning options available, plan implementation, monitoring and evaluation and feedback. GIS can be used in these different stages of urban planning to achieve the desired goals. Different stages, scales and sectors of urban planning require different GIS uses (Yeh, 2008). However, the purpose of this chapter is to give a general overview of the application and use of GIS in some of these sectors in urban planning in general with reference to Zimbabwe giving as much as possible City of Harare as an example and then show GIS urban applications by way of a pilot project.

Globally GIS has been used within a number of disciplines ranging from the army in USA, forestry, agriculture, environmental systems and natural resources (Lang ,1998), mining , geology to navigation , education (Ludwig , 2000 ; Palmer , Anita ,Malone and Voigt , 2010) , health (Lang , 2000) , industry , marine , town and urban planning (Batty, 2013), urban poverty (Rosario, 2008) , real estate , land administration and management (Williamson , Enemark , Wallace and Rajabifard, 2009) , tourism , water management (Maidment , Strassberg , Norman, Jones , 2011), conservation geography (Convis , 2001) , cartography (Imhof , 2007 ; Rumsey and Punt , 2004) , architecture (Peters , 2012), transportation amongst others. Nowadays GIS related technologies are also increasingly being used in business entities (Maguire, 2008), main institutions such as Local and central government e.g. GIS in e-government (Greene, 2001; William, Huxhold, Eric, Fowler and Brian, 2004). A lot of literature is being put together to show GIS applications in disaster management (Amdai, 2001, Greene, 2002), telecommunications, enterprise GIS (Harde, 1999), Web GIS (Tang and Selwood, 2003), archaeology and landscape (Jacobson, Tepfer and Meacham, 2009), mapping (Bewer, 2005), transportation (Butler, 2008) urban and regional planning (McElvaney, 2012), environmental management and urban environment (Scally, 2006).

Use of GIS in urban planning is quite varied. Industrial location modelling (Cwen, Mitchel and Meyer1990), supply and demand forecasting in real estate markets (Gurd, 1990), redistricting (Sullivan and Chow (1990), land suitability assessment facility, siting (Siderelis, (1992), Berry (1991), Cowen and Shirley (1991) and many more are some of the uses.

Developments in technology especially in America in the 1980s led to the emergency of new digital data sources and GIS techniques such as GRASS. With the increased use of GIS applications in the 1980s a wide variety of urban GIS modelling approaches were invented such as TransCAD (1983), GRASS (1983) ArcGIS Spatial

Analyst Extension (ESRI, 2004). This meant that spatial planners had new platforms for analysing urban planning scenarios. New techniques for data acquisition, processing and manipulation, management and visualisation were created (Nyerges, 1995; Nu, 1996; Suin, 1998), Openshaw and Openshaw 1997). Urban development was now looked at differently other than the dependence on the neoclassical version of urban development (where only supply and demand forces determine urban development). The urban development process itself became an open and complex self-organising system with a constant exchange of goods and energy within cities and also within the hinterland. The urban development process became a spatially dynamic process with self-organising features, taking cognisance of the emergency thereof, of suburban centres variously known as "cities without cities" Sieverts (2003: 44), "edgeless cities" (Lang and Knox, 2008: 22), outer cities (Herrington, 1984), edge cities (Garreau, 1991) *expolis* (Soja, 1989) *metroburbia* (Knox, 2008) and *boomburbs* (Lang and Lefurgy, 2007) within the suburban areas of the main city. It is about the same time in the 1990s that the new urbanism concepts were also invented with the emergence of compact city and smart city ideas. Environmental planners today try to interlink GIS techniques to smart city development ideas.

According to ESRI (2012), GIS has been used practically since the 1980s, in the production of maps, determination of human settlement densities and the optimal provision of related social services such as clinics, hospitals and schools. The spatial planning and allocation of these facilities using ARCGIS has given opportunities to determine where there is greater need. Globally it has been shown that GIS has been used with greater success in the field of environmental planning, landscape design, eco-city planning and smart city planning. Throughout different countries; especially in the developed countries, GIS has now been used in the reclamation, rerouting, siting and design of facilities. Since cities are becoming more and more complex in the wake of rapid urbanisation and consisting of an intricate collection of elements such as infrastructure, machinery and materials, it is becoming more and more imperative for spatial planners to use more sophisticated tools to help in the management and design of these cities.

GIS stands for Geographic information system. The simplest definition is that it is a computer system that is capable of holding and using data describing places on the earth's surface. It is a system for capturing, storing, checking, integrating, manipulating, analysing and displaying data which are spatially referenced to the earth. This is normally considered to involve a spatially referenced computer database and appropriate applications software. A GIS contains the following major subsystems, data storage and retrieval subsystem, a data manipulation and analysis subsystem and a data reporting subsystem. GIS has been found to be a means of storing, retrieving, sorting and comparing spatial data to support some analytical process, It is a system of computer hardware and software programmes which store, analyse and display information about places on the earth' surface. A GIS is able to integrate spatial information and tabular information (database) thereby enabling users to visualise and analyse relationships, patterns and trends. There is a narrow definition that means an integrated collection of software and data that is used to visualise and organise place-based data for the purposes of performing geographic analysis and creating maps (Wade and Sommer, 2006). In broader terms, GIS also includes, the group of people whose role is to create and share the data, the activity of using GIS for problem solving and knowledge creation (Longley, 2008). GIS allows urban planners to use and perform spatial planning analytical functions such as buffering, connectivity and map overlay (Berry, 1987, Tomlin, 1990). Planners have a long history of applying map overlay in land suitability assessment which is a key component of urban planning (McHarg, 1969; Steinitz, 1976; Hopkins, 1977). Figure 10.1 is a diagram showing thematic layers that may be overlaid to create a composite layer.

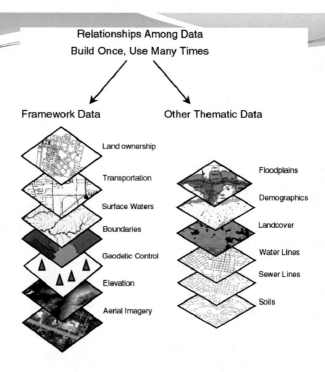

Figure 10.1: Thematic maps that can be created and combined together (Adapted from National Spatial Data infrastructure-USA, 2003)

The above diagram shows a lot of thematic maps that can be created and combined together. This land-use overlay method has been found to be the most efficient GIS technique in urban planning. For years, the method has been used manually but now it is being applied within a GIS with much efficiency and quicker output. GIS integrates various thematic layers to create one composite layer. GIS can be simple, complex or anything in- between. Users can use simple map or perform detailed and in-depth spatial analysis, modelling, transportation routing, reporting, charting, image processing and analysis, GPS tracking, remote sensing and aerial photo applications and usage. There are different types of GIS software that can be used for spatial planning purposes. There are different types of GIS packages within the market in this modern time. There are the commercial ones which could not easily be accessed unless procured through a certain licence for a use over a period of time and there are open sources which could be accessed easily by anyone without even purchasing the package. These packages could be uploaded from the internet for use.

Forthcoming is a list of both open source GIS software packages and the commercial ones, but this list is not exhaustive as there are many software packages outside these ones.

- *Commercial Source*
  o **ARC GIS** software-is powerful in mapping and spatial data analysis.
  o **MapInfo** software-is desktop tool for mapping and locational analysis.
  o **Intergraph** software-is a tool for enterprising engineering mainly for businesses and organisations.

These software packages have been the products of Environmental Systems Research Institute (ESRI) and are well known for their support of vector based spatial data and their operations, user interface and map production. The software are a product of America's invention. ARCGIS software package is well known internationally with very strong functions in overlay and vector based spatial data analysis. It has become the leading software package providing consultative training work and publications across the globe.

- *Open source*
  o **Quantum GIS-**supports both vector and raster data and provides a collection of plugins for geo-processing, analysis and visualisation. It is multi-platform i.e. can be used with window, Linus and Mac operating systems.
  o **GRASS-**Geographic Resources Analysis Support System. The software was created by USA army in the 1980s as a low-cost, user friendly and public domain alternative for resource management applications (Mitasova and Neteler, 2004).
  o **Udig-**This is a Canadian software package. It was created by Refraction Research Company of Canada in 2004.

177

The Zimbabwean context

Within the Zimbabwean context, GIS use and application within the field of urban planning have been relatively low. There is limited literature in Zimbabwe in terms of the application and usage of GIS related technologies. Part of the reasons has been cited as the lack of adequate resources on part of Government to finance GIS projects. Comparatively GIS is being applied more within neighbouring countries like South Africa, Namibia and Botswana than in Zimbabwe. However, there are now indications of Central Government embracing GIS technology.

In Zimbabwe open source software's such as GRASS and QuantumGIS are now freely available on the market and can be uploaded from the internet for GIS related use. In terms of mapping, a lot of geological maps of Zimbabwe have been created via vector map analysis, thereby enhancing the map database. Different types of maps that include aeromagnetic atlas maps, geological maps indicating unconfirmed underground aquifers are now being created in a GIS format. Harare wetland map was developed from GIS technologies. Cities which have already embraced the technology in Zimbabwe include Harare, Bulawayo, Gweru, Kadoma, Chinhoyi and Kariba and a host of other rural district councils. Bulawayo was assisted by the Australian Government in 2015.Hunter (2014) helped the establishment of GIS in these urban areas with the assistance of Australian aid and German Society for International Cooperation (GIZ).

Although the literature is somehow limited, GIS related courses are now being taught at most state universities in Zimbabwe. The following universities are already teaching GIS related courses in their curricular: National University of Science and Technology (NUST), Chinhoyi University of Technology (CUT), University of Zimbabwe (UZ), Bindura University of Science Education (BUSE), Midlands State University (MSU), Great Zimbabwe University (GZU) and the Harare Institute of Technology (HIT).There are already research organisations that are involved in GIS such as the Scientific and Industrial Research Centre (SIRDC). However, these organisations are not directly involved in the application of GIS in spatial urban planning. This has left a knowledge gap between practising spatial planners and those that may have little knowledge about the practicability of GIS in town planning. In terms of research and literature, a vigorous effort is therefore needed to make GIS accessible and applicable to both practising and upcoming spatial planners in Zimbabwe.

The spatial growth of Harare Metropolitan City can be measured using GIS technology, remote sensing and aerial photos. Under remote sensing, newly formed settlements or buildings can be identified and measured against the original boundary to detect the rate of growth over time, of either residential, commercial or industrial areas. Normally residential exponential growth is more pronounced than the growth of other land-uses. GIS has been used to analyse the growth of an urban area over time. This analysis can be done through the use of remote-sensed data and or aerial photos which are taken at consistent time intervals such as five years. Knowledge of the rate of growth of urban settlements is an essential equipping tool to a spatial planner in the hunt for a spatial solution. GIS can be used in the planning of a new railway or a road route. There are packages that can be applied in highway road engineering for the benefit of town planning, for example the GROUTES algorithm application programme. In developed countries, some planners have been using such programmes in the determination of flattest route, least damage to surrounding people and least disturbance routes in highway planning. GROUTES algorithm programme has been used for the determination of the least-cost route in road highway planning in India and northern parts of Nigeria (AKinyede and Ellis, 1990).

In developed countries such as the Netherlands, highway roads in both towns and the countryside are coded according to their lifespan and the information is computerised. Each road is monitored through the use of a database monitoring system that is GIS related. Real estate as one sector of urban planning within the municipality of a town is concerned with the administration and planning of property. Land administration deals with how land and property rights are administered properly. The registration and management of property rights need some modern-day GIS operations for the process to be effective and efficient. Information pertaining to land value, land ownership and land- use needs to be properly documented. In a GIS, such information is recorded in a non-spatial attribute format as tabular data showing who owns (name of property owner) what (stand or property number it is, the name and location of street name and location, large is the size and value of stand or property. As shown in table 1.This information is related or covers spatial issues linked to master plans, land -use plans, detailed site development plans, engineering infrastructure as well as other survey information .The information in the real estate office may also include records of all legal transactions such as deed of transfer, power of attorney, leasehold (leases and subleases) commonage or state-land beneficiaries, freehold ownership or double share of flats or compartments. This whole information is practically cumbersome to manage using the traditional manual filing approach. GIS; being computer-based systems therefore is being used to handle such a big amount of data and information in a manner not only effective and efficient, but also transparent, faster and user friendly.

The data that may be handled by the real estate office may be spatial or attribute data. Spatial data refers to the data which is location based with respect to the earth's surface and normally geo-referenced (in terms of geographical latitudes and longitudes)or geo-coded, while attribute data refers to spatial data that is described in terms of characteristics or qualities in an attribute tabular format as in table1 overleaf .This simply means a GIS dataset system may have a property parcel or land unit or property stand described in its spatial database and have qualities such as name of property owner , plot number ,plot size , use , property value in its attribute database. Therefore, GIS is able to handle both spatial data as well as attribute data that are interrelated for the benefit of a spatial planner, in order to solve the urban planning problem.

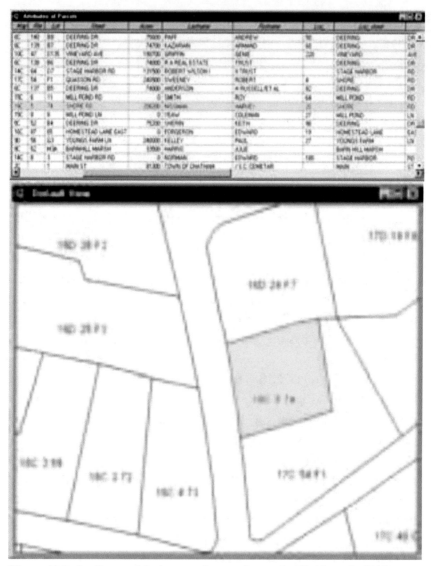

Figure 10.2: Attribute table 1 geo-referenced parcels (Field work, 2018)

The above attribute table is linked to the parcel identified with the yellow colour. The land parcels, units or property stands are geo-referenced while the attribute data are non-spatial and kept in a database format.

Electricity, telecommunication network and the cooking gas can be measured on a daily basis to help in the mapping of data, in inventory systems, track maintenance, monitor regulatory compliance, or model distribution analysis, transformer analysis and load analysis. GIS can be used by business organisations within urban areas as technical tools to market themselves, increase and determine their clientele base. GIS can keep a track of where the customers of a company are located, site business targets marketing campaigns, optimize sales, territories and model retail spending patterns. This makes prospective companies more competitive and successful in their businesses.

In managing real estate in urban planning, taxation has become really an issue as most property owners try to evade the payment of taxes. However, with the introduction of digital taxation, it becomes easier to follow up all tax evasions. The use of GIS in digital taxation system also makes it easy to determine the amount of taxes to property owners. This type of information can be created in a non-spatial tabular database system that is linked of course to the spatial data system. Accurate pipeline route selection brings about risk and cost reduction, as well as better decision-making process. GIS least cost path analysis has been effectively used to determine suitable oil and gas pipeline routes. An example of the route that may require the use and application of GIS if further extended to Bulawayo city is the Feruka, Beira and Harare pipeline in Zimbabwe. In Harare City, the current upgrading of sewer pipelines may be further enhanced through the use of GIS.

GIS has been used together with Remote Sensing especially in areas requiring the quantification of housing units and other urban community services (Polle, 1996). In the computation of housing densities in urban areas (number of houses per hectare) considerations or planning indicators such as type and number of houses, size of an area with specific type of residential land-use and population size are considered. The relationship between population size and number of dwelling units or houses is the number of people per housing unit which is the occupancy rate. The relationship between the residential land area and population size is the number of persons per hectare which is the density. The third relationship is the residential floor space per person. The relationship between population and their income is shown by the type of houses or the type of residential land-use. In Harare, types of houses and the value of the land in Borrowdale are more expensive than in Mbare residential areas. With this assessment model a spatial planner may go from the indicator housing to population and from population to need for services and then compute the data modelling process via GIS.

Satellite images with a resolution of 10 m (e.g. the French Spot pan) are comparable to aerial photographs at 1:200 000 scale and can therefore be used for counting housing units to calculate number of houses. Residential area (in hectares) and residential floor space in square metre can be calculated. Types of houses, population statistics per area, social and economic class of the population and number of dwellings per area are indicators which may be used in an ARCGIS to create thematic map layers for various uses. GIS and remote sensing can assist town planners to determine housing density, type and number of housing units, occupancy rates, type and size of residential area and net housing densities (Polle, 1996).

In many developed countries domestic energy use is monitored and controlled overtime. Such monitoring is done for sustainable energy usage and in conformity with UN goal number 7 of 2015. Domestic Energy, Carbon Counting and Carbon Reduction Model (DECORUM) are a GIS based programme that is used for regulating carbon emissions in towns and cities on the United Kingdom. This GIS related toolkit can estimate energy related emissions (co2) and the impact of mitigation strategies in UK residential buildings, grouping the results to a street, district and city level (UN-HABITAT, 2016). There is enormous potential for the use of this GIS model in developing countries. Such methods of designing for energy economy using GIS in urban areas need to be adopted also in cities of the developing world for prosperity and sustainability. This also shows the use and application of GIS in urban planning. It implies that with the current global environmental climatic change, the impact of urban heat island on the urban human settlements can be controlled.

The location identification technique is used to find new locations for retail outlet. It helps to find out what exists at a particular location. Information such as name of place, postcode and geographic reference in terms of exact xy coordinates is generated.

Location based GIS is particularly important in the real estate industry where it has a bearing on the value of property.

When querying information in a GIS, determination of, for example, stands which are 60 m away from a railway or from a major road can be detected using the 60m buffering technique. A list of all properties that are within this 60m from the centre line of the road can be drawn. Such properties may be demolished and property owners compensated to pave way for a major highway that addresses congestion problems within the city. Figure 10.3 is a diagram showing this technique.

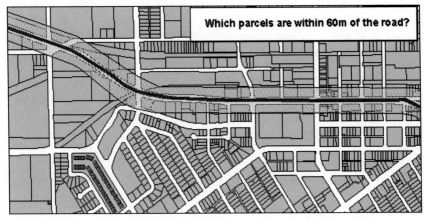

Figure 10.3: land parcels (ESRI, 2003)

This layout shows properties that could be demolished and the detection was done using GIS querying and buffering technique. GIS can be used to determine the under-provision or over-provision of social services such as schools, hospitals, clinics, community halls or libraries. In GIS this can be done through a buffering technique. Coupled with statistical data from the statistical office and from other sources, a solution can be found to either increase the number of social services within an area or to reduce them. In planning for schools, the buffering method has been found more useful in the determination of minimum walkable distances of children of school going age. The determination of catchment areas or areas of influence for the schools, clinics and hospitals can easily be identified through this buffering process.

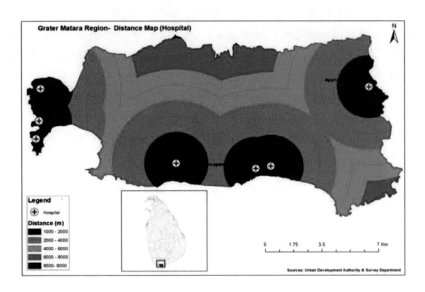

Figure 10.4: Distance Map (ESRI, 2003)

Figure 10.4 shows the concept of buffering that is frequently used for the determination of areas of influence or catchment zones. These zones are created using GIS with the formation of minimum distances patients are travelling to seek medical attention. This map may not be adequate unless it is superimposed by another layer indicating population distribution. The resultant map after map overlay may show areas in need of more hospitals.

3D GIS visualisation in urban planning

The growing urban population especially in Asia, South America and African cities, aging infrastructure, complex urban development are the driving factors that compel modern day city planners to be more creative and innovative in the hunt for urban spatial solutions. Detailed and comprehensive 3D GIS applications come in handy in the search for these solutions. 3D application model is seen as a beneficial expansion of the existing 2D for the urban planner.

With 3D GIS models available on the market, planners can now assess new spatial development proposals to be put up in certain urban area locations. Spatial planners in town planning can now add proposed building development into the model for simulation purposes. The development of a new town such as Mt Hampden

185

centre in northern Harare can be shown in a 3D indicating how individual buildings proposed are going to look like in future. A 3D solid model can be used to visualise and analyse the impact for the proposed urban development at the conceptual design stage. 3D models are also used to show visual designs of existing buildings in their length width and height images. 3D visual images of both existing and proposed settlement influence decision-making of city governments. Community participation is also enhanced with the introduction of the 3D model as people seek to find the best alternative physical outlook to the benefit of the society at large. Nowadays spatial planners need to show new town models in 3DS in order to visualise proposed future designs and also impress upon the authorities the need for effective land and space usage.

3D GIS functions (such as Bentley 3D) also include build, utilise, manage and maintain operations. There are now advanced 3D operations which are used for navigation, spatial analysis and visualisation. Spatial analysis that goes beyond the usual 2D such as flood analysis and noise analysis may need these advanced 3D applications. In urban or town planning 3D models are usually associated with architecture. Below is a picture of office buildings that were constructed on top of a tunnel in the city of Hague in Belgium. Such pictures are better visualised in a 3D model showing different types of land-uses and efficient use of urban space.

Figure 10.5: Office building constructed over the road in the city of Hague: typical 3D building in a city centre (Stoter, 2004: 122)

186

Figure 10.6: Paris -showing a railway tunnel underneath building from one corner of this rectangular picture to another (Stoter, 2004: 126)

The picture depicts the importance of 3D complex property situation in urban.

Figure 10.7: Simulation 3D model with different urban land-uses (Stoter, 2004: 88)

GIS is used and applied by land cartographers, land surveyors and geographers in mapping and coming up with other alternative scenarios of different thematic maps. The current land- uses are usually in paper form and are outdated. They need to be upgraded. These maps take a lot more time to create. With GIS, mapping time saved is about 90 %. GIS mapping or cartography has been found to be very useful in the production of base maps or other user maps for application or as outcomes of GIS applications. Some of the common maps that are web-GIS related are Google maps and internet maps. When the old maps usually in the surveyor general's office are digitised and stored in a GIS, it will become easy to retrieve and update them to meet current demand. The following are the suggested maps and the usual scales adopted:

- Topographic maps 1: 25000
- Cadastre base maps 1: 1000 – 1:2500
- General Master plan 1:5000
- Master plan and building regulations 1:2000
- Detailed urban plan 1: 1000-1:500

Urban planning is an activity that requires planners to be innovative to meet the current urban demand. Land-use strategies are therefore needed to combat a wide variety of spatial problems associated with current rapid urbanisation in most cities of the developing world (UNHABITAT, 2009).Prevention of urban sprawl, efficient transit system , intensification of urban centres (a concept called gentrification in Europe and America) and redevelopment, conservation of historic areas, improvement or upgrading of informal settlements and maintenance and improvement of suburbs are some of the diverse types of land-use strategic activities to be carried out by the spatial planner. All these can be achieved through the strategic use of GIS enhanced master plans, development plans and local subject plans. With the development of modern-day GIS technologies such as ARCGIS, a variety of land-use plans can be created to achieve desired goals. For example, ARCGIS can create master plans indicating plots and blocks (*lines*), blocks and plots (*polygons*), banks, manholes, bus stops (*points*) and a general zoning (*polygon*). Layout depicting historic areas of interest such as Monomotapa, Makombe, Parliament and Lonrho buildings (*Herald*, 19 June, 1997) can be created as either *points* or p*olygons* depending on scale and purpose for use. City of Harare development plans 19, 21 and 22 showing mix of land-uses and a master plan for transport can be developed indicating use of point and line polygon ARCGIS analysis. Master plans are usually created for the duration of ten to twenty years. All features in a GIS are represented either as point, line or polygon.

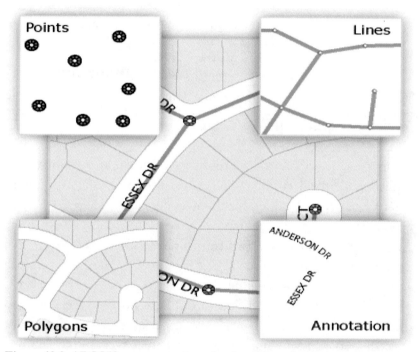

Figure 10.8: ARCGIS representation of point, line and polygon (GIS Handbook for Municipalities UN-HABITAT, 2013)

The diagram depicts an urban layout development plan with stand parcels shown as polygons, access road as lines and bus stops as points.

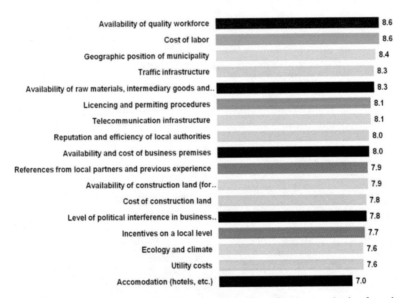

Availability of quality workforce	8.6
Cost of labor	8.6
Geographic position of municipality	8.4
Traffic infrastructure	8.3
Availability of raw materials, intermediary goods and..	8.3
Licencing and permiting procedures	8.1
Telecommunication infrastructure	8.1
Reputation and efficiency of local authorities	8.0
Availability and cost of business premises	8.0
References from local partners and previous experience	7.9
Availability of construction land (for..	7.9
Cost of construction land	7.8
Level of political interference in business..	7.8
Incentives on a local level	7.7
Ecology and climate	7.6
Utility costs	7.6
Accomodation (hotels, etc.)	7.0

Figure 10.9: An example of GIS based multi-criteria analysis for the establishment of new industrial facilities in Serbian city. (Graded 1-10, where 1 is the least important) (Lazarevic, 2013:54)

In choosing a site for a project in an urban area, GIS can be applied to aid the decision-making process through a rigorous multi-criteria analysis. The method involves assigning value to a wide variety of factors that determine or have influence to the site. Each factor is given a weight chosen from a range of one to ten as shown above with 8.6 being the highest value. The sites are grouped according in their rankings depending on their relative weightings. The end result is the evaluation of different possible scenarios and then a selection of optimal site is then made. This is an oversimplified procedure of this method as it is in actual fact a complex and technical procedure that involves an array of social, economic, environmental, political and ecological issues that may conflict each other. GIS is important in linking all these factors together and assisting decision-makers to come up with the best solution in site selection and suitability multi criteria analysis.

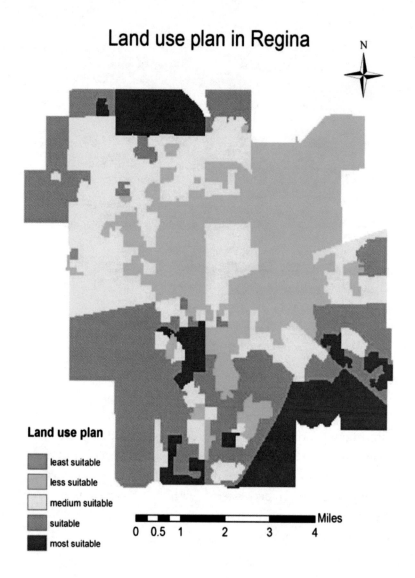

Figure 10.10: Land-use plan (Chen, 2014: 23)

The land-use plan/map in Figure 10.8 shows how GIS can be used in land-use map production. Master plans, development plans and local subject plans that are more localised and detailed can be produced after all the data input and necessary sources are in place. The above key shows categories of land-use suitability levels.

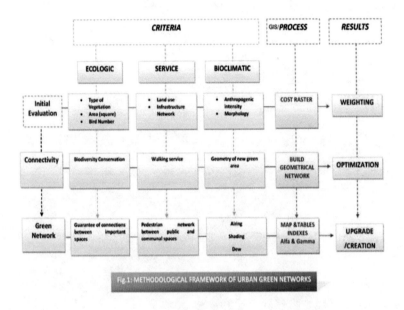

Figure 10.11: Framework of urban green networks (Pigani 2008: 45)

Figure 10:11 is showing how GIS can be applied in environmental design linking ecology, biodiversity, land-use infrastructure network, pedestrian and public spaces and the green space. Environmental urban designers today are concerned with balancing the urban ecosystems with environmental and human settlements needs in a harmonious way and thereby creating environmental sustainability.

Figure 10.12: The trammers system (UNHABITAT, 2011: 22)

Figure 10.12 in the previous page shows the use and application of the trammers system whereby train-like buses travel along the same road used by normal public transport vehicles. A 3D GIS visualisation modelling is the appropriate tool for this picture. It is worth noting that it such a means of public transport is adopted in the City of Harare, it will promote environmental sustainability. This reduces the number of people using individual cars and therefore reducing carbon footprint. Riding and walking to work ease congestion along the road and promote smart city development concept or the new urbanism idea.

A smart city is defined as a city that uses ICTs infrastructure in all its activities. Angelidou (2011) defined a smart city as a city equipped with some technology allowing interaction and analysis among its citizenry, businesses and information systems. Information technology connectivity, urban transport system, good governance that includes e-governance and the involvement of the community are all ingredients of a smart city. Thomas (2015) identified healthy people, safe city, smart country, resilient city, sustainable city, liveable community, smart communities and resilient people as some elements of smart city within the urban populace. There is no universal definition to the concept of smart city. However, the general consensus is that a smart city leads to the provision of smart services by a smart government that uses e government networks, have some smart businesses, with smart environment (eco city designs), greening the city and infrastructure with a digital enhanced environmental design, which is sensitive to the needs of the people. A sustainable city is a city whose inhabitants seek to live in harmony with the surrounding nature for the benefit of the people, the economy and production. In a sustainable city, all the people, irrespective of colour, creed or income have equal opportunity and access to a healthy environment. The search for social and environmental justice needs no emphasis.

GIS can link all the above facets of smart city /compact city concepts together to achieve sustainability within the city. In Sweden, for an example, an underground GIS and ICT enhanced waste collection infrastructure system is used to collect different types of residential industrial and commercial waste through an underground pipe that will eventually empty the waste to a digestive plant used to generate electricity for the people. With GIS in smart city design, or compact city design, some models can be created using GIS 'What If 'approach to determine the impacts of various projects upon the environment and the desired outcomes. With this approach, the Mbare waste digester plant, in the City of Harare, that is already nearing completion, can be linked to the beneficiary households through a GIS enhanced system for a smart city urban environment.

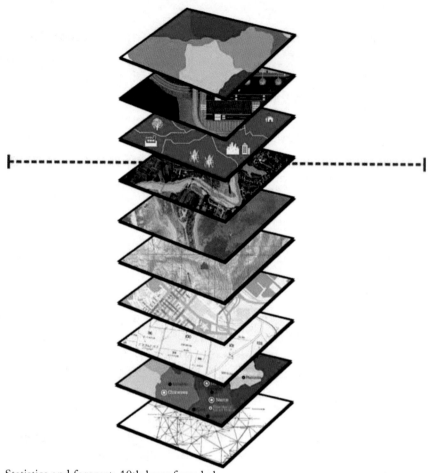

Statistics and forecast -10th layer from below
Physical Planning-9th layer from below
Usage of area-8th layer from below
     Environmental protection- 7th layer
     Orthophoto- sixth layer
     Topographic maps -5th layer earth surface with natural and
     man-made features
     Administrative boundaries – 4th layer from below
     Cadastre index map- 3rd layer showing details of ownership
     and value
Place names-2rd thematic layer from bottom
Geodetic map-first map from the bottom

Figure 10.13: Once geodetic thematic bottom layer is in place other corresponding data layers can be used for many applications and uses. The diagram shows the overlaying technique of ARC GIS in town planning (UN-HABITAT, 2008)

The application of GIS in urban planning in Zimbabwe

With environmental challenges bedevilling the urban areas in the developing world today, spatial planners need to find ways of militating against negative externalities and other environmental problems and plan for the public benefit with greater efficiency and capability. The use of fossil powered cars is still on the rise in developing countries' cities, thus contributing to the rise of urban temperatures and carbon footprint, eventually leading to the ozone layer depletion. This has a net effect of affecting human life. The City of Harare gets at least 100,000 cars per each working day (*Herald*, 2015) and most cars are second hand from Japan. Diesel 50 which is environmentally friendly and which the Government of Zimbabwe is encouraging motorists to use and has not been well embraced by the general road users. Additionally, its availability on the market has been limited. With the use of GIS and GPS tracking systems, it can be made easy to find out which vehicles are already using the required type of fuel for the benefit of the environment and the public. The appropriate GIS and ICTs methodologies can also be used to detect un-roadworthy vehicles.

Harare water drainage system is currently malfunctioning. Most of the drains are clogged up with uncollected garbage to the extent that surface runoff flows in large volumes along the road surfaces during the rainy season. The City of Harare water drainage network system needs to be upgraded and made functional. This can be aided through the use of an ARCGIS analytical network system (using *line analysis*) at city broad level, to curb this environmental spatial problem.

The use of GIS in environmental planning is on the rise globally. A lot of spatial problems are now tackled through GIS environmental modelling. GIS comes as an aid in the supply of much needed spatial information on the suitability of land for infrastructural development and for determining levels of contamination of certain urban areas. GIS can be used in the feasibility studies of waste disposal and treatment activities. Detection of the number, nature and sizes of existing wetlands in Harare can also be done through the use of GIS and Remote Sensing. Most of the wetlands in the City of Harare have been taken up by encroaching human settlements, including the one upon which the Long- Cheng mall was constructed. This is despite a concerted effort from the controlling body, EMA that penalises anyone (including councils) who uses these wetlands or destroys them to the detriment of the environmental biodiversity (flora and fauna) and ecology.

GIS has been used as a monitoring tool in the development and growth of urban areas. The use of GIS in Environmental Planning is on the rise globally. In Zimbabwe, the Environmental Management Agency (EMA), works under Environmental Management Act chapter 20, inter alia, to manage and control the use of toxic substances throughout the country. Water and air pollution as well as solid waste mismanagement are punishable under this environmental Act. The detection of the illegal activities is aided through the use of remote sensing and GIS. Chemical pollutants stemming from household waste, pesticides and fertilisers (from Msasa plant in Harare), industrial waste and polluted runoff need to be controlled and some others banned altogether. The control of the use of the toxic or hazardous chemicals is done through the use of GIS. In Zimbabwe, EMA was one of the first organisations to use GIS.

Throughout developing cities, it is estimated that about 50% of urban garbage remains uncollected. In the City of Harare, it was estimated that 11000 tonnes of garbage are deposited everyday (*Herald*, 15 October, 2016). The solid waste problem has increased mainly because of rapid industrialisation of many developing cities resulting in a deteriorating health situation. Toxic gases, diseases, ground and surface water contamination become prevalent. In the circumstances, GIS becomes a necessary monitoring tool to detect the amount and effects of toxic material on a dumping site. GIS can also be used to identify a list of suitable areas to be used as dumping sites for industrial waste and other electronic waste coming from electronic gadgets. A list of several dumping sites is drawn up in order to choose the appropriate ones after some further investigations which may include the use of GIS. In the City of Harare, Pomona and Golden Quarry dumps are the well-known two dumping sites. GIS can be used to determine the environmental impact of these sites with the possibility of choosing better sites that pose no harm to urban human settlements. GIS technology has determined that Pomona dumping site has impacted negatively to the surrounding Mt Pleasant and Borrowdale inhabitants and also beyond, to as far as Mufakose (*Herald*, 26 November, 2016).

Waste disposal and treatment feasibility studies can be aided through GIS applications. The determination of levels of contamination at, for example, Mt Pleasant Pomona dumping site can be done using GIS. Below is an example of solid waste dumping area that was identified using GIS technologies.

Figure 10.14: St Louis Country Solid Waste Department Parcel Boundary (St Louis County USA, November 2010: 55)

The advantages of GIS and related ITCs gadgets make it an attractive option to use GIS in transport planning and management. The types of data that is related and that can be used in transit-oriented development (TOD) include traffic flow density, speed data, road geometry and urban transport systems analysis related data. In Harare for example, such data can be compiled along major arteries of the roads namely Harare-Mutare road, Harare –Bulawayo road, Harare- Masvingo road, Harare-Mutoko road, Harare-Chinhoyi and Harare-Bindura road for the determination of traffic volume and number of cars entering the City or Harare CBD. With the increase of urban population within the developing world and an increase in the car ownership by urban dwellers, this type of study is gaining a lot of traction this twenty first century. GIS technologies have been found to be very useful in transport-oriented development studies in towns and cities of the developing world.

Site selection

GIS can help the spatial planner to find the right site for the corner shops, neighbourhood centre or urban shopping centres. Residential subdivisions or sites to put up industrial plants under special economic zones can easily be detected using GIS technical methods of site selection. In town planning or real estate new trading areas with new potential could be detected. With knowledge of GIS, remote-sensed data can be combined with aerial photos, customer surveys and census data.

In Harare, identification of areas affected by water pollution can be made easy through the use of GIS and remotely sensed data. Manyame and Mukuvisi rivers are some of the heavily polluted sources of river affecting urban settlement and its populations. Right from Cleveland dam (source of Mukuvisi River), all settlements downstream to Lake Chivero may directly or indirectly be affected by the polluted Mukuvisi and Manyame rivers (Herald, 16 March, 1999). It is estimated that all settlements South of Harare (including Waterfalls, Sunningdale, Houghton Park, Glenview) are already affected. The level of the impact to the settlement can be assessed or be established through the application of GIS and remote sensing.

The following is the suggested procedure that can be followed in this analysis:
- Step 1: Identify affected area. This includes the mapping of the contaminated reservoir, rivers, streams and urban areas.
- Step 2: Identify all streams flowing from this reservoir, any portable water abstraction points, boreholes and wells dug within the identified area and all areas that can be possible sources of contamination. Within the City of Harare along Mukuvisi River, the fertiliser plant in Masasa area and the sewerage plant are the possible

sources of further contamination as waste from the fertiliser plant is allowed to flow into Mukuvisi River.

• Step 3: Identify urban areas and settlements supplied by the contaminated water. This can be done through laboratory tests of water selected from representative points selected and sampled within the affected area. Data on the portable water supply networks emanating from the extraction point at the reservoir are mapped out and the urban areas thus supplied are identified.

• Step 4: Inform affected homes and businesses of appropriate action to take.

• Step 5: Establish a buffer around the affected water bodies and streams. In a GIS application procedure, buffering has been found useful in the analysis of catchment areas, extent of areas affected, mean travel distances and the over and under supply of urban services.

• Step 6: Initiate the supply of clean water to affected areas. In this final analysis it shows that GIS has now found a solution to an urban planning problem of catastrophic proposition.

Site selection using GIS can also be done to determine the best site for the construction of Kunzvi Dam for example. This will facilitate the provision of equitable and sufficient water supply to the population of Harare Metropolitan City. Factors to be considered include economic, social, engineering as well as topographic and other environmental site-specific considerations.

Some GIS applications could be used in order to assess the number of buildings or houses in need of demolition in an urban slum settlement upgrading. Settlement upgrading has been done in Tanzania's Dar es Salaam Manzese area through the use of GIS as pilot project under the auspices of ITC in the Netherlands (Sliuzas, 1998). In Harare, areas in need of settlement upgrading include Hopely, Southley Park and Caledonia. These areas are housing a lot of urban people under slum and sometimes squalid conditions not suitable for human habitation. Forthcoming is a general GIS methodology that can be followed for slum settlement upgrading for Hopley.

a) Survey of all slums (e.g. in ward 6 of Hopley after some fieldwork were done) which are the most affected settlements

b) Mapping of slums using GIS related technologies

c) Planning the area and the creation of thematic maps e.g. unplanned settlement layer, planned settlement thematic layer.

d) Map overlaying to determine the houses and buildings which need demolition or regularisation.

e) Integration of geospatial and socioeconomic data

f) Identification of development model proposed for Hopley slum settlement.

g) Production of base maps, satellite images from Google Map, aerial photos and statistical data from the ward. Maps should have appropriate scales.

Methodology in GIS Applications

The following is the methodological outline that was applied in the production of the maps below using desktop Quantum GIS

a) Land-use characterisation and classification-digitisation, polygonisation of areas through vector layer creation analysis

b) Measurement of layout drawings from the window icon draw

c) Creation of thematic boundary map- roads using vector line analysis

d) Creation of thematic map- existing buildings using vector point analysis

e) Creation of thematic line map sewerage

f) Map overlaying and integration of geospatial data

g) Attribute table analysis

h) Entering of stand values, stand numbers and IDS

i) Querying the data

j) Annotation and labelling

georeferenced area taken from satellite-Chinyuka

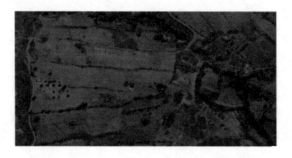

Figure 10.15: Geo referenced map (Google Map, 2017:12)

Figure 10.15 is satellite image geo referenced and extracted from a certain area in Manicaland province with the use of ARCGIS. This map is taken in its prevailing state. A GIS pilot project was then initiated to do practical work on residential layout designs using some desktop Quantum GIS applications. The first stage was land characterisation and suitability assessment to determine the land classes or areas suitable for settlement and construction of residential and commercial buildings for a small urban settlement. The results of this characterisation and suitability assessment yielded a map which is in Fig 10.16. The resultant map can also be used as an environmental impact map showing different layers of land capability classification.

land suitability classification map

Figure 10.16: Environment (Google Map, 2017)

The green areas indicate that it is class five that is wetland area not suitable for building or settlement. The green pattern also shows that the area may be a river or a stream where urban settlement is not possible. In GIS application a buffer zone may be applied along the proposed green area showing the boundary to which urban settlement may occur. The other colours blue, light green yellowish colours indicate various levels of suitability.

residental layout design –high density and medium density

Figure 10.17: Urban settlement (Fieldwork, 2018)

After determining areas suitable for an urban settlement, a residential layout design is created using QGIS vector layer creation analysis methodology. The stand sizes created are according to current approved planning design standards. For high densities 150m^2 and for medium densities 300m^2 were designed and drawn through GIS as shown above. The stands were drawn upon areas that were detected to be suitable for urban settlement as in Figure 10.16.

sewer reticulation network

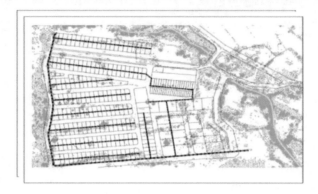

Figure 10.18: Sewer reticulation in urban settlement (Fieldwork, 2018)

Fig 10.18 shows a sewer reticulation network as is provided in an urban settlement where back to back houses are provided by one line within the servitude. The network was created using vector line analysis in a QGIS. Manholes and inspection eyes can be created in the sewer network using GIS and some detection of problem areas can be done through querying method.

a combination of sewer and road network

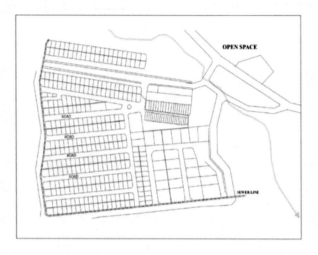

Figure 10.19: A combination of sewer and road networks in urban settlements
(Fieldwork, 2018)

Figure 10.19 indicates a combination of a sewer network as well as road network. The green line on the map indicates the main sewer line that is parallel to the district road. The blue line is the illustration of an existing river and the direction of its flow is shown by an end arrow. This mixed residential layout plan was created through GIS techniques. The fig 10.20 below shows the location (exact geo-referenced spatial area on the earth) of the identified properties and their sizes and value.

Land administration: stand size and value

Figure 10.20: Land administration (Fieldwork, 2018)

The value of the property at the corner in green colour is higher than that in orange because of different sizes and location. This type of information is analysed through querying attribute data. With the use of ARCGIS property number, property size, type (high, medium, low) value, property owner and tenure (leasehold, freehold, mortgage), can all be linked together to create a database for land administration purposes in an urban area. By means of simple click on the computer the whole range of querying and answers appear for example as to who owns what property and what value, where? How many properties need relocation or demolition and where are they situated? How many houses are valued at 25000 us dollars and above among others?

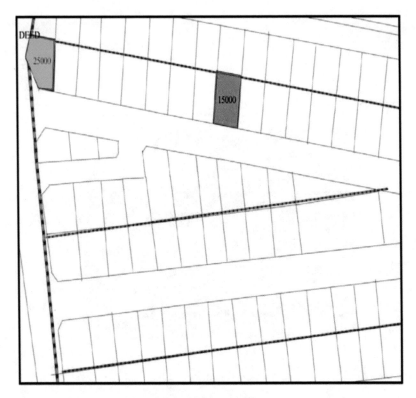

Figure 10.21: Land tilting and property record purposes (Fieldwork, 2018)

Figure 10:21 shows how GIS can be used for land tilting and property record purposes. Properties that are with title deeds are recorded together and those under some leasehold. GIS makes the urban land registration and cadastre easier. A multi-purpose cadastre in simple terms means a record of interests in land consisting of a register and a map (land-use plan) within a city, country or district; showing properties, units, parcels or stands (Hensen ,1996). The table below is a simplified analysis of how GIS can be used in urban areas.

Table 10.1: A Simplified analysis of how GIS can be used in urban areas (Fieldwork, 2018)

Activity/GIS question for urban planning	Data requirements	Spatial unit Point, line or polygon	Temporal time frequency	Applicable procedure and GIS package
How to plan for master plans, development plans and local subject plans	Estimate land requirements, remote-sensed data, aerial photos or mosaics, corresponding base maps	City level (for Harare is Metropolitan level –polygon	10 year Or 20-year duration	Raster based GIS Digitisation Land-use classification
Where are hazardous lands located and how much area is affected by what types of hazards	Hazardous zones-remote sensing and aerial photos	Hazardous zones (for Harare it is Pomona and Golden quarry Dumpsites) polygon analysis	Once a year	Remote sensing and Raster based GIS
How many houses are located on hazardous land?	Geo-coded housing units affected, statistical data	Houses as polygons or as points in zones (polygon areas of hazards)	Once a year	Buffering, see figs 3and 4 above ARC GIS
Where is urban land conversion taking place?	Land-use units Base maps Remote sensing	Land-use units Admin zones	Once a year	Polygon analysis
What is the spatial distribution of public toilets in Harare CBD?	Thematic public toilet map Total number of functional and dysfunctional toilets	Toilets as points	Once a year	ARCGIS point vector analysis
What is the length of Harare Drive road?	Harare road network thematic map and other base maps	Road as a line	Once a year	ARC GIS Line Vector Analysis
What is the bird's eye view of proposed Mt Hampden Harare New City?	Simulation modelling data	Simulation 3Dmodel	Three times a year	3D ARC GIS Bentley 3D See figs 5, 6 and 7

Table 10.1 is an oversimplified summary sheet to show some basic questions and urban activities that may trigger the use and

application of certain datasets, spatial entities and appropriate GIS technical software tools.

Conclusion and Recommendations

With increasing rapid industrialisation, globalisation and urbanisation of developing cities in Asia, South America and Africa, the use of GIS and ICTs has become very essential in seeking for possible spatial solutions to problems prevalent in these cities. This chapter has already shown (although not exhaustive) urban spatial planning areas which need the application and use of GIS in order to solve the urban spatial planning problems. GIS and related technology have been involved and can be used in Zimbabwe, in the analysis of urban spatial and temporal growth, site suitability assessments, transport planning and management, solid waste management issues, environmental sustainability planning, smart city development issues, housing ,3D visualisation, land-use and urban design planning, infrastructure planning and land and property management issues. However, there are quite a lot more areas where GIS can be very useful and applicable in urban planning which are not covered under this chapter. Suffice to say that this chapter has given an overview of applicability of GIS in urban planning which forms the basis upon which further research and analysis may be carried out. GIS has managed to create maps and layout designs and allows the public and specialists to answer spatial related questions such as how many buildings are affected by the rerouting of the road, what is the best site for the establishment of a primary school? Environmental and demographic data can be integrated, overlaid and the results visually attractive, with well explained graphics. It is a means of assessing different types of given alternatives. A planner using a GIS software package solves a planning problem faster than a planner using old methods of solving the spatial problem. This chapter has shown that GIS can be applied in urban planning in order to solve spatial planning problems that bedevil most urban centres of the developing world. It offers a quicker means of addressing spatial related problems. Rather than dwell on the cumbersome, time consuming and outdated methods of urban development planning,

210

town planners today need to become more sophisticated and technologically capable of handling large spatial databases that are used to aid decision-making.

GIS provides the necessary platform for the development of spatial based database systems. When an attribute table is created in a GIS already the system develops a database for future references and storage. A Database Management System software package is then provided to help synthesize the database already in the system. With 3D GIS modelling as shown in fig 10.7, collaboration and public participation from the general public, policy-makers and Government is enhanced due to the visualisation and the map –like design that they discuss and relate to for decision-making processes. GIS provides the necessary applicable technology for internet-based tools such as web GIS to aid in the decision-making process. Currently spatial planners no longer depend on GIS alone but also utilise current Information and Communication Technologies (ICTS) that includes telephones for data acquisition purposes. According to ESRI (2012) the combined use of GIS and related gadgets and web or cloud GIS is collectively called Geospatial Technology or Geographic Information Technology (GIT). GIS provides the opportunity to do further spatial analytical research and in-depth spatial queries for decision-making processes e.g. the determination of the number of housing units to be affected by toxic waste within 60 km radius of the site (Figure 10.3).

In the field of housing statistical data such as stand no, size, value and property ids are enhanced with the use of GIS. As already stated, this type of information is necessary for land administration and management purposes (Figure 10.20). Information that is location based (geocoded) is easily made available with the use of GIS. With the use of GIS there is improved mapping-ESRI estimated that since the use of GIS mapping has increased to more than 90% with a better product. Thematic mapping enhances analysis. There is an improved analysis of spatial planning data. With GIS, there is efficient and effective analysis of data. GIS applications aid pollution and toxic information reports related to hazards and poisonous chemicals. Tax evasions are easily traceable since GIS relates to fixed parcels (home ownership units) and the data are easily available as it is up-dated continuously. GIS can assist decision-makers to formulate public policies that are more effective for improved resource allocation, for economic development, for better urban community as well as efficient delivery and use of public facilities. Quality of planning service to the people is improved. With the use of speed access to planning information by the general public for example vacant space, slum settlements, wetland areas, retail growth amongst others. GIS has proved to be user friendly. GIS saves time and improves customer service. The theoretical background has already indicated at the beginning of this chapter, that GIS enhances Decision Support System (DSS). Thematic mapping that is generated by GIS (FIG 10.13), usually for overlaying purposes, enhances data analysis, processes manipulation and visualisation. The link to organisations and to Government entities can easily be increased through the introduction of e-government facilities that are GIS related.

For GIS to be successful in Zimbabwe there must be pilot projects carried out by planners or professionals working in urban centres. Government must institute a deliberate policy for supporting the initiation and management of GIS policy. The policy must be augmented by the financial budget for it to be implementable. There must be a strong financial backing both from both inside and outside the country for the programme to be successful. One reason why Rwanda Land Information System was successful was a strong financial backing from the International Community and the political will by its government. A monitoring mechanism also needs to be created for the continuous updating of new technologies. It is critical that all institutions of higher learning must adopt and adapt GIS technologies. Before such spatial application models are adopted there is need to carry-out a needs assessment to determine the amount of work and the general work flow patterns and data processing activities needed. Capacity training for staff members working in municipalities, government institutions that relate to spatial issues is required. There must be adequate skilled manpower to gather relevant spatial data for data capture, storage, manipulation, analysis, visualisation and map production.

References

Bentley. (2009). *The benefits of a 3D city, GIS for Sustainable City Infrastructure*: A Bentley white paper, Bentley Systems Incorporated. www.bentley.com

Chen, J. (2014). GIS-based multi-criteria analysis for land-use suitability assessment in City of Regina. *Environmental Systems Research*, 3(1), 1-13.

Dimitrova E., Burov, A and Nikolovh. (2010). *GIS in Urban Planning Education: Support for Integrated Approaches to Sustainable* Urban Development paper, 2010, Bulgaria.

ESRI. *GIS for Cadastre Management*, ESRI, GIS Technology in Europe, Rotterdam: The Netherlands.

ESRI. (2006). *GIS Solutions for Urban and Regional Planning*, Designing and Mapping the Future of your Community with GIS. www.esri.com/international.

GIS for Housing and Urban Development http://www.nap.edu/catalog/10674.html

Held, G., and Zlatanova, R. (2017). *Introducing GIS modelling*: Web 3D GIS for Urban Environments.

Herald. (24 February, 2017). Decentralisation to return Harare's glory? *Herald*, Zimpapers, Harare Zimbabwe.

Herald, (11 May, (2016). Biogas Project curbs Mbare waste wars: *Herald*, Zimpapers Harare, Zimbabwe.

Herald. (15 October, 2016). Harare: Littering in the Sunshine*: Herald*, Zimpapers, Harare, Zimbabwe

Herald. (26 November, 2016). Effects of Garbage burning at Pomona Dumpsite: *Herald*, Zimpapers, Harare, Zimbabwe.

Herald. (16 March 1999). Sewage pollution threatens city's main water supply: *Herald* Zimpapers, Harare, Zimbabwe.

Herald. *(29 June*, 1999). Harare's Ground water raises scare: *Herald*, Zimpapers, Harare, Zimbabwe.

Herald. (19 June 1997). Hope for Historic buildings: *Herald*, Samara publications, Harare, Zimbabwe.

Haughton, G and Huntor, C. (1996). *Sustainable Cities*, Routledge Publishers, London and New York.

International Institute of Aerospace Survey and Earth Sciences (ITC), Journal (1996). *Planning Urban Services* Special HABITAT 11 Issue, Enschede, The Netherlands.

Kohsaka, H. (2012). Applications of GIS to urban planning and management: Problems facing Japanese local governments. *Geo Journal*, 52(3), 271-280.

Liu, Y. (2009). *Modelling Urban Development with Geographical Information Systems and Cellular Automata*, CRC Press, London, New York.

Sliuzas, R. (1998). *Unplanned settlement Upgrading*: Manzese area, Dar es Salaam, Case Study, ITC.

Simon D. (2016). *Rethinking Sustainable Cities*: Accessible Green and Fair, Policy Press, University of Briston, UK.

Stoter, J. E. (2004). *3D Cadastre*, published PHD thesis, Netherlands Geodetic Commission, Delft: The Netherlands.

Tarik, G. (2017). *Smart Cities through a Geospatial lens*: The Planning Institute of Jamaica, 16 Oxford Road, Kingston 5, Jamaica West Indies.

The use of GIS in Urban Planning, Volume 2: *Urban Planning and GIS*: Implementation Issues, Helsinki Consulting Group, Skopje. Available online: http:\Applic\MK_GIS\6_My_\materials\GIS_trainingVP_3e dited2.doc. [Accessed on 08 May 2018]

UN-HABITAT. (2009). *Sustainable Urban Planning Handbook for Cities and Towns*: Unon Publishing Services Section, Nairobi, Kenya.

United Nations. (2000). *Handbook on Geographic Information Systems and Digital Mapping*: Department of Economic and Social Affairs Statistics Division, Series F No79, UN, New York.

UN-HABITAT. (2013). *GIS Handbook for Municipalities*: UN-HABITAT, Nairobi, Kenya.

UN-HABITAT and UNEP (ICLEI), *Sustainable Energy Planning*, A Handbook for Cities and Towns in Developing Countries: UN-HABITAT and UNEP.

UN-HABITAT. (2011). Annual Report, UN-HABITAT.

Yeh, A. (2008). *GIS as a planning support system for the planning of Harmonious Cities*: UN-HABITAT, lecture Award Series 3, UN-HABITAT Nairobi Kenya.

Chapter 11

Negotiation in real estate

Motive Baloyi and Innocent Chirisa

Introduction

This chapter is about how negotiation in general and then how the same is applicable in real estate in Zimbabwe. It goes beyond describing what negotiation is and the process involved in introducing pressure points in negotiation as well as the strategies one needs to embrace when negotiating. The chapter goes beyond simple description of negotiation as one of the alternative dispute resolution methods to explain where one negotiates in real estate and the rationale for reaching agreements. The existence of plenty dispute areas in real estate makes negotiation a crucial art and skill which every player should possess. The conflict areas range from inheriting a property, lease terms, rent offers that landlords usually place, condition of the property versus the renovation pace, price placed on a certain piece of land or a property versus its location and services; dispute among property management agents and landlords on issues such as the agent fees, collection of rents and termination of the property manager's contract among the endless list. These are issues that motivate planners and realtors to understand conflict areas in real estate and proffer solutions on how to resolve the conflict through the art of negotiation in a transparent and traceable way through written documents in the presence of duly authorised representatives. However, focusing on negotiation in real estate context alone does not make negotiation in other fields less important. According to Schatzki *et al.* (2005), we are all negotiators, what differs is what we negotiate for. The variations include negotiating for a car, long lunch breaks, a wife, house, a raise, a contract and rental among many things one might think of. The list shows that negotiation is a crucial subject across all fields, hence the planners and realtors in the case of this chapter are not lost in

215

developing interest in the negotiation subject to show how people can be able to survive in the real estate field.

Literature indicates that many scholars vary in explaining what negotiation is. According to Ary *et al.* (2014),' a negotiation or bargaining process attempts to reach an agreement or a consensus.' However, these scholars highlight that it is not an obvious case that an agreement or a consensus always reflects the best interests of all players involved. In some cases, the best result is only achieved if there is no agreement at all. Gosselin (2010)'s definition of negotiation is detailed in that there is an indication of the reason of wanting to negotiate not just a mere agreement. The definition shows that, 'negotiation is the moment in which two or more agents are confronted in a game of interest adjustment, each agent trying to reach their objective: to maximise tangible or intangible gains, those profits being of economic, financial, political, diplomatic or military nature. Schatzki *et al.* (2005) edify the definition by saying, 'negotiation is the art of getting what you want through trading in order to meet your needs under a condition where there might be a 'no' or a maybe or as long as there is an absence of total acceptance. The definition of variations is only in the wording but all of them have something in common which is conflict resolution through dialogue with the goal of maximising benefits to all parties involved.

Models of Negotiation

According to Fisher *et al.* (1981) negotiation models are frameworks or strategies that try to guide the negotiators towards a successful conflict resolution. The models include ZOPA (zone of possible agreement), BATNA (best alternative to a negotiated agreement) and value creation through trades. The models according to Alfredson (2008) work perfectly well for weaker negotiators so that they become successful when dealing with strong and talented negotiators.

ZOPA
Raiffa (1982), admits that successful negotiation agreements are the ones that contain a ZOPA (Zone of possible agreement) in them.

A ZOPA is a range or an overlap that is between the maximum purchase prices the buyer is willing to accept versus the minimum price the seller will be willing to get. The overlap range between the points according to Fisher *et al.* (1991) is the ZOPA. For example, if a buyer is willing to pay 250 000 dollars as the maximum purchase price and the property owner is willing to take 200 000 dollars as the minimum price, the range between these two reservation points is the zone defined as the ZOPA. Therefore, if the negotiations are said to be successful according to Raiffa (1982), the agreement should fall somewhere in the demarcated ZOPA zone. Therefore, in this case, a successfully negotiated agreement would result in the purchase price between 200 000 and 250 000, where 250 000 will be the maximum limit of an expensive property according to the buyer and 200 000 the lowest benchmark price for a cheapest property according to the property owner. Fisher *et al.* (1991) explain that in the cases where the reservations do not overlap, then there is no ZOPA. Such cases may exist. Using the above example, the seller would be expecting to accept a lowest limit price of 250 000 dollars from the property whilst the buyer would be willing to offer 200 000 dollars as the maximum purchase price. Raiffa (1982) identifies such no ZOPA scenarios as problematic in that they end up being a win-lose situation where one party in the deal may have to take a decision which is not favourable or result in no agreement at all. However, in other cases it is better to reach to a no-agreement decision than getting into risky agreements that leave the other party paying more by too much compromise.

BATNA

BATNA (best alternative to a negotiated agreement) is a concept developed by Roger Fisher and William Ury in 1981 as a solution or a way out or a preferred course of action that will be an alternative to a negotiated agreement in most cases in the absence of a deal. Having a BATNA means somebody knows what to do or a pathway to take in the case of failing to reach an agreement. Fisher *et al.* (1981) argue that having a BATNA or a bottom line can be very costly and can cause inflexibility and prevent parties from getting a negotiated favourable position. However, to talented negotiators BATNA's is an opportunity to evaluate their options during and after the

217

discussions to see if the deal will be worth taking or rejecting Anderson *et al.* (2008) urge negotiators to always improve their BATNAs and to know the other side's BATNA so that the negotiations are better placed in the boundaries of the bottom line alternatives. Knowing the other person's BATNA can be very powerful in a negotiation especially when dealing with experienced and powerful negotiators.

Value creation through trade-offs

The concept stressed that negotiating parties can improve their negotiated agreements by trading their values at the disposal of the property. Such arrangements help each party to something it wants in return of something it values less. This concept dismisses the assumptions that a fairly negotiated deal should end with both parties getting equal quantities. The idea of the concept is to enlighten the negotiators that sometimes negotiating from the position point of view result in each party losing much than negotiating on the basis of interest. Professor Chirisa in one of my undergraduate classes once gave an illustration of this concept using an orange example. He said, "If an orange juice maker and a gardener were to negotiate for an orange using the position approach, that they both want an orange they would probably cut it into two halves but would it be the best solution given that the juice maker is only concerned with the juice and the gardener with the orange peels. Isn't it a loss to both of them because they will throw away what they are not interested in? Therefore, the best option is for the juice maker to take away the juice and give the peels to the gardener who can use them in the composite to produce organic fertiliser." Therefore, given the example, an interest-based negotiation approach is very useful in that the parties trade their values and little or no losses are incurred.

Raiffa (1982) argues that inevitable conflict scenarios in real estate make negotiation a life and a survival skill every involved party should own. The dispute areas differ with what is at stack. One reason why people negotiate is that without negotiation they will not get what they desire to have. Diverse interests exist in different instances in the real estate context. For example, lease terms and conditions require both the landlord and tenant to identify their needs as well as to communicate them especially when they are obviously subdued or in cases where there are slim chances that the needs may be fulfilled. Therefore, negotiation is used to communicate subdued needs which may be met through adjustments of the initial agreements. Headley (1995) agrees that negotiation is again used as a process of exchange where the parties trade and reach a mutually beneficial agreement. Through this trade-off, where for instance a tenant can be able to negotiate a reduction in the rentals for a certain month in the exchange of labour that the tenant may be able to provide; for example, fixing old ceilings and painting. It is the provisions of labour in this case that will lead the landlord to accept a reduction in the rentals for the expense will be unavoidable. The other reason why negotiation is crucial in real estate is that people are usually bound to put their interests first such that if the other interested people do not communicate their interests so that adjustments are made to benefit everyone, decisions are bound to serve the interests of decision-makers or those who have an upper hand in any given scenario. Therefore, to avoid serving the interests of one player in real estate issues, objection and negotiation is a required skill in the process of negotiating a trade-off so that everyone at the end.

What to negotiate for in real estate and the players involved

There are a number of cases where one needs to negotiate in real estate. The main reason for negotiating is that the interested parties in every scenario have diverse interests and it is so rare to find parties which have the same interests. The main categories where people negotiate in real estate include lease negotiations, property sale negotiations, land sale negotiations, execution of a deceased's property and property management negotiations.

Negotiations with the landlord

Lease Negotiations
According to Pruit (1993), lease negotiations are done between the tenant and the Landlord. These two parties normally have

diverging interests. The landlord is usually interested in realising value of the property through normal rentals as well as getting a good tenant who does not bring headaches in negligence and carelessness in terms of handling property. The tenant is also interested in getting an understanding landlord and reasonable rentals that match with the condition and location of the property. Therefore, given the different interests the parties involved have, reaching an agreement where both parties benefit is only done through negotiation. For example, a tenant may have looked around town in search of an ideal apartment to rent but finds it difficult to get one. Then there is a scenario where the tenant got some favourable places but the apartments in those areas are too expensive.

The rule of negotiation shows that the tenant should not give up in those areas. Instead, it is an opportunity to negotiate with the property owner for the type of rentals that suit the tenant ideally. Rental reduction is one example that has been identified so far under lease negotiation but there are a lot of other things the tenant may need to negotiate in that scenario. However further negotiations usually require the tenant to build a good rapport with the landlord so that it becomes hard for the property owner to quickly brush the tenant and say no. The other examples of further negotiation on lease negotiation may include repairs. Depending with the landlord, repairs may provide the tenant with an opportunity for rental reduction since some property owners may choose to give the tenant the authority to repair or renovate anything and subtract that cost from the monthly rentals. However, this option depends with the faithfulness of the tenant since it will be hard to trace the actual cost incurred from getting the equipment to the labour costs. The option is usually to trusted tenants, not a mere tenant. On repairs, the other option is that the property owners may choose to fix the things on their own. Therefore, in that scenario, the rentals won't be affected since the expense is on the landlord, not the tenant. Therefore, depending with what the landlord chooses as the best option, negotiation is inevitable either way.

Besides repairs, permission for pets and any other allowances can be further negotiated with a tenant that would have built a relationship with the property owner. These further negotiated issues are only granted after an examination of the kind of a tenant one is. For example, permission for pets is granted to someone who is smart and follows orders in terms of where the pets should be kept so that they do not roam around and mess up everywhere. Lease negotiations on rental reduction at first depend on the first contact that a tenant has with the landlord. However other further negotiations are conditioned to the tenant behaviour and the skill of learning whether he is suitable to be in a position of a successful bargaining process.

Property management negotiation

Property management is another example of real estate negotiation which includes the involvement of many parties into play. These include the lawyers, property owner, tenants and property manager. The property manager and owner are directly involved participants in this kind of negotiation. Thompson (1990) shows that, the first stage in this negotiation process is the contract negotiation where the agent will be bargaining for a job as a property manager, especially in the cases where the owner is absent and requires someone trustworthy to leave the property under custody. The contract negotiation also involves the discussion of the agent fees so that the offer is left on a reasonable amount which the property owner can afford to pay at the same time being one which the agent is willing to accept. After negotiating the contract, the two parties have a number of things to discuss and agree on. Failure to agree brings tension and confusion, with the tenants spicing up the relationship; especially when they cause either the property manager or owner to violate the rules they agreed on. The conditions of this kind of contract is usually written and is witnessed by duly authorised representatives since the issues involved may result in serious civil cases and in extreme cases result in criminal cases Dawson (2005).

Feri *et al.* (2011) identify problematic areas in property management negotiation and one of the cases that may arise because of property management negotiation. They include the violation of the code of ethics in real estate by the property owner through hiring another property manager during the term of the initial manager if there is no properly written document which clarifies the date of commencement and expiration date of the first hired property manager. Therefore, the written agreements on the start and finish date helps protect the property manager from unethical behaviour of the property owner. Therefore, property management negotiations in Zimbabwe seem to be crucial in that they require proper paper work or written agreements as compared to the lease negotiations which can be discussed and finalised without any proper documentation Dawson (2005). The lease negotiations especially on single houses is more casual, the issue only gets serious if the lease negotiations involve commercial buildings and residential flats and clusters. However, property management negotiations are stricter and they require legally crafted documents since the disposal of the property into the property manager's custody involves much risk as this include strangers who work in a long-distance context as property management in Zimbabwe is usually for properties that have their owners outside the country. Despite that, the lease negotiations process is easy it is usually problematic because many negotiations in the lease context are not written and it is hard to depict what was initially agreed on if the parties are by any chance in conflict and have decided to go to court as a resolution.

The other area of conflict in property management negotiation is the limit which both parties have as far as the disposal of the property is concerned. If not discussed and clearly laid out, both parties have the potential to go overboard and overlap into the duties of one another. For example, a property manager is usually given the permission to manage the property not to lease it and the owner is also mandated to lease the property with the manager's knowledge Dawson (2005). Therefore, if these duties are not performed correctly with the rightful persons mandated to carry the work, it becomes an issue can make the relationship of the two directly involved parties very rough. The violation of the duty by the property owner is an ethical issue but leasing a property without the owner's knowledge on the side of the property manager can attract criminal cases as that can be equated to stealing. Therefore, a clearly written document will specify that the agent is only given the permission to manage the property, but not to lease it. The above condition does not mean that there are no agents who are given permission to manage and lease the property as well, but this depends on the rapport between the owner and the manager and the levels of trust they have in each other.

Collection of rentals is one problematic issue. The owner and the agent at first have to clarify on what happens because if this is not made clear, the owner in most cases tends to lose the money to the agent as it is hard to trace funds which are not documented. Therefore, as part of negotiating the conditions of the contract, the agent's duty is specified as the one to collect the rentals and deposit security deposits from tenants into a trust account (Anderson *et al.* 2008). To secure that the money will surely be deposited in the trust account; the agreement will also specify that the agent is held monetarily responsible for inability to collect rents. Depositing the rentals in the trust account helps avoid unethical practices by the owner in cases where he might decide to lie that the money was not received and make the agent to pay Dawson (2005).

The other problematic issue in the property management negotiation is repairs, renovation and redecoration. These again need to be discussed so that it is specified on who has the authority to decide when to repair, renovate, redecorate; how it will be done and who will be hired for the job. The agent can be given the permission to redecorate or repair but this is done with the owner's consent. The agent in some cases is even allowed to terminate leases, serve notices of termination but with the owner's consent. Therefore, given the conflict zones in the property management negotiation, a legally written document is required which specifies every discussed issue and how it's supposed to be handled. A summary of the issues discussed that should appear in the document include the commencement date and expiration date, permission to manage not to lease, collect rentals and deposit it into the trust account, renovate or repair or redecorate with the owner's consent, terminate leases and serve notices of termination with the owner's knowledge (Anderson *et al.* 2008). The owners' duties are also specified in the document which includes not negotiating with tenants without the agent's knowledge, not looking for another agent within the agreement period with another agent and shall not lease the property without the agent's knowledge. All the do's and don'ts are mandated to be performed within the context of the agreed conditions and both the parties have roles to play in order to make the relationship smooth. The lawyers are only available as witnesses as the agreements are crafted so that the document will be a reference in case there are conflicts and the other party is failing to comply with the abiding rules Dawson (2005).

Property sale negotiations

The bargaining process involves lawyers, the buyer, the seller, estate agencies who act as go –between in the case of a buyer and a seller. According to Farthing (2002), the negotiation process begins when the property owner disposes a property into the custody of estate agencies so that they value and advertise it. The seller (owner of the property) is involved in a negotiation process on the offer price which lies in the limits of what the owner is willing to accept, the market price and the value of the property or what the property is worth (Anderson *et al.* 2008). The estate agent and the owner will have to negotiate on the offer price and also provide a written document which is called the agreement of sale which is the permission the estate agent would be given to sale the property in exchange of a negotiated commission. The estate agent advertises the property as well as negotiates the buying price by those interested. The buying price is mostly negotiated on the basis of the form of payment in Zimbabwe. Properties that are bought in cash transactions tend out to be cheaper than that of a transfer transaction. Property sale negotiations end up with legally written documents that specify the name of the owner of the property, for how much it has been sold, on which date and the name of buyer and witnesses which are duly authorised people Dawson (2005).

The process of negotiation

According to Ary *et al.* (2015) negotiation in real estate is a very complex process with abundant stages and issues, which demand a substantial input of time and money. The negotiation process is iterative in such a way that the stages normally do not follow the sequence that is said to be there Anderson *et al.* (2008) show that the response one gets after identifying determines the pace of negotiation and how to negotiate. Therefore, four stages have been identified to be processes in which every negotiator follows when faced with a situation of wanting to negotiate. The first stage is to prepare. The preparation stage is where needs are identified and objectives are assessed. For instance, using a land acquisition example between a certain local authority and a farmer, the local authority might be the one to go through the first stage of preparation if it is planning to take the farmer's land for house development projects. The authority is also supposed to assess the farmer's needs, which are mainly about farming. The assessment of the authority and farmer's needs will help determine the position that the authority will decide to take for negotiation with the farmer. The position of the planning authority is to relocate the farmer and compensate him to another plot.

According to Anderson (2008), if the respondent agrees to the demands, there is no negotiation to talk about. However, if the response is no or maybe, then negotiation is a requirement so that there is a discussion on why the answer is no or maybe and see if the reasons can be subject to change. Still, in the light of the example, the position of relocation will trigger areas of discussion. The farmer may argue that the land is fertile and the location is so strategic and close to the city centre and water sources. The reasons that the farmer gives will determine areas of possible flexibility or not. If the farmer shows that relocation is an impossible situation, the planning authority may have to reconsider its position and adjust to the response. The new direction is to negotiate on part of the piece of land, not the whole plot. The new direction may provide a new positive working climate where the farmer gives in if he stands to benefit from the development. Therefore, such a win –win situation may lead the farmer to compromise and give away part of the land as a condition to benefit from the development. The negotiation process is subject to iteration because people's needs change over time and they might need to reconsider some of the agreements that were made, especially if they are no longer beneficial.

Negotiation Pressure points

Dawson (2005) identifies that power negotiators should know how to apply negotiating pressure points so that they are successful in the bargaining process. One of the critical areas in pressure points is the options button. The point as explained by Dawson is to convince the sellers about the different alternatives you have. Sellers are usually clever in that they use the options button to have an upper hand in the negotiation process. A seller who has six buyers waving 300 000-dollar cash transactions has more options that it will be hard for someone who has 250 000 dollars and there is no way that kind of buyer will be able to convince the seller to leave the 300 000-option to go for a lower price. A talented negotiator, even if with a lower offer price will be the only one to make the seller think twice if there is a demonstration of the option power by the buyer who might trap the seller by highlighting that he has other properties in mind which are lower priced and situated in a better location. Therefore, the option power drives those who have the option power to negotiate. The options the buyer has is a threat to the seller since the options are cheaper and better located which may, in any way make the other buyers to reconsider their offer prices and their option.

Time pressure is said to have significance in negotiation in general. However, in real estate, this pressure point has more impact. Children know how well to use this pressure point to get what they want from parents. If a parent is running late, children know that it is the time to ask whatever they might need because the really know that unknowingly, the parent will agree to the demands because when people are under pressure, they become flexible. However, in real estate it is hard to know if a seller or an owner of a property is under time pressure unless the buyer does some little research to find out the time pressures that the seller will be under. Examples of time pressures in the context of the seller include, retirement and the seller want to quickly move, the seller may be behind on his mortgage payments and is failing to catch up, might need money urgently to pay other mounting debts and in foreclosure and in danger of losing the property. Therefore, if a buyer is able to identify such pressing

226

issues, he is in a better position to win a deal since time pressures make people flexible with something they would not do in a normal situation.

Strategies to use when negotiating

One of the critical strategies every negotiator embrace is the information strategy. According to Urbanaviciene *et al.* (2009), 'efficient negotiations on products of construction and real estate demand awareness of the current economic situation and understanding of the main factors affecting the supply and the demand'. The macro environment factors affect negotiations differently. Some have a direct impact, others an indirect impact. Currently in Zimbabwe, the cash crisis has affected the real estate market, especially on the side of buyers of real estate as they are made to pay more if the transactions are to be transfers. The cash form of payment is the most favourable one and has led many properties in the country to be relatively cheaper as compared to the different price that the same properties have if transfers are involved. Therefore, getting such information is critical for the buyer to decide the form of payment and a strategy to negotiate the price down if it is in cash. Real estate is an expensive product and does not fall into the daily or monthly purchases, thus information to use when negotiating real estate needs to be researched since it is so easy to win the heart of someone who does not have information. Urbanaviciene *et al.* (2009), explain this thought by identifying that real estate is not a homogeneous item, even identical properties can sell differently in the market depending on the information diversity of the estate agent and the negotiation skills of the one buying the property.

The other strategy that every negotiator involved in real estate transactions should have, whether buying, selling and contracting or renting is the ability to walk away from the table when the deal is not worth to take. Hale (2017) shows that having a bottom line which according to Fisher and Ury (1981) is a BATNA is very critical when negotiating because it protects the parties from avoiding useless deals that a no agreement state will be much better than getting a deal. Hale explains it as skill to be able to identify what is not right for you. His document even goes to the extremes of protecting a bottom line by sharing it with trusted friends or family such that it will be embarrassing to give in to the emotions of the negotiation and stray from the bottom line which was published to family and friends. The point is to protect any party from getting into a bad deal since it is far less beneficial to have a bad deal than walking away without losing anything. Successful negotiations come with favourable deals.

A narrative is again one of the negotiation skills that every negotiator should possess. This is all about being a good story teller. People are subject to follow people who have information and those that know what they will be doing. Therefore, storytelling in real estate involves knowing the list of properties that sold much on the market or in the area and the ability to do the comparables and to clearly articulate the differences when it comes to the subject of a particular property in question. The differences that sell in real estate may include the unique finishings, the lifespan of the building and the zoning rights. These specifics according to Hale (2017) help the negotiator to make a fluff story why the property is being sold to win the minds of the other negotiating counterparts.

References

Allred, K. G., Mallozzi, J. S., Matsui, F and Raia, C. P. (1997). The influence of anger and compassion on negotiation performance. *Organizational behaviour and human decision processes*, 70(3), 175-187.

Samsura, D. A. A., van der Krabben, E., Van Deemen, A. M. A and Van der Heijden, R. E. C. M. (2015). Negotiation processes in land and property development: an experimental study. *Journal of Property Research*, 32(2), 173-191.

De Pauw, A. S., Venter, D and Neethling, K. (2010). The effect of negotiator creativity on negotiation outcomes in a bilateral negotiation. *Creativity Research Journal*, 23(1), 42-50.

Ennis, F. (1997). Infrastructure provision, the negotiating process and the planner's role. *Urban Studies*, 34, 1935–1954.

Farthing, S and Ashley, K. (2002). Negotiations and the delivery of affordable housing through the English planning system. *Planning Practice and Research*, 17, 45–58.

Feri, F and Gantner, A. (2011). Bargaining or searching for a better price? An experimental study. *Games and Economic Behaviour*, 72, 376–399.

Fisher, R and Ury, W. (1981). Getting to Yes: Negotiating Agreement without Giving In. *Penguin Books,* New York: USA.

Fisher, R., Ury, W and Patton, B., (1991). Getting to Yes: Negotiating Agreement without Giving In. *Revised 2nd edition. Penguin Books,* New York, USA.

Nigro, G. L., Bruccoleri, M and Perrone, G. (2006). Negotiation in distributed production planning environments. *International Journal of Production Research, 44*(18-19), 3743-3758.

Goldman, A and Rojot, J. (2003). *Negotiation. Theory and practice.* Kluwer, The Hague.

Gulliver, P. H. (1979). Disputes and Negotiations: A Cross Cultural Perspective, Studies in Law and Social Control. *New York and.*

Hale, J. P. (2017). Negotiating a real estate contract. Real Estate, Inc. in Westminster, Maryland.

Healey, P., Purdue, M and Ennis, F. (1995). Negotiating Development: Rationales and Practice for Development Obligations and Planning Gain (Spon, London).

Jicai, L and Charles, Y. J. (2009). Real option application in PPP/PFI project negotiation, *Construction Management and Economics*, 27(4), 331-342

Northcraft, G. B., G. A., Van Kleef and L. Wang. (2012). Beyond negotiated outcomes: The hidden costs of anger expression in dyadic negotiation. *Organizational Behaviour and Human Decision Processes* 119: 54-63.

Pruitt, D. G and Carnevale, P. J. (1993). *Negotiation in social conflict.* Thomson Brooks/Cole Publishing Co.

Raiffa, H. (1982). *The art and science of negotiation.* Harvard University Press. Research, 44:18-19, 3743-3758, DOI: 10.1080/00207540600575787

Ruming, K. J. (2009). Development configurations and planning negotiations: *A case of fringe development in Sydney*, Australia. Urban Studies, 46, 1461–1483.

Schneider, H. (2016). "Emotions in Real Estate Negotiations," *Joseph Wharton Scholars.* Available online http://repository.upenn.edu/joseph_wharton_scholars/4

Thompson, L. (1990). Negotiation behaviour and outcomes: Empirical evidence and theoretical issues. *Psychological Bulletin,* 108(3), 515-532.

Thompson, L. (2005). The mind and heart of the negotiator. Pearson Prentice Hall: New Jersey

Vita, U., Artūras, P., Edmundas, K., Zavadskas and Mark, S. (2009). The web–based real estate multiple criteria negotiation decision support system: A new generation of decision support systems, *International Journal of Strategic Property Management,* 13:3, 267-286.

Zeckhauser, R. J., Keeney, R. L and Sebenius, J. K. (Eds.). (1996). Wise choices: Decisions, games and negotiations. Cambridge, MA: Harvard Business School Press.

Chapter 12

The scope and issues in property maintenance

Geraldine Usingarahwe and Chipo Mutonhodza

Introduction

The main concern of the construction industry is to satisfy its clients by delivering projects that achieve their set goals, meet their expectations and provide the best value for money (Barrett and Stanley, 1999; Watson and Asher, 1999). Maintenance plays an important role in retaining, restoring or improving the built environment to perform its planned function. Property in this context it refers to the built environment thus buildings. The Committee on Building Maintenance (1972) defines maintenance as work which is done to keep, restore or improve every facility of the building, i.e. every part, it services and currently acceptable standard to sustain the utility and value of the facility. This definition takes into account the notion of value, which is linked with life expectancy and relevant is the consideration of the complex mechanisms which either erode or enhance the value of a built environment over time. The building offers different services to the clients who include heating and lighting, air conditioning and ventilation, lifts in the case of vertical construction and other installations. Therefore, all these facilities should be working property every time because they are used daily by the clients and breakdown of any will cause problems to their daily routines thus causing dissatisfaction.

The construction industry contributes to the social and economic development of societies through provision of building and infrastructure projects, causing major impact on the environment. The industry consumes a very large amount of non-renewable resources, being a substantial source of waste, a polluter of water and air and also a contributor to land dereliction (Friends of the Earth, 1995; Roodman and Lenssen, 1995). The awareness of sustainability has increased in construction projects worldwide attention towards saving the environment, improvement on building performance, achieving client satisfaction and enhancing value for money (Addis and Talbot, 2001; Thomson *et al.* 2003; Abdellatif and Othman, 2006). The construction industry should make efforts to improve client satisfaction through continual improvement and flexibility when responding to their requirements, meeting the needs of the end-users, coping with changes of the regulations, exploiting new business opportunities, adapting to technological improvement and providing best value for money (Othman *et al.* 2004). This is done to keep customers satisfied, loyal. Maintenance is a key function in sustaining long-term profitability for organisations (Parida and Kumar, 2006). This recognises that an effective programme to control maintenance costs must start at the design stage of the building and must eventually justify itself, not only by minimising the costs of maintenance, but rather maximising the benefits of the investment (Son and Yuen, 1993).

Theoretical underpinnings

Historically, buildings were ageing and constantly being renovated in a way where actions were taken at different times or ways rather than being planned for from the beginning. The scope of many renovations was limited due to restraints in funding and ended up resulting in cosmetic change that had few or no infrastructure improvements. This could further lead to inefficiency of the mechanical systems, customer complaints due to dissatisfaction with their property or surrounding environmental conditions and higher utility bills and maintenance costs (Kumar and Ellingsen, 2000). Facility managers did not generally consider any management process because they relied on reactive actions according to the clients' or users' complaints. It can be concluded that the managers preferred carrying out reactive maintenance rather than proactive works (Schmberger and Knod, 1997). Concerns have been raised on maintenance management being unprofessionally applied by managers in many cases. Attention towards management and upkeep of properties has been seen extending substantially from macro to micro level as private property owners realized the importance of maintaining and enhancing the value and use of their capital assets. Macro-level initiatives especially in developed countries as such as those in Europe were directed at maintenance activities in order to prevent the deterioration of public pre-war housing stocks which were occupied mainly on a rental basis. Developing countries concentrated on the construction of new homes with little or no planning for the after-care of the buildings.

Design decisions affect the building's performance throughout its life cycle and faults in building design place a heavy burden on the infrastructure for rest of its life as there is no compensation for it. In such situations, the responsibility falls on the designer because they must think carefully and consider long-term effects of their design projects. Explaining the link between maintenance and building design, Ramly (2006) suggests four sectors of building design that should be considered and regarded as important to avoid the need for unplanned maintenance at the post-occupation stage. These sectors are the main fabric or walls, floors, roofs and internal finishes which include ceiling and wall finishes such as; special design features like decorative elements for the doors, windows, glass; cleaning and housekeeping elements of all building components. Structure or design faults on buildings impose heavy financial burdens to the occupier or owner of premises later.

The completion stage of the construction project represents a critical milestone for evaluating building performance. While occupying, operating or using the building, design deficiencies and construction defects can reduce the building's sustainability and endanger the surrounding environment (Gibson, 1979). The importance of maintenance management is highlighted to assess building performance, define areas that require attention from the design and construct teams to generate sustainable values and improving the performance of their new projects. The project team should aim at delivering buildings that enhance quality of life, achieve client satisfaction, ensure flexibility and allow for user changes in the future, provide and support favourable natural and social environments as well as maximise the efficient use of resources within the built environment.

A property is an investment to the owner; therefore, he or she expects a return from it through receiving the best value his money. If the property is being leased with poor performance and defects attached with, clients will not be satisfied with such conditions and may decide to relocate. As a result, this will create losses to the owner as there is no income being generated from the property. Therefore, an excellent practice of maintenance management is greatly required to increase the life cycle of the property and to minimise unexpected breakdowns or deterioration effects. The most sensible approach to take is to see maintenance practice as that which enables the building to continue to perform efficiently the functions for which it was designed. This may also include some upgrading to raise the original standards, where appropriate, to contemporary norms and the rectification of design faults. Therefore, building maintenance needs to be seen as a part of a larger property management function.

Literature review

There is an increase in the use of property as collateral for business loans which provides further motivation to maintain buildings. Occupational health therapists and other researchers investigated 'building related illness' and 'sick building syndromes' which were, amongst other things, often attributed to poor operation and maintenance of sectors like HVAC systems in energy conserving 'sealed' buildings. Significant positive changes were seen in the attitude towards maintenance and modernisation of private sector building stock and rising standards of living began to register more fully on the electorate. The building life cycle should be considered at the early stages (Wood, 2003). Early major repairs and demolitions in the expected life of a building are always associated with faulty design. A properly maintained building is expected to have a good life span provided that the design does not/or impose excessive maintenance costs. Several defects can appear on a building at the post-occupational stage. For example, cracks in a building can result from design faults which in turn cause partial or total collapse. The main sources of defects are the mistakes which would have been made at the design stage, construction phase and maintenance practice. Construction faults may include poor material selection.

Researches from developed countries like Singapore, analysed defects of buildings constructed in wet areas of buildings by Chew (2005) reported faults in design and material selection. Faults made during construction include tile debonding, mastic failure, water leakage through cracks, pipe leakage through walls, paint defects, water ponding, spalling of concrete and unevenness of tile surface. Mistakes at maintenance phase include staining tiles. Moreover, in England, research by Olubodun (2000) on housing stock reveals problems of similar nature in the housing stock under study. Present are various implicating factors of design and construction in the United Kingdom. These defects are as a result of faults of design, construction, supervision and workmanship. For example; rising dampness that affects both exterior and interior surfaces due to poor supervision and workmanship has resulted in poor flow in waste pipes. Also, communication gap can influence building design while creating the need for extensive maintenance of the building at post occupational level. Communication in design allows for the discharge of the ideas during design stage or corrective ideas during the construction phase.

In Malaysia, there is a huge number of buildings requiring maintenance, irrespective of the sector, size, location or ownership. The government made efforts to emphasise its commitment to the performance of public assets and facilities by establishing the National Assets and Facilities Management, (NAFAM) in 2007. It is a government initiative that seeks to advice on ways in which the public assets and facilities can be managed. According to the former Deputy Prime Minister, Najib Tun Abdul Rasak, large amounts of funds have been provided for improvement, maintenance and development of public facilities like schools and police stations (*The Star*, 25 April 2009; *The New Straits Times*, 16 June 2009). For university buildings, maintenance management procedures are planned contingency measures made and corrective maintenance implemented (Ishak 2006). Similarly, Zakaria and Ali (2006a and 2006b) and Zakaria *et al.* (2008) identified the procedures of maintenance management as service, corrective, routine and

235

preventive maintenance. Even so, there are continuous realisations that the best value cannot be obtained from any of these approaches to buildings maintenance but when maintenance is not properly managed, it often leads to buildings that will be very expensive to own or operate in the long run (Spare, 2001; Christian *et al.* 2002). In Hong Kong, The Hong Kong Mortgage Corporation Ltd extended its Mortgage Insurance Programme to cover properly maintained older buildings and also agreed to introduce a ten-year building management and maintenance scheme for the owners. It encouraged the public to implement proper maintenance management procedures to maintain their buildings regardless of their age.

In Poland, property management is the task of qualified managers, also known as property administrators. They are granted a property management licence which is required of them to provide property management services. Property managers are obliged to keep a building log book by the Polish Legislation that is a documentation of any inspection or repair of a building object conducted at the stage of exploitation (Lewandowski 2005; Bryx 2009). This obligation is imposed on subjects managing a particular building object, or on its owner. Polish building law also requires them to make periodic inspections once a year and every five years. Definitely, these are not all the procedures developed to ensure safe use of a building object. It is a basic and compulsory mechanism designed to ensure proper technical condition of a building object. Unfortunately, if the inspections are conducted at such long-time intervals it would be difficult to avoid an undesirable situation in the long run. Along with the technological advancement, there has also been a development of software branch that supports facility management. However, none of these programs practically include technical factors which are in fact, the most important when it comes to the maintenance of a facility. These programs only allow the keeping of an electronic version of a building log book or record of any notification of damage by a user and activities done by the property manager to respond to damage. Moreover, nearly 100% of widely available software supports the management of residential properties (Kaplinski 2009; Kaplinski 2008). This is so because residential properties are many and the issues occurring in their management are common.

This part examines the structure, conduct and performance of the Sub-Saharan Africa's construction sector in order to understanding its capacity to facilitate maintenance management. With the exception of South Africa, the rest of Sub-Saharan Africas' construction sector is very fragmented and underdeveloped, hence limiting its potential to evolve into a functional industry (ILO, 1987). Apart from being a highly fragmentary structure, the other noticeable feature of the construction sector, is the lack of co-ordination in the industry. This has hindered the development of professional cadres of trades and management personnel, rather making it difficult to subject the sector to regulatory policies and improvement programmes. Most construction firms are owned and managed by sole traders with little knowledge of the workings of the construction industry (Ofori, 1991). They operate largely in the informal sector of their economies and are unregistered. This shows the lack of corporate approach to management, thus further explaining the transient nature of most construction firms in the developing countries (Ofori, 1991). This has severely affected skills training and retention of expertise in the industry as construction workers become highly mobile, entering and exiting the industry depending on performance in other sectors of the economy. The impact reveals the rigid adherence to management techniques and practices handed down from colonialists, which emanated from inadequate skills. This lack of capacity has remained unchanged and irrelevant to immediate requirements.

Poor building maintenance in Ghana is widely regarded as the result of peoples' apathetic attitude and a poor "maintenance culture" (Ghana News Agency, 2001). According to the United Nations Educational, Scientific and Cultural Organisation (UNESCO; 1997), the problem of maintenance affects Africa as a whole resulting in being termed the "African Poor Maintenance Culture". Perhaps this is why in a BBC discussion titled "Is Africa's architecture dying?" those who commented felt that the problem with Africa is not its architecture but the poor maintenance culture (BBC 2006). Regarding to this view, the dwellings in Ghana are in poor condition because the occupants do not have a responsible attitude toward maintaining their buildings. The attitude towards proper maintenance could have its roots in some traditional cultural beliefs. Deborah Pellow (1988, 2001) discovered that maintenance in Ghana is of secondary concern to some ethnic groups. They believe that homes should have sentimental value instead of market value. The condition or state of repair of buildings does not matter but the set of social relations that a building embodies matters. For example, a family house, is not for sale and thus maintenance which increases the market value, but not necessarily sentimental value –is not usually a major concern (Tipple, 1987; Willis and Tipple, 1991; Geest, 1998). Researchers have unveiled several reasons which result in poor maintenance. In Ghana there is insecurity of tenure where many land transactions are not well documented (Abdulai, 2006, 2010). When people do not feel secure in their homes, they under-invest hence not maintaining them (UN-HABITAT, 2003). There is lack of rental payments by occupants of the buildings. The willingness and ability of landlords to maintain buildings also depend on the revenue streams they receive from renting. However, it is believed that tenants tend to pay more for a property that is better managed because a building will be offering higher-quality services (O'Sullivan 2003). Therefore, in theory, when demand and supply raise rentals for higher-quality housing, landlords or owners can be able to spend more on maintenance to improve the quality of their properties in order to make them "filter up" on the rental market (Somerville and Mayer 2003).

Methodology

Results of this research were collected mainly from secondary sources published by different researchers. It includes different reports from maintenance managers and maintenance service providers companies of different parts of the world. Maintenance managers gave a brief on the building background, their maintenance services provided, the systems which were used, manpower, subcontractors as well as problems and improvements that have been completed or that are still in progress for the building. Researchers conducted interviews which were then analysed for the research evaluation on the systems applied by the maintenance managers.

Results

Most post-colonial governments inherited economies from their colonialists which were structurally weak and introduced very little radical change. Trade patterns determined during the colonial period relied mostly on the production and export of raw materials and agricultural produce. However, it experienced a decline in world market share during the 1970s and 1980s (Rakodi 1995). Zimbabwe's economy is agro-based relying on primary production of agricultural produce and manufacturing. At independence in 1980, the government inherited a controlled economy that had suffered from years of isolation and under-investment during the period of the Unilateral Declaration of Independence (UDI) and international sanctions. In 1980, the majority of Zimbabwe's urban workforce was employed in the formal economy which was unusual for Southern Africa, partly because a formal sector job had been a condition of urban residence and partly because planning controls restricted commercial activities on residential plots (Rakodi 1995). At the end of 1980s, increasing unemployment, rising inflation and difficulties in financing the spiralling budget deficit, led to the recognition of the need for major structural change.

Property boom was one of the most surprising results of the ESAP era in the city centre between 1991 and 1997, having a development of more than 30 high-quality new office blocks and an increase of 60 per cent in the amount of office floor space for rent. Several factors contributed to this growth. First, there was a belief in the long- term improvements in the economy as a result of ESAP by soaring inflation and negative real interest rates made the money markets unattractive for investment and made real estate the best choice of involvement. Restrictions on international investment were still present and strict controls on the remittance of dividends by foreign companies. As a result of cash-rich companies were looking to protect their portfolios through safe investments in the local economy. Pension and insurance funds led the investment boom.

Due to progressive relaxation in the amount of discretionary funds they could invest, almost two thirds of the new floor spaces were built by the institutional investors. By 1996, investment in the commercial office sector had slowed, partly as a result of high interest rates. Investment returns on the money market reached up to 25 per cent and they were more attractive than the 10 per cent yield from property investment partly because of excessive building costs resulting from high inflation (Matisma 1996; Mugiyo 1996; Munjoma 1999). The property boom transformed Harare city centre into a modern high-rise city with a dramatic skyline. It also created a powerful lobby among those interested in promoting continuity in control of the urban space of the city centre, retention of high levels of parking and restriction of informal activities. In 1998, commuter bus services were restricted from stopping on the roadside in the city centre and were relegated to outlying terminuses. An introduction of one-way system of traffic management eased traffic congestion, but did nothing to make it better for pedestrians to get around. By then public buildings and utilities were properly maintained and managed because the population was still low, with ease movement to walk in the central business district unlike today.

There is an increase on the pressure on urban space in Zimbabwe, particularly because the rate of people moving to urban areas in search of greener pastures has risen. Currently, the informal sector is very significant in its contribution to the development of the economy of Zimbabwe as jobs in the formal sector are showing negative growth. Several factors have led to the increase of informal trading. Formerly, informal activities were prohibited by the legislation of the colonialists but presently, a large number of people are earning a living from it because of lack of employment. Restrictions which includes licensing, zoning and other requirements, as Mupedziswa (1991) observes, some of the legislation and by-laws have been detrimental to the development of the informal sector. Government should relax registration requirements because the bureaucratic registration procedures drive many businesses into the informal sector. The public has seen it cheap to operate as informal traders since they cannot afford to rent a property because of the current state of the economy. Others are even moving out of the properties before the expiry of the lease because of default payments. Review of all policies pertaining to informal sector activities is required so that the operators can work in a more conducive atmosphere. However, there is still need for the monitoring of these activities to ensure that health and other standards which may compromise the welfare of the population are adhered to.

Zimbabwe's' property market is characterised by a lot of occupational voids because of the economic meltdown. Economic meltdown has affected rental payments; hence most tenants are in default they cannot meet their rental obligations. Moreover, because the property is not generating income, there is lost tax revenue for the government meaning fewer financial resources for the local government to devote to public improvement projects and maintenance of public buildings (Accordino and Johnson, 2000). Vacant properties tend to lose value due to lack of maintenance as property owners cannot fund cost of maintenance since the same are not performing. Occupational voids have led to property abandonment because the owner has no income stream to continue maintaining the property to keep it in a good condition. As the economy of Zimbabwe is now characterised by informal traders the demand for property to let is now low. Abandonment has been viewed as an indicator of market failure, a symptom of urban disinvestment, or the result of a neighbourhood's life cycle, instead of being viewed as a problem itself (Accordino and Johnson, 2000). This view is a justification of the urban researchers and policy-makers to focus on policies that stimulate market demand and urban investment. Occupational voids have mostly affected the commercial buildings thus causing disinvestment. Also, studies found that nearby vacant buildings affect other properties within a neighbourhood by lowering property values (Shlay and Whitman, 2006; Griswold and Norris, 2007; Mikelbank, 2008).

Discussion and synthesis

As shown by the study, the Zimbabwean economy is characterised by more informal activities which have affected the property maintenance practice. Vending activities should be supported by the local government enough resources like well-maintained premises to operate in and finances. They cannot obtain short term loans for they do not have security to provide the lender with. The aim could be to allow those who currently operate illegally to make a small increment in security and level of formality, until they reach a level where they are happy and able to pay rent, which can then be used to fund further management initiatives like maintenance of their premises. The local planning authorities have provided regulations which should be adhered to by both the practitioners and those who require the services to guide them. For instance, the urban planners and the building inspectors are required to inspect a building at certain stages during the construction phase and make approvals where possible. The building has to be sustainable, not constructed with intention for renovation. Therefore, the urban planners should continue making a follow up on those completed buildings to see if the agreed terms are being practiced and check it the building is being properly managed. Among the property markets in Zimbabwe building constructions are unregistered and tend to operate like that because of the current status of the economy. They can exit the market anytime with no profits being realised. The property market firms now work together with no specialisation to reduce the risk of failure.

Conclusion, policy options and future direction

In conclusion, several factors have been unveiled which affect the practice of property maintenance mainly in Zimbabwe. The local government can be seen as an actor which can try to help and curb the problems. There is a strong request for proper monitoring of the operations of the property management companies, particularly if their engagements are made mandatory, starting from strengthening the current self-regulation system, implementing a licensing or registration system of the companies as well as drawing up rules and codes of practice to guide their operations local government introduce a grading system also for these companies according to a performance assessment system. Government authorities have to increase the quality level of maintenance companies in order to improve buildings' sustainability and enable them to perform their intended function. They should be responsible for the construction sector to establish rules that organise the relationship between clients and design firms making sure that the role of clients has to be activated and design firms should not take decisions on their behalf. The design firms should encourage and specify locally made materials to support the local industry, improve the economy and society to avoid the problem of maintaining imported materials. This chapter concludes that maintenance management guidelines should be put in place to standardise the practices of office building maintenance managers (Wireman, 1998). Consultations with the end-users should be a mechanism to establish a proactive management process, thus valuing the important roles of their clients.

References

Abdellatif, M. A., and Othman, A. A. E., (2006) 'Improving the sustainability of low-income housing projects: the case of residential buildings in Musaffah Commercial City in Abu Dhabi', in Emirates. *Journal for Engineering Research*, 11(2), 47–58.

Accordino, J and Johnson, G. T. (2000). Addressing the vacant and abandoned property problem. *Journal of Urban Affairs*, *22*(3), 301-315.

Addis, B and Talbot, R. (2001). Sustainable Construction Procurement: A Guide to Delivering Environmentally Responsible Projects, CIRIA C571, London, CIRIA.

Akcamete, A., Akinci, B and Garrett, J. H. (2010). Potential utilisation of building information models for planning maintenance activities. *In Proceedings of the international conference on computing in civil and building engineering* (pp. 151-157).

Barrett, S and Stanley, C. (1999). Better Construction Briefing, Oxford, Blackwell Science Ltd.

Chew, M. Y. L. (2005). Defect analysis in wet areas of buildings. *Construction and Building Materials*, 19(3), 165-173.

Christian, J., Newton, L and Gamblin, T. (2002). A comparison of the roof maintenance management systems of two public sector organizations. In *Annual Conference of Canadian Society for Civil Engineering* (pp. 5-8).

Damen, T. (Ed.). (1980). Research in maintenance and modernisation, Proceedings of the CIB W70 1979 Rotterdam Symposium, CIB Publication 54.

Friends of the Earth, Prescription for Change: Health and the Environment, Brussels, Friends of the Earth.

Gibson, E. J. (Ed.). (1979). *Developments in building maintenance 1* (Vol. 1). Applied Science Publishers.

Griswold, N. G and Norris: E. (2007). Economic impacts of residential property abandonment and the Genesee County land bank in Flint, Michigan. Flint, MI: The MSU Land Policy Institute. Industrial Press, New York, NY. *Journal of Urban Affairs,* 22(3), 301–315.

Kapliński, O. (2008). IT applications in Polish construction sector. In *25th the International Symposium on Automation and Robotics in Construction, ISARC-2008, Vilnius, June* (pp. 26-29).

Kaplinski, O. (2009). Problems of the information technologies use in Polish construction sector: state of the art. *Archives of Civil Engineering,* Vol. 55, No 2, pp. 173-198.

Kumar, U and Ellingsen, H. P. (2000). "Development and implementation of maintenance performance indicators for the Norwegian oil and gas industry", Proceedings of the 15th European Maintenance Conference (Euro Maintenance 2000), Gothenburg, Sweden.

Quah, L. K. (1992). Facilities management, building maintenance and modernisation link: Evolution of facilities management traced suggesting a need to re- divert attention back to underlying issues such as improvements in maintenance, modernisation systems and feedback procedures. *Building research and information,* 20(4), 229-232.

Lewandowski, K. (2005). Property management (in polish). Lexisnexis, Warsaw.

Matisma, K. (1996) 'Major trends in commercial office development, 1990-1995', unpublished dissertation, Harare: Department of Rural and Urban Planning, University of Zimbabwe.

Mikelbank, B. A. (2008). Spatial analysis of the impact of vacant, abandoned and foreclosed properties. *Federal Reserve Bank of Cleveland.*

Mugiyo, I. (1996). 'The role of insurance companies and pension funds in the commercial property market: a case study of Harare', unpublished dissertation, Harare: Department of Rural and Urban Planning, University of Zimbabwe.

Mugwindiri, K and Mbohwa, C. (2013). Availability performance improvement by using autonomous maintenance–the case of a developing country, Zimbabwe.

Munjoma, T. (1999). 'Property investment under an economic structural adjustment programme: the case of the Harare central business district office development', unpublished PhD thesis, Aberdeen: Department of Land Economy, University of Aberdeen.

Mupedziswa, R. (1991). "The Informal Sector with Particular Reference to Zimbabwe. Functional Role and Prospects for Growth," *School of Social Work Staff papers,"* Harare.

New Straits Times. (2009). RM3.2 billion contracts to be awarded. Prime News.

Olubodun, F. (2000). 'A factor approach to the analysis of components' defects in housing stock', Structural Survey, 18 (1), 46 – 58.

Othman, A. A. E. (2004). Value and Risk Management for Dynamic Brief Development in Construction, PhD thesis, Loughborough University, UK.

Parida, A and Kumar, U. (2006). 'Maintenance performance measurement (MPM): issues and challenges', *Journal of Quality in Maintenance Engineering,* 12(3), 239–251.

Quah, L. K. (1991). Building maintenance and modernisation research and practice trends, Proceedings of European Symposium on Management, *Quality and Economics in Housing and Other Building Sectors,* Portugal.

Quah, L. K. (Ed). (1990). Building maintenance and modernisation worldwide, Vol. I and II, Proceedings of the CIB W70 1990 Singapore Symposium. Longman, Singapore.

Rakodi, C. (1995). *Harare: Inheriting a Settler-colonial City: Change or Continuity? Chichester.* John Wiley.

Ramly, A. (2006). 'A link between design and maintenance'. *Journal of Building Engineers,* 81 (5).

Roodman, D. M and Lenssen, N. A. (1995). Building Revolution: How Ecology Health Concerns are Transforming Construction, Paper 124, Washington, DC, World Watch Institute.

Ruben, R., Queru, G and Monteil, E. (2006). U.S. Patent No. 7,143,048. Washington, DC: U.S. Patent and Trademark Office.

Schmberger, R and Knod, J. (1997). Operations Management: Customer Focus Principles, Irwin, Chicago, IL.

Seeley, I. H. (1987). Building Maintenance, Palgrave Macmillan, Basingstoke, UK.

Shlay, A. B and Whitman, G. (2006). Research for democracy: Linking community organising and research to leverage blight policy. City and Community, 5(2), 153–171.

Spare, J. H. (2001). Building the business case for condition-based maintenance. In *Transmission and Distribution Conference and Exposition, 2001 IEEE/PES* (Vol. 2, pp. 954-956). IEEE.

The Star. (2009). Billion riggit projects. 23 March 2009, N4

Thomson, D. S., Austin, S. A., Mills, G. R and Devine-Wright, H. (2003). Addressing the subjective view of value delivery.

Watson, P and Asher, H. (1999). Implementation of value management in construction. *Construction Information Quarterly, 1*(2), 1-9.

Wireman, T. (1998). *Developing performance indicators for managing maintenance.* Industrial Press Inc.

Wood, B. (2003). Approaching the care-free building. *Facilities, 21*(3/4), 74-79.

Zakaria, Z, Ali, N.M., Abd Hamid, M.R., Othman, N and Haron, A.T. (2008). Exploring on issues of maintenance management at higher learning institution in Malaysia. In: *Proceeding of the International Conference on Civil Engineering 2008 (ICCE '08): Challenges in Facing Natural Hazards for Future Engineering Practice,* University Malaysia, Pahang.

Zakaria, Z and Ali, N. M. (2006). Assessment of implementation of maintenance works at Kolej Universiti Kejuruteraan dan

Teknologi Malaysia (KUKTEM). In *Proceedings of the National Seminar on Civil Engineering Research.*

Zakaria, Z and Ali, N. M. (2006). Maintenance management approaches in public higher learning institution in Malaysia: KUKTEM's perspective. In *Proceedings of the 1st Malaysia Technical Universities Conference on Engineering and Technology.*

.

Chapter 13

The role of real estate practitioners in the financial market

Mike Juru

Introduction

This aim of this study is to explore and assess the contribution of realtors in the financial market, particularly given in the background that the financial markets are the backbone of an economy. There is an opportunity to address finance market challenges using the realtor services in Zimbabwe particularly given the infancy nature of real estate education and practice in the country. The aim of study was to explore the role that a realtor could play in improving performance of financial markets in Zimbabwe. The key questions are: what is the structure of the financial market and the link the real estate? What is the role of the realtor practitioners? How did the real estate evolve in each of the country? What financial market challenges can be addressed by the realtor? The results of the study are significant in informing policy-makers on how they can harness the potential capacity of real estate practice to address challenges in the financial markets and increase awareness on the hidden impact of real estate on the financial markets. The results will also be useful to real estate professional bodies and academic institutions responsible for training realtors on structuring their education programmes to develop realtor who are competent in the financial market sector.

The described the methodology and first part of the paper develops the conceptual framework for understanding financial situation and real estate practice. A theory of institutions is provided which helps in exploring the role of relators and the evolution of real estate practice in the institutional context. The next section explores financial market and real estate practice at global, regional and national context. After this, presentation of results is done and made in the light of global and regional practices. The final part is a conclusion of the study.

Methodology

The research is an exploratory and explanatory research. It seeks to assess the practice of real estate management in the context of the financial markets. The research used both primary and secondary data sources. For primary data collection, key informant interviews were conducted to solicit the opinions of realtors in different capacities and fields in Zimbabwe. Therefore, key informants interviewed were from the valuation division, consultancy and facilities management, insurance and marketing fields. The reason for engaging realtors in different fields was to a cross cutting view of the impact of real estate practice on the financial markets. Secondary Data sources such as the government financial policies and quarterly reports from the financial sector were used. Literature was also reviewed for experiences in other countries within the region. The results were analysed based on themes that were emerging.

Theoretical perspectives

A realtor has to provide advisory services to real estate investors. This link exists where investors rely on loans with high leverage and therefore have to match the income flows to the cost of the loan to ensure that the benefits are congruent (Baker and Chinloy, 2014). Therefore, since their investment is linked to loan availability in the long run and interest rates, this shows that the financial sector is linked to real estate investment. The realtor as a broker has to go between, advising the investor on investment decisions based on the interest rate conditions in the market. This covers issues of rental capitalisation and management of returns on investment for developers. Mortgage terms for repayment of interest and principles are best designed with an insight from a realtor where mortgage lenders have to decide on how to efficiently price a mortgage, basing on many factors such as the understanding of the returns' expectations for real estate investors (White and White, 2014). Real estate agents also act as conduits in selling mortgages (Ball, 2006). The banks look upon the real estate sector as a market for selling their products. The link is made effective through the realtor who organises information and advises on mortgage issues. The real estate practitioners' skills of property investment appraisal are also integral in influencing the real estate transactions on the property market. These transactions have an important input on the viability of financial markets. In addition, the status of financial markets has an impact on the viability of the real estate markets (Idowu and Filho, 2009). This can be explained in terms of interest rates and inflation and their impact on real estate finance. For example, when interest rates are low, this tends to stimulate more investment in the real estate sector since cost of borrowing will be low too. Another link also exists in terms of the financial markets aiding as a source of investment for real estate in terms of debt, securities, securities, equity, bonds or mortgages (White and White, 2014). It is the role of a realtor to facilitate the organisation if these systems which are important on the financial sectors lending system.

Realtors are also important in the financial sector in the issuance of bonds which financial sectors are entitled to purchase (Boleat and Coles, 2012). Realtors have a role to play in the management of investment risks since they transfer real estate risks from the investors through securitisation (Tunaru, 2017). Investment banks use it for hedging; insurance companies use the real estate derivatives for portfolio management and diversification. Pension funds use it for portfolio diversification and mortgage lender for hedging risks (Tunaru, 2017).

A typical form of risk is the credit risk. This explains the capacity of the borrower to repay a loan of a specific amount. Under this case, consideration is given to the value of collateral security pledged by the borrower. Collateral is defined as the assets pledged by the borrower to recover the loan given to the person in case the borrower fails to repay the loan (Brandl, 2017). Under this case, the real estate agents establish the value of assets if real estate property or land is pledged as security. This is an important factor in the loan management sectors of banks. The real estate practitioner is also important in the financial market with regard to real estate loan decisions. The realtor is vital for the processing of loans when lending mortgages (Sirota and Barell, 2003). This involves the realtor determining the ability of the borrower to pay based on the value of property pledged as collateral as well as establishing the marketability of the title in the market. This is done using what (Glickman, 2015) refers to as the leverage metrics which involves computations of value of real estate assets against the total amount that a developer interns to borrow. This information forms the basis and foundation for processing and approving mortgage applications.

Other than acting to process mortgages, a realtor can also be engaged as a mortgage insurer providing mortgage insurance services. They are also involved in the calculation of asset liquidation values. This involves securitisation of real estate under the capital market (Himes, 2001). In addition, property has been identified to be an integral part of the real estate capital markets. Therefore, with capital markets comprises another part of the overall financial system. As a result, the realtor profession is imbedded with and calls for the understanding of financial systems and principles (Brown and Matysiak, 2000).

Real estate practice

The theory of institutions helps in understanding the focus, rules and responsibilities of real estate practitioners as an institution. Institutions have been defined as human created or naturally evolving conventions which shape interactions between society and the methods for enforcing these interaction mechanisms (Mooya, 2016). Shaping interactions and behaviour is done using a system of rules, regulations and procedures that dictate the actions to be taken and resultantly direct action in a predictable manner. In the context of real estate practice, these are provided by professional codes of conduct such as RICS, REIZ, Valuers Council and the Estate Agents Council among other actors. The main reason for the emergence of institutions is to address problems in societies. It is important to note that once they come into operation, they are not static but evolve as per demands and dictates of the institutional context (Furusten, 2013).

The institutional theory in this context is critical in understanding the birth of the real estate profession as well as the scope role and responsibilities of realtors as it explains how real estate institutions are governed by professional codes well as the evolution of the real estate society from the traditional era up to present day. This is the institution responsible for property brokerage and property management. They are also responsible for transformation of the theory of property management into practice. In addition, conduct is guided by laws of professional ethics which vary from one country to another. The real estate practitioner can come in the form of agents or brokers, real estate developers, valuers and real estate property managers, consultancies and financial advisors (Schulte, 2012). Common duties of real estate practitioners include property brokerage and property management. Property brokerage includes marketing and the facilitation of transactions between buyers and sellers while property management involves building maintenance, leasing and rental management. While the practitioner areas of speciality can vary from one country to another and are also based on individual preferences, the common denominator is that the first practitioners were drawn from law, business management, engineering, surveying and the building industry (Schulte, 2012). This remains the field commonly linked to the real estate practice to date. Thereafter courses and programmes have been development to acquit professionals with the relevant skills desired in the real estate practice. Basing in this view, real estate practice is a multi-disciplinary field that calls upon the practitioners to understand urban planning, surveying, building design, business management, finance, law and social psychology among other disciplines.

Real estate practice existed long back in the period of socialism in the 1800s. Though it was informal, it was later legalised after the liberalisation of the economy (Schulte, 2012). This saw the development of ethical codes governing the practice of realtors. The main aim of these professional bodies was to increase cooperation, improve quality of services offered by realtors, open activities to the world and to build collaborative power to force government to reform laws to increase their influence as well as promote development of modern management practices in the field (Schulte,

2012). To date these institutions still exist in the form of international realtors' associations, an example of which is RICS to which real estate management and valuation is part of. In this regard, the profession of real estate has its birth in the private sector (mainly market driven). This is supported by the review of development of real estate profession in America where it rose among the middle class and properties (Hornstein, 2005).

Changes in the global nation of economies, ICT and the social aspects had an impact on the practice of real estate practice hence realtors need to constantly adapt their skills to meet new emerging needs in the market. Under this regard, the profession can be regarded as dynamic (Teifonov, 2012). The evolution of the real estate practice in Singapore was driven by globalisation and the integration of real estate and capital markets (Huat *et al.* 2016). Innovations such as REITS are a way through which real estate embrace technology. While real estate practice developed long back in the developed continents such as Europe (Teifonov, 2012), it is important to note that there is great variation in terms of the development in Africa where reports are that real estate is rarely regarded as a business due to the fragile structure of land tenure and property rights arrangements (Ghyoot, 2012).

A real estate practitioner needs to be knowledgeable on aspects of accounting, law as well as psychology and behavioural studies since this has an impact on influencing investment decisions in the capital markets (Levy, 2004). On this note, a real estate practitioner can be regarded as a professional that integrates different fields together (law, architecture, accounting, business management as well as psychology). An understanding of these issues has an important input in shaping the practice by a professional realtor. The client for realtors has been identified to include banks where the capital markets and monetary institutions lend to developers and therefore require the service of the realtor. Likewise, the financial system innovations also have an impact on the realtor service provision. In addition, complexity in the financial sector has also called upon the adjustment of the roles of the realtor to maintain a profitable link between real estate and financial systems. One of the manifestations of the dynamics has been a requirement for more information and advice from the realtors (Weiss, 2002). Information has been identified as one of the critical components for market efficiency in economics where private information is aggregated for the public benefit to eliminate inefficiencies associated with lack of information (Barucci and Fontana, 2017).

The change in the role of realtors as dictated by the markets has also meant a change in the learning and training of real estate practice. In the case of Singapore, the curriculum has evolved from a narrow focus on business management to a broader focus which deals with issues of real estate securitisation, finance and ICT (Huat *et al.* 2016). Real estate education has been evolving not only in Singapore, but in countries like the UK and the United States which has been identified as the cradle of the profession. These innovations in estate education were meant to capture changes in the industry so that the services realtors provided remain relevant. Though they are variations between the demand of the markets and the type of real estate practice by country, the common services offered by the realtor include valuation, brokerage, facilities management, fund management and capital markets advisory services. A major change has been the shift from the traditional roles of valuation and brokerage towards the expansion of the roles to include fund management and capital market advisory services. This has been a result of the innovations in the real estate products; innovations such as the introduction of REITS and the integration of the real estate and capital markets.

Globalisation has also seen the rise of global cooperate real estate consultancy. Transformation which has been noted that has an impact on changing the scope and methods in the real estate practice includes a change in client profiles, ICT innovations, the globalisation of real estate and the integration of real estate in the financial markets. These changes call upon the reform of the services offered by realtors such that they remain relevant in facilitating the flows of capital and meeting the needs of investors in domestic and global markets.

In developing countries where real estate is an emerging practice, realtors have to understand real estate from the finance and returns perspective (Ming, 2016). This is based on the background that a properly developed property tenure system is key to capitalism and the creation of wealth (De Soto, 2010). Integration of real estate and financial markets calls upon the service providers to provide financial services. Real estate services include equity placement, loan management, debt finance and financial consultation, hence the need for real estate education to emphasises on finance. In the cases of developing countries in Southern Africa, education on finance has had less emphasis as compared to that in developed countries such as the UK, US, Australia and Singapore (Schulte, 2012). In the case of Singapore, UK and US, real estate education has been evolving to meet changes in the demands of the industries among which are globalisation and the integration of real estate and financial markets (Ming, 2016). In the case of developing countries, emphasis has remained in the traditional roles of the realtor related to design and construction with an emphasis on the physical aspects of real estate investment. It is pertinent to note that technology is having an impact on real estate and real estate profession, particularly with the introduction of online platforms that reduce the demand for physical property inspection which erodes and the physical thrust of real estate management (Ming, 2016). This has transformed the roles of a realtor.

The financial market

By definition, financial markets are regard as a type of market in which financial assets such as bonds and security are traded. These assets include liquid money, stocks, shares, securities and bonds. Financial markets play a distributive role of transferring funds from those who have excess and may not be willing to use it to those who need it. This is done by financial institutions which include banks, pension funds, credit associations and real estate investment trusts (REITS), (Madura, 2015). There are a variety of forms of the financial markets. These include the money, bond, stock, mortgage and the securities markets (Brandl, 2017). Real estate interests are traded on the capital markets, bond and securities as well as the stock market (for REIT stocks) (McCoy, 2006). Real estate interests and securities are also traded in a real estate capital markets (Glickman, 2014).

The portfolio theory of financial market was first developed by Markowitz in 1952 and seeks to solve the optimal portfolio problem. It allows for the establishment of optimal portfolio, insurance and investment combinations in a risky setting. This is because agents, corporates and individuals in the money markets seek to invest their wealth by trading on risk free and risk prone assets. The aim of the agents is to maximise the expected utility form their assets (Barruci and Fontana, 2017). However, investors on the financial market the markets are riddled with risks such as interest rate risk, credit- risks, liquidity risks, structural and leverage risks, legal risks and political risks among other investment risks (Kritchene, 2012). It is a theory of investment behaviour under uncertainty where the investor is faced with different investment opportunity under uncertainty. In such conditions, the decision on how much to invest into which assets or markets and how to form an optimal investment portfolio is made under uncertainty where the investor does not know the probability of success for each particular market, they are willing to invest in. Therefore, decisions on investment, according to this theory, are based on expected returns on investment subject to environmental risks and the corresponding opportunity cost of foregoing the investment (Kobold, 1986). The implication of this theory is that it provides an understanding of the investment motives of property owners; both individual and corporates on the financial markets. It also provides an appreciation of the uncertainty inherent in investment context and how decisions made have to factor these in.

Literature Review

One global case study of real estate and the financial markets is the United States. There was a great change in the perception of the link between real estate and the financial sectors after the Great Depression where a federal housing association was created as a government intervention in the financial market (Peca, 2010. Secondary mortgage markets later on emerged in order to stimulate investment in real estate. This was facilitated by the government policy in the late 2000 which permitted the engagement of financial institutions in real estate. This was based on the fact that real estate activities were identified as largely financial (Eubanks, 2011). The common roles to be played included brokerage as well as property management which has to do with negotiation of leases, managing and service rentals and maintaining security deposits.

Similarly, the real estate practice in Europe emerged concurrently with the establishment of urban planning in America (Weiss, 2002). It was an activity initiated by the private small-scale agents who later collaborated to form associations and demanded recognition by the government in the public sector. The primary and traditional speciality areas of the profession in America was to deal with matters in the subdivision markets which included issues of title insurance wherewith, the employment of strict deed restrictions was intended to control the development of the real estate properties (Weiss, 2002). Therefore, like its sister profession; urban planning, the practice of real estate in America was largely concerned with the control of property development. However, changes in the institutional, political and land-use dynamics such as suburbanisation in America in the 1940s saw a change in the role of the realtor. Events of the Great Depression in the 1930 marked a turning point in the profession of real estate management in America. This led to the consideration of the role of real estate in mortgage- lending institutions, investment trusts, insurance companies and banks. This was due to business failures and real estate foreclosures which placed much of the nation's real estate in the hands of mortgage institutions, financial companies, banks and investment trusts. The realization by property owners that there has to be more to property other than letting out and receiving rental collections brought an increase in the demand for real estate professional services. This resulted in the creation of realtors' associations for collective voice and service quality control by regulating code of conduct of realtors (Kyle *et al.* 2000). It is important to identify that the practice of real estate and the real estate profession in America is continuously evolving, given the changes in the complexity of properties on the property market.

The financial market in the U.S is diversified and includes the debt, private or public equity, bonds, loans and the securities markets (McCoy, 2006). The financial system development of a viable financial system was pertinent to support a viable economy through accumulating capital and efficiently distributing it to those who wanted it (James, 2015). Equally important were the institutions governing the activities of the financial markets such as the banking and monetary policies. A variety of financial intermediaries were formulated to deal with the financial demand of the increasing population of America to meet its financial needs. Deregulation of the financial system was one of the positive developments. These adjustments were meant to stimulate effective flow of funds within and outside the economy. However, regulations that were passed such as the Bank Act imposed limitations on capital mobility in terms of high interest rates, ((James, 2015). The financial crisis in America in 2006 was attributed to failures in the housing market from the 1990s. The rise in the real sector stimulated increasing demand, which rose in 2006. The decline in home prices stimulated an increase in mortgage loans defaulting, resulting in foreclosures (Jarsulic, 2010). REITS emerged as an innovative form of financial institution that has its birth in Australia. In the context of America, REITS are an innovation that aims to meet the financial challenges of commercial property owners where banks were unwilling to lend to them (Huat, 2016). In terms of the operation of this market, they raise finance by issuing real estate backed bonds and securities. REITS provide a mechanism for owning and managing commercial property assets and it is also their mechanism through which these assets have access to the capital markets (Parker, 2012).

The dynamics of the realtor profession are associated with the rise of urban planning where; to ensure that houses are of a particular value and standard, minimum requirements are made on building materials (Doucet and Weaver, 1991). There are other important considerations in understanding the roles of real estate management in the evolution of the financial markets in America. The global financial crises in 2007, was largely a result of the failure of the real estate markets. The link is provided through real estate financial markets such as the real estate agent capital markets and REITs. The trade of real estate securities has an important impact on the viability of the financial markets. The financial crisis was attributed to the decline in returns on the REITS markets (*International Financial*

Markets, 2017). The lag in the returns on REITS were affected by volatility in the stock markets of America.

Real estate practice in Singapore and elsewhere in the world has evolved from preconception with 'brick and mortar', where real estate practice was disconnected from financial markets towards full integration into the financial markets (Huat, 2016). Globalisation has also had an effect of integrating real estate at local level to the global systems. The transformation of the real estate practice was mainly driven by changes in the real estate sector. These changes include the integration of real estate and financial markets which increased investment choices.

Globalisation of real estate was also facilitated by laws that promoted internationalisation of investments. A major change in the 1970s was the inclusion of real estate among the investment portfolios of banks as a means of risk diversion and as a hedge against inflation. This calls for a distinct type of realtor practitioner who specialise in investment portfolio management for the financial institutions such as banks and insurance companies. Further interest and investment in real estate called for the increase in real estate professionalism with better skills in investment management. This brought a change in the practice of real estate in Singapore (Huat, 2016). Under this context, Singapore institutions and developers played a role in globalising real estate investments (Huat, 2016). Investment in real estate in Singapore by foreign companies further expanded the traditional roles of the domestic realtor. The increase in demand for intermediaries such as banks, asset managers, fund managers, lawyers and accountants to meet the demands by overseas investors- gave rise to investment analysts, portfolio managers, economists and consultants to provide information (property indices- these are used by portfolio managers to compare the performance of real estate to other assets within the portfolio.) to external investors (Huart, 2016). This broadened the scope for real estate practice. Further innovations in which the real estate industry, stimulated by the capital markets included REITS (REIT managers as a new profession) and mortgage backed securities brought major changes to real estate investment. These real estate products are tradable in the financial market.

Core focus of real estate education is in economics (land economics, property and facilities management, with a link to business administration which has its core foundation in the US. Real estate practice in the U.S placed emphasis on business management and the administrative side of real estate while in the case of UK, emphasis was on the physical property and hence programmers focused on the survey field, including aspects of valuation, building construction and planning (Ming, 2016). These were the traditional sources of real estate practice and with the passage of time, new aspects have been incorporated.

In the case of Japan, there is a strong link between real estate valuation and financial markets since real estate assets form key collateral for the country's loan portfolio. In addition, land value has been identified as a fundamental component in bank lending. Furthermore, the link between the real estate market and the financial markets in Japan is in term of trading of real estate interest and securities. Decline in real estate assets prices seriously affects the value of collateral security held by banks and therefore the functionality of the financial system. For example, a decline in land prices in the 1990s in Japan had an adverse effect on the banking system (Mikitani and Posen, 2000). In addition, real estate asset prices affected the development in the capital market in Japan (Mera and Renaud, 2016).

As far as the real estate practice in South Africa is concerned, it is important to note the existence of a dual property system. In urban areas title and the property markets are well defined while in the peri-urban land, markets are poorly defined (Simons, Malmgren and Small, 2009). Real estate developments in the tribal lands remain outside the formal financial systems, which have proven a challenge in integrating them in the formal real estate capital markets. This is against the background that formal land tenure forms the basis for capital formation in an economy (Desoto, 2010).

Like in the case of Zimbabwe, the financial markets in South Africa, were decentralised in the 1980s. Deregulation of the financial markets has been reported to have resulted in the formulation of secondary mortgage markets (Acton, 2013). The mortgage banking sector has been riddled with challenges of inappropriate legal systems in dealing with defaulters as a result of its issuance of long-term fixed rates mortgages (UNHABITAT, 2008). To hedge against the bank losses in case of changes in interest rates, these mortgages backed loans were traded to third parties on the financial market. Integration of the mortgage and financial markets was reported to have a positive impact on the economy of South Africa where mortgage loans and mortgage backed securities are traded. This reduces the bank risks – particularly associated with fixed rate mortgage lending (Un- Habitat, 2008). Securities based on residential mortgages can be traded on the stock exchange. The mortgage banking industry in South Africa, post 2000, is well developed. This is attributed to sound laws and favourable economic environment since 2000. These conditions have promoted the rise in securitisation of residential (RMBS) and commercial mortgage loans (CMBS) in the form of commercial mortgage backed securities which were developed in the post 2000 period (Freybote and Karoly, 2008). The CMBS provides an innovation in the dynamic commercial real estate sector. This mortgage securitisation innovation arose in South Africa out of the attempts of nonbank actors. In terms of the bond market, bonds are subject to global rating. This shows the effect of globalisation on South Africa's bond market (Freybote and Karoly, 2008). The economy is construction-driven hence the importance of real estate finance. Finance and the construction sector were identified as fast-growing sectors of the South Africa's economy since the 1990s (Saul and Bond, 2014). Hence the existence of well-developed real estate backed financial systems within the economy. Challenges on residential financing include the unavailability of transaction information to the public and legal laws on the use of mortgage bonds as inappropriate.

The practice of real estate management in South Africa has a long tradition under which the activities were regulated by the Real Estate agents of the Transvaal in early 1900. The main purpose was to regulate the code of conduct for professional realtors in South Africa. In addition, the board was also responsible for controlling the quality of real estate education (Miller, 1995). The role of a realtor in South Africa as given under the Real Estate Agents Association of South Africa, of 1995 falls under the traditional category in which the real estate agents have the responsibility of production of the physical property (Huat, 2016). The practice is also embedded in the legal matters through the legal and moral responsibility of realtors to ensure fairness in executing transactions between agents. The legislative aspects of real estate transactions in South Africa led to the recognition of the importance of the realtor in maintaining a good relationship with the attorney. Marketing has been identified as one of the traditional responsibilities of relator in South Africa.

This relationship in South Africa exists in terms of the provision of mortgages and bonds. Real realtors from the Association of Real Estate Agents were traditionally engaged by banks and building societies as home loan consultancies (Estate Agents Association of South Africa, 1995).

The financial market in Zimbabwe since 1980

Regarding the history of financial system in Zimbabwe, the financial system was a simple one which was structured based on the need to facilitate foreign trade with little focus on the domestic market (Gelbard and Leite, 1999). In addition, the financial market operated under strict control by the government. However, reforms on the financial system were made after independence. Like in other economies in Africa, these reforms were meant to stimulate economic growth. The financial markets in Zimbabwe are reported to have changed significantly, particularly following liberalisation in the 1990s. The impact of liberalisation was an increase in financial intermediaries in the sector. Another important change cited included the liberalisation of bank interest rates. This increased the attractiveness of interest-bearing deposits. Increase in intermediaries led to sophistication of the market from the simple one before 1980 ((Mugwati, Nkala and Mukanganiki, 2013).

Governance of the financial sector is fragmented. This is because various bodies like the Reserve Bank of Zimbabwe and the Registrar of Insurance and Securities Commission regulate the stock exchange market (Mugwati *et al.* 2013). In addition, political intervention is one of the challenges to Zimbabwe's financial sector. This results in an increase in financial demands beyond the capacity of the financial markets from the domestic sector (Kovaven, 2004). As a result, this shunned private sector credit and led to an increase in interest rates. Investment in treasury bills became more attractive as opposed to bank deposits. The restructuring of the domestic public debt by government has an impact of further collapsing real interest rates which became negative. This led to an increased demand for foreign currency in the post 2000 era. In addition, inflation was a common phenomenon. The central bank had no policy autonomy in setting interest rates in the money market (Kovaven, 2004). In terms of the money market, the private sector and the black-market activities have increased.

Reform through the liberalisation of the financial markets affected the stock market positively since it increases trade of stocks on the stock exchange market (Oyama, 2004). With regard to the impact of deregulation on foreign investment activity, international banks were engaged and by 1995, the Zimbabwe currency was more convertible to facilitate repatriation of earnings and dividends to foreign investors (Bond, 1998). However, stock prices have been reported to have immediately fallen during the 1991 to 1992 period as a result of liberalisation of interest rates. This gave rise to companies listing on the ZSE (Tsaurai and Odhiambo, 2012). Positive changes were reported for the period soon after implementation of the liberalisation policy. Investment flows in stock from the international investors increased. This is supported by the view by Bond (1998) explains that deregulation of the financial system was mainly intended to improve the functionality of the stock market to promote economic development in the country. However, recent reports indicate that activities of the ZSE from 2017 to 2018 first quarter have declined. This resulted in huge losses in market capitalisation (Reserve Bank of Zimbabwe, 2018).

Other than the interventions in the monetary and stock markets some changes involved the creation of new intermediary financial institutions such as venture capital companies and group credit schemes (Bond, 1998). The reform was meant to stimulate innovations in the capital markets among which included encouraging new, riskier lending activities by new institutions. Despite the immediate positive changes, recent reports indicate that the positive contribution of the stock market remains limited given that it is constrained by host of factors among which include, a poor institutional framework and a narrow portfolio as reports that lack of diversity in the type of securities traded increases risky proneness (Tsaurai and Odhiambo, 2012). The overall impact has therefore been limited capacity in mobilising investment for development.

Deregulation of the interest rate and exchange rates was identified as a premature policy intervention which negatively affected savings and investment in the economy (Bond, 1998). Deregulation of interest rates has resulted in instability of interest rates on loans as they are subject to upward and downward adjustment as per conditions on the money and capital markets. This brings instability in the financial markets. The after-tax interest rate on deposits on money market dropped to negative (Harvey, 1998). This discouraged investment on the money market due to market interest rate. Inflation from 2000 to 2008 has had a negative impact on interest rates. Interest rate charges by financial institutions and building societies vary depending on type of financial institution and the location of a property (Mutekede, 2009). Despite some positive aspects after the adoption of the multi- currency era that resulted in stability in the money market, the financial sector in Zimbabwe remains fragile (Dzomira, 2014). The financial service sector has been on a declining trajectory since 1980 and particularly after the unplanned for liberalisation of the market, not considering the fragmented governance of the sector (Mugwati et al. 2013). Other than poor governance, the failure of the banking systems in Zimbabwe, poor risk management and high levels of non-performing loans as a result of poor selection criteria for borrowers has brought negative effects (Dzomira, 2014). This poses challenges in the credit management sector for banks and financial institutions in Zimbabwe as evidenced from the Reserve Bank of Zimbabwe (2014). Illiquidity in the financial sector has been reported as a common characteristic as money supply declines.

As far as the roles of the realtor in Zimbabwe are concerned, practitioners prior to independence were governed by the provisions of the Estates Agents Act (Chapter 27: 05) which is administered by an Estate Agents Council. The range of responsibilities for the realtor under this provision included sale of property, negotiation, property valuation and assessment of rental values of properties (Real Estate Agents Act, section 52 of 1970). With the recognition of professionalism and the need to secure realtors, a later act such as the Valuers Act (Chapter 27: 18) of 1996 was enacted which provides for the registration requirements for practicing valuers as well as bestowing the council with powers to regulate the practice of valuers in Zimbabwe. The qualifications for registration as a recognised valuer under this statute requires that persons hold degrees in valuation and estates management or land economic of some related fields as well as demonstrate some required level of practical experience (Section 25 and 26 of the Valuers Act Chapter 27:18). Like in the case of America, real estate practice in Zimbabwe polio to independence existed in the private sector. Less emphasis was required for professionalism. Hence, members could enter the field easily. However, the requirements for education in Valuers Act brought a change in real estate practice. Real estate education in Zimbabwe places emphasis on the building, planning and engineering related aspects of real estate (Paradza, 2015). This has a negative implication on the capacity of these realtors to deal with financial matters, given the important role of real estate in financial system. Furthermore, like observed earlier, the discipline is yet in its infancy stage in Zimbabwe.

The decline in the performance of Zimbabwe's economy is attributed to land reform and collapse of the property rights system. This shows the influence of property rights and real estate on the financial aspects of the economy (Richardson, 2015) where land could be used as equity for development. The disruption of the property rights system through the land reform programme reduced the borrowing activity thereby affecting the functionality of banks and other financial institutions in Zimbabwe (Richardson, 2016). It also contributed to a loss of investor trust in the country as witnessed by a decline in the stock exchange activities by a drop of 88 % in the value of stocks traded on this market from 1993 to 1998 when the intention of the government to compulsorily acquire property was declared. The loss of land equity by resettled farmers since banks could not foreclose on land had negative impact because land remains owned by the state. This negatively affected the banking sector; hence collapse of the financial activity in Zimbabwe.

Perspectives of local real estate practitioners

The interviewees engaged raised a number of perspectives in as far as they understand the industry in a local context. Realtors determine rental values which will influence the property value through capitalisation. Rented properties (commercial properties) are capitalised at the market rate of interest to establish property returns and that is value of the property. They determine the best return on investments that developers can measure against the return from other competing investments on the financial markets such as stocks, bonds or securities (Acton, 2013). Therefore, it is important in investment analysis. Therefore, it helps to pull finance and investment towards high yielding portfolios. This is based on calculation of yield and returns using IRR, NPV.

Advisory to banks is on mortgage lending. On the same practice of valuation, another observer notes the importance of real estate valuations to determine the market values of property. This is important to prevent over-lending risks (when the value of real estate properties is overestimated or under- lending when the value under-estimated) on the basis of collateral. Over-landing may result in foreclosure of loans which has been reported to be one of the challenges in the bank loaning sector during the financial crises of Zimbabwe's banking sector in 2008. Therefore, the valuation services for property serve for securitisation of financial products (CBMS, RBMS). The impact of politicians has been analysed as political risks factor particularly for long term investments. This is based on the political nature of real estate investment projects in Zimbabwe particularly land. An important note provided was the difference of the property markets in Zimbabwe and those abroad.

Interviews also indicated that the role of the realtor was to provide consultancy service to potential investors towards the choice of investment projects and the assets on which to invest. Their role is to convince an investor on the portfolio combination that yields the highest returns. How and to what extent can they convert an investment? In terms of advice, they would also inform about the on securitised products such as CBMS or RBMS. Another interviewee indicated that the roles of a realtor were largely advisory. Where investors are advised on balancing their investment portfolios in situations where real estate is one of the portfolios, they help investors on decision on investment based on returns and time risks. Consideration is given to the type of investment that brings the highest returns within the real estate sector, for example, investment targeting clients with low levels of default (Boleat, and Coles, 2012). On the same note, another interviewee indicated that they help through the presentation of business ideas for funding to the insurance companies. They also aid in identifying growth opportunities in real estate for financial industries and opportunities with high returns and untapped markets.

Real estate practitioners have a role in valuations for financial reporting which is a prerequisite where financial institutions are required to publish their reports and financial statement. The transactions in real estate form an important factor on the financial market (money market, bond or securities).

It was further observed that they play on informational role as a source on the real estate market. Information has been identified as a pertinent component for the functionality of financial markets. Another key informant insisted that realtors keep information on trends and asset values which is important for the financial markets. In addition, they interpret the real estate market signals to the sellers and buyers of real estate products. Furthermore, they provide information on risks which is a source of imperfection in the real estate financial markets. Brokerage is the link between investors to the financiers. In facilities management, real estate practitioners help preserves the value of assets through maintenance. Moreover, another observer notes that property managers ensure there is durable finance throughout the life time of the assets by managing lease agreements and adjusting lease terms where appropriate. They are also critical in the raising of finance for real estate through issuing shares on the stock exchange.

Based on the findings, it appears that property valuation and facilities management as well as brokerage to a lesser extend are the specialist real estate areas that are crucial in enhancing of the realtor in the financial market.

Discussion and Synthesis

One of the challenges observed in the global context has been lack of securitisation of mortgage loans which has culminated in the global financial crises that had contagious impact on financial markets across the globe. In the case of Zimbabwe, the banking sector crises of 2008 have been attributed to a narrow product portfolio. This is contrary to the case of Japan where land and real estate assets form the bulk of the investment in the banking sector. As such, the employment of realtor services in the sector of managing the investment portfolios is a key to sustain the financial markets. However, the major challenge is that most of the real estate assets in Zimbabwe lacks private tenure (dead capital) and therefore cannot be used for investment. This is contrary to the case of Japan where the property system is well developed and institutionalised. On the other hand, financial defaulting by mortgage borrowers has been identified to be another reason for defaulting of the Zimbabwe's financial market. This further call for the need for a realtor's service in evaluating the market value of collateral offered before a mortgage can be extended so as to prevent over lending. Over-lending to residential developers has been one of the causes for the financial crises in the United States in 2006. Assessment of market value of collateral against loan required reduces change of defaulting and the credit risk of banks (Brandl, 2017).

Following the post liberalisation era in 1990, Zimbabwe's financial markets have been characterised by unstable interest rates. Interest rate fluctuations are detrimental to the functionality of the financial system since they erode investor confidence. The interest rate risks can be countered through securitisation of mortgages. This has been successfully done in the case of South Africa. Likewise, in Zimbabwe, the opportunity to engage realtors in hedging against interest rate risks remains (Brandl, 2017). This is despite the difference in the level of development of the property markets of South Africa and Zimbabwe.

Changes in the demands of the markets, globalisation of financial real estate markets and ICT innovations are some of the factors that have seen the evolution of real estate to meet new needs. These have also resulted in innovative real estate financial mechanisms such as REITS. This has broadened the scope of the realtor's focus throughout the world despite the fact that the speed of innovations in the property markets tends to be slower in developing economies. These innovations have implications on developing the capacity of the realtors, in terms of the education systems to meet the competences required in the financial market (Brandl, 2017). Beyond the influence of the realtor government policies and political interventions also influence the success of the real financial sector. This is based on the view that real estate (housing and infrastructure) and land remains an area of interest for politicians.

Conclusion

Realtors have an important role to play in the financial markets across the globe. This has been made eminent in history by discovering that one of the causes of the well documented global financial crises in history had its source in poor regulation of residential lending mortgages in the USA. This led to a renewed interest in real estate planning as an integral part to the wellbeing of financial markets, both at domestic and global level. The findings indicate that the traditional roles of the realtor such as property valuation, facilities management and brokerage earned a higher position with regard to regulating the financial markets. However, based on the context, the realtor's suitable policy environments have to be provided to enhance capacity of realtors particularly with regard to institutional environment. Depending of the level of complexity of development of the financial markets, they may also need to revolve the skills of realtors align them to needs of the market.

References

Acton, A. (2013). *Issues in Housing and Real Estate, 2013 Edition:* . Georgia: Scholarly Editions.

Baker, K and Chinloy: (2014). *Privates Real Estate Markets and Investment.* (K. Baker and P. Chinloy, Eds.) New York: Oxford University Press.

Ball, M. (2006). *Markets and institutions in real estate and construction* (Vol. 17). John Wiley and Sons.

Barucci, E and Fontana, C. (2017). Financial Markets Microstructure. In *Financial Markets Theory* (pp. 583-659). Springer, London.

Boleat, M and Coles, A. (2012). *The Mortgage Market.* London: Routledge .

Bond: (1998). ,*Uneven Zimbabwe: A Study of Finance, Development and Underdevelopment Africa* . Eritrea: World Press.

Brandl, M. (2017). *Money, Banking , Financial Markets and Institutions.* USA: Cengage Learning.

Brown, G and Matysiak, G. (2000). *Real Estate Investment: A Capital Market Approach.* Financial Times Prentice Hall.

Desoto, H. (2010). *The Mystery of Capital* . Transworld Publishing.

Doucet, M and Weaver, J. (1991). *Housing the North American City, .* London: McGill-Queens University Press.

Dzomira, S. (2014). Analysis of the Bank Failure During the Finacial Tumult in Africa- Zimbabwe: A Historical Review. *Journal of Governance and Regulation , 3*(3), 75-80.

Eubanks, W. (2011). Should Banking Powers Expand into Real Estate Brokerage and Management? In S. Lombardi, *Real Estate Investment Markert* (pp. 169-175). Nova Science Publishers.

Freybote, J and Karoly, V. (2008). Secondary Mortgage Markets in South Africa. In D. Ben- Shahhar, C. Leung and S. Ong, *Mortgage Markets World Wide* (pp. 179-214 I). Oxford: Blackwell Publishing.

Furusten, S. (2013). *Institutional Theory and Organisational Change.* Cheltanham: Edward Elgar.

Gelbard, E and Leite, S. (1999). *Measuring Financial Development in Sub-Saharan Africa.* InternationalMonetary Fund.

Ghyoot, V. (2012). Africa. In K. Schulte and K. Schulte (Ed.), *Real Estate Education Throughout the World: Past, Present and Future* (pp. 463- 488). New York: Springer.

Glickman, E. (2014). *An Introduction to Real Estate Finance* . Amsterdam: Elsevier

Harvey, C. (1998). The Limited Impacts of Financial Sector Reforms in Zimbabwe. In M. Brownbridge and C. Harvey, *Banking In Africa* (pp. 163-186). Oxford: James Currey.

Himes, M. (2001). *Japan Real Estate Investment.* Greenwood Publishing.

Honohan: and Beck, T. (2007). *Making Finance Work for Africa* . Washington D.C: World Bank ,.

Hornstein, J. (2005). *A Nation of Realtors: A Cultural History of the Twentieth Century American Middle Class.* USA: Duke University Press.

Huat, S. N. (2016). Singapore Commercial Real Estate Industry in a Global Context. In S. Huat, S. Foo, Y. Ming, S. Huat, S. Foo and Y. Ming (Eds.), *Singapore's Real Estate: 50 Years of Transformation,* (pp. 113-158). London: World Scientific Publishing .

Idowu, S and Filho, W. (2009). *Professionals Perspectives of Corporate Social Responsibility.* (S. Idowu and W. Filho, Eds.) New York: Springer.

James, A. (2015). *Money and Capital Markets in Post- Bellum America.* New Jersey: Princeton University Press .

Jarsulic, M. (2010). *Anatomy of a Financial Crisis: A Real Estate Bubble, Runaway Credit Markets and Regulatory Failure.* . USA: Palgrave.

Kobold, K. (1986). *Interest Rate Futures Markets and Capital Market Theory: Theoretical Concepts and Emprical Evidence.* New York: Walter-de Gruyter.

Kovaven, A. (2004). *Zimbabwe: A Quest for A Nominal Anchor* . International Monetary Fund.

Kritchene, N. (2012). *Islamic Capital Markets: Theory and Practice.*

Kyle, R., Baird, F and Spodek, M. (2000). *Property Management: 6th Ed.* . Chicago: Dearborn Publishing.

Levy, D. (2004). *Behavioural Real Estate.* Bingley: Emerald Publishing.

Madura, J. (2015). *Financial Markerts and Institutions* (11 ed.). USA: Cengage Learning.

McCoy, B. (2006). *The Dynamics of Real Estate Capital Markets: A Practioner's Perspective*. Urban Land Institute.

Mera, K and Renaud, B. (2016). *Asia's Financial Crisis and the Role of Real Estate*. London: Routledge.

Mikitani, R and Posen, A. (2000). *Japan's Financial Crises and It's Parallels to the US Experience*. Washington DC: Institute for International Economics.

Miller, D. (1995). A Short History of the Institute of Estate Agents of South Africa. In I. o. Africa, *The New Real Estate Sales Guide: A Practical Manual of Applied Techniques for Real Estate Agents. The Institute of Estate Agents of South Africa* (pp. 3-9). Kenwyn: Juta.

Ming, Y. (2016). Role of Real Estate Service Providers in Growing the Real Estate Industry. In S. Huat, S. Foo, Y. Ming, S. Huat, S. Foo and Y. Ming (Eds.), *Singapore's Real Estate: 50 Years of Transformation* (pp. 101 – 112). London: World Scientific Publishing.

Ming, Y. (2016). Real Estate Education. In S. Huat, S. Foo, Y. Ming, S. Huat, S. Foo and Y. Ming (Eds.), *Singapore's Real Estate: 50 Years of Transformation* (pp. 239-252). London: World Scientific Publishing.

Mooya, M. (2016). *Real Estate Valuation Theory: A Critical Appraisal*. Verlag: Springer.

Mugwati, M., Nkala, D and Mukanganiki, C. (2013). The Composition and Regulation of the Financial Service Sector in Zimbabwe. *Asian Economic and Finance Review, 3*(4), 483-489.

Mutekede, L. (2009). *Housing Finance Mechanism in Zimbabwe, 2009*. Nairobi: Un-Habitat.

Oyama, T. (2004). *Determinants of stock prices: The case of Zimbabwe*. International Monetary Fund.

Paradza: (2015). *Undergraduate Real Estate Education in Zimbabwe: A Comparative Study*. University of Pretoria: Faculty of Engineering, Built Environment and Information Technology, .

Parker, D. (2012). *Global Real Estate Investment Trusts: People , Processes and Management*. Oxford: John Wiley and Sons.

Peca, S. (2010). Real Estate Development and Investment: *A Comprehensive Approach* . Wiley and Sons.

Reserve Bank of Zimbabwe, (2014). Banking Sector Report for Quarter Ended 30 June 2014. *RBZ Quartely Review*, pp. 1-15.

Reserve Bank of Zimbabwe. (2018). Quartely Economic Review: March 2018. *Quartely Economic Review*, pp. 1-28.

Richardson, C. (2015). The Loss of Property Rights and the Collapse of Zimbabwe. *Cato Journal, 25*(2), 1-35.

Saul, J and Bond: (2014). *South Africa: The Present as History from Mrs Ples to Mandela and Marikana,* . New York: James Currey.

Schulte, K. (2012). *Real Estate Education Throughout the World: Past,Present and Future* . Springer .

Simons, R., Malmgren, R and Small, G. ,. (2009). *Indigenous People and Real Estate Valuation* . Springer.

Sirgy, M. (2014). *Real Estate Marketing: Strategy Personal Selling, Negotiation, Management and Ethics,* . London: Routledge.

Sirota, D and Barell, D. (2003). *Essentials of Real Estate Finance* (10 ed.). Chicago: Dearborn Financial Publishing.

Teifonov, N. (2012). Central and Eastern Europe Countries. In K. Schulte, *Real Estate Education Throughout the World: Past,Present and Future* (pp. 61-88). Springer.

Tsaurai, K and Odhiambo, N. (2012). The Dynamics of Capital Market Development in Zimbabwe. *Cooperate Ownership and Control* , 9(2), 355-363.

Tunaru, R. (2017). *Real Estate Derivatives: From Econometrics to Financial Engineering* . OUP Oxford.

Tunaru, R. (2017). *Real- Estate Derivatives: From Econometrics to Financial Engineering.* UK: Oxford University Press .

Un- Habitat. (2008). *Housing Finance System in South Africa.* Nairobi: Un- Habitat.

Weiss, M. A. (2002). *The Rise of Community Builders: The American Real Estate Industry and Urban Planning.* Washington DC: Beardbooks.

White and White. (2014). *Real Estate Issues: Real Estate Finance in the New Economy* . John Wiley and Sons.

Chapter 14

Factors influencing property values: The case of Harare

Wendy Tsoriyo and Geraldine Usingarawe

Introduction

Property values are the estimates of the market value for which a property can be exchanged on the market after taking into account all the underlying factors. The values are obtained from the process called valuation or appraisal. These property values are determined by a host of factors which include the property's characteristics, locational attributes and the permitted use of property. The property values are used for various purposes after being obtained from a valuation for purposes such as sale, a purchase, mortgage, insurance among others. This practice is also guided by regulations which govern the actions of the practitioners known as the valuers. In the case of Zimbabwe there are various factors which hinder the proper practice of valuation resulting in manipulation of property values. These factors are to be discussed in this chapter as the main objective of this study. Property values differ from property to property because of difference in characteristics which include their types, location and purpose. Furthermore, in literature there is a phenomenon called NIMBY which stands for *Not in My Backyard* and is defined as an attitude of opposition by local residents against certain risk-generating facilities that have been chosen to accommodate either government or industry. It keeps striking every time a community has been chosen to host a hazardous facility or a facility that will carry some cost for local residents. These facilities can be landfill sites, nuclear waste repositories, new railways, especially for high-speed trains or transportation of dangerous goods, mental health facilities, prisons or rehabilitation centres and affordable housing (Heiman 1990; Schwab 199 1). The concerns expressed by local residents are due to fear of physical damage or stigmatization of the community, which may result in a decline in the values of property (Popper 1985). The article begins with discussion on the general factors affecting property values and the attitude of the population towards developments made by different agencies. Provided in the article is literature on different countries on the factors which they face and how they managed to overcome them. Following are data collection methods which were used in this study. Factors affecting Harare are also examined and are the main focus of this article. Furthermore, recommendations on future directions for the town to prevent property values from continuous decline are presented.

Theoretical underpinnings

The value of real estate property depends on several sets of factors. These factors, as mentioned above, differ according to the type of property, for example a house. It can include structural attributes such as the size of the living space, the size of the lot, the age of the house, the number of rooms and bathrooms, the quality of the structure and other amenities and features. The other set of factors includes location attributes, such as the slope of the landscape, traffic noise, air pollution, scenic views offered by the house, such as a lake, a mountain, a river, a park or open space (Ding, Simons and Baku, 2000). The third set of factors includes the quality of neighbourhood and city-level infrastructure and services, such as the road quality, public transportation, police, fire protection and emergency medical services, schools. Fourth, the set includes city-level attributes that affect housing demand and supply (Masocha, 2003). On the demand side, it includes employment opportunities, growth in population and property tax rates, while supply includes government regulations such as limits on urban growth and large lot zoning. Finally, economic and demographic factors at the regional and national levels affect housing prices and may include unemployment rates, structural changes in the labour force, cost of construction, demographic change and mortgage rates (Ding, Simons and Baku, 2000).

The NIMBY phenomenon is the motivation of residents who wish to protect their turf. These are the protectionist attitudes and opposition tactics adopted by community groups in the face of unwanted development in their neighbourhoods. The residents usually consider these facilities necessary, but not close to their homes, hence the term "not in my back yard (Masocha, 2003). The NIMBY phenomenon is usually associated with similar acronyms, all comprising of a relatively negative connotation. Examples include NIABY (not in anybody's backyard), LULU (locally unwanted land-uses), NIMTOO (not in my term of office), BANANA (build absolutely nothing anywhere near anyone), NOPE (not on planet Earth) and CAVEs (citizens against virtually everything). NIMBY views or thoughts can have an overwhelming effect on the provision of human services, leading to the decrease of tax revenue for needed programs or to the closure of a particular facility. Consumers will then, either have to do without the service, or travel long distances to obtain the service (Masocha, 2003). However, neighbourhood complaints can result in valuable improvements to the proposed programs; and customer-led voice opposition can lead to positive adjustments to the program plans of human service providers. Opposition arguments, generally express three specific concerns which includes the perceived threat to values of property, personal security and neighbourhood amenity (Dear 1990). In recent decades, the principal concern of opponents was that values of property in their neighbourhood would decline. Therefore, planners are usually on the front line when addressing NIMBY responses and face challenges of responding to public opposition, promoting inclusive engagement processes, participate in project reviews, assist developers with the unwanted development and in some cases bring together evidence to challenge development proposals. NIMBY asserts that individuals have the right not to be unfairly exposed to risks, with the sole justification that it is in the interest of the collective.

Literature review

In the United States, concerns raised about the affordable housing program by the opposition, feared a decline in the value of properties nearby. At the end of the twentieth century, the country experienced unprecedented levels of economic prosperity, characterised by such trends as rising per capita income, low unemployment and the expansion of the stock market. At the same time, the country also faced some of the biggest challenges in providing adequate housing for its people. The reduction in housing expenditures (Basolo 1999), combined with the increase in housing prices in metropolitan areas of the country due to the rise of the new economy (Landis, Elmer and Zook 2002), posed problems for households at all income levels, especially those at the bottom of the socio-economic hierarchy. Households with extremely low or very high incomes have experienced severe housing problems, for example, paying a large portion of their income in exchange for rent and / or living in substandard housing. The construction community has sought to go beyond profit, to mitigate the housing affordability crisis (Power, 1999). The lack of affordable housing is not just the only factor that has contributed to the housing crisis. However, opposition from community members to the development and construction of affordable housing in their community has interrupted and / or completely blocked the development of affordable housing projects (Pendall 1999). The reasons for the opposition to affordable housing were diverse and complex. They concern the quality and design of structures, the character or image of the neighbourhood, negative externalities such as congestion and environmental degradation, the entry of undesirables into the neighbourhood and anti-childhood feelings in general. (Downs, 1992, California Planning Roundtable, 1993, Turner, Popkin and Cunningham 2000). These concerns are related to the fear that the value of their property will be affected.

In Chicago, a measure of the impacts of foreclosures on nearby property values was done with neighbourhood characteristics data. Their conservative estimates indicated that each conventional foreclosure within a distance of an eighth of a mile of a single-family

278

home resulted in a 0.9 percent decline in the value of that home. Cumulatively, it means that for the whole city of Chicago, it is estimated that the 3,750 foreclosures reduced nearby property values with more than $598 million, or an average of $159,000 per foreclosure. This did not include the effects on the value of condominiums, multifamily rental properties and commercial buildings (Skogan, 1990). Foreclosures can also result in significant costs and hardships for those most directly affected. One of the potential impacts of increased foreclosures in a community is crime. Criminals flock to such communities because they do not fear being caught, thus causing social and physical disorder. Moreover, recent literature has addressed the impact of deteriorated or vacant residential buildings on property values or, conversely, the impact of rehabilitation on values of property. Shlay and Whitman (2004) analysed the impact of vacant housing units on nearby home values in Philadelphia and revealed that properties located within 150 feet of an abandoned unit sold for over $7,000 less than other properties. Ding, Simons and Baku (2000) found that housing rehabilitation and, in particular, new constructions have a positive effect on values of nearby property and that this effect is high in low-income neighbourhoods and predominantly white neighbourhoods.

Ghana, like many countries in sub-Saharan Africa, does not have well-designed landfills. Increased urbanisation and real estate growth are driving landfills to compete with other land-uses, particularly residential areas, resulting in greater proximity between landfills and residential neighbourhoods. The analysis indicates that although landfills depress nearby residential property values, the effects depend on the location of the property relative to the level of urbanisation of a community. Technical landfills are scarce in many parts of the developing world, while rapid urbanisation and urban growth have outstripped the waste management and sanitation capacity of municipal authorities (Fobil et al. 2008, Owusu et al. 2012). As a result, generated solid and liquid waste generated may be left uncollected or, once collected, disposed of in open dumps and left exposed (Chaplin 1999, United Nations Population Fund (UNFPA), 2007; World, 1999). Landfills in Ghana are generally not well designed and their operations tend to be below the required environmental and health standards. As a result, there are manifestations that generally arise from the perception that landfills will have negative effects on health and the environment in adjacent neighbourhoods (Owusu *et al.* 2012). The results of the landfill sites examined in Ghana showed that the presence of the landfill did not result in a reduction in land prices or rent, but rather a reduction in the number of people who come to buy or rent square to live. However, using a basic analysis of supply and demand, we infer that land prices and rents could have been much higher than they were, otherwise the presence of landfills in Mallam and Oblogo communities. In short, we infer that more people would have looked for land and shelter in these areas, which would have affected rents and land prices even higher than their current levels.

With regard to values of property in South Africa from the mid-1980s onwards, South African newspapers constantly reported massive housing price declines in suburban areas located near either expanding black townships or new informal settlements (see for example, Krige 1991; Saff 1994). These news reports uncritically accepted the view of the white residents, realtors and some property economists that the mere presence of squatters in an area resulted in property declines. Beyond the headlines, the newspapers tended to base their entire analysis on interviews with one or two local realtors. Typical of this trend are the comments by a realtor in Noordhoek who recounted that homeowners were losing at least25% of the value of their houses due to the establishment of the informal settlement (called Site Five). The same realtor also noted a general difficulty in selling houses in the area and the reluctance of some financial institutions to grant mortgages in the area (Weekend Argus, 21 March1992; see also Cape Times 7 February 1992). Two detailed studies of Hout Bay and Noordhoek partly confirm the realtors' comments, noting that the houses closest to the informal settlements lost value and became much difficult to sell (Oelofse 1994; Sowman and Gawith 1994). According to Oelofse (1994, 329) realtors suggested that property prices in Hout Bay had dropped by 15% in some areas. In the late 1980s, informal settlements were established in or around affluent Cape Town suburbs. Despite objections by suburban residents that these settlements would result in a rapid escalation of crime and a dramatic fall in the property values, the authorities allowed the settlements to remain.

The effects that the informal settlement of Marconi Beam had on house prices and housing turnover within Milnerton, the adjacent suburb was examined. The results showed that most of the objections to the effect of Marconi Beam on the value of the properties were unfounded because the by-law had only a negligible effect on the value of properties in the adjacent suburbs. From the late 1980s onwards, a handful of informal settlements were established in the boundaries of some affluent white suburbs in South Africa. Within the Cape Town Metropolitan area, the three most notable examples occurred in the suburbs of Hout Bay, Noordhoek and Milnerton. In all three cases the white residents objected vociferously to allow these settlements to permanently remain within their areas. The most commonly voiced suburban concerns were that the informal settlements would increase crime in the adjoining suburbs, decrease property values and cause environmental degradation. In January 1991, a newspaper report appeared in the major Afrikaans language newspaper (Burger 17 January 1991) under the headline "People hesitate to buy houses in Milnerton." This article quoted the chairman of the Milnerton Ratepayers Association as saying that, because of the squatter situation, about twenty houses for sale in Milnerton could not be sold because potential buyers were hesitating to make purchases in the area. This assertion was contradicted in interviews with local realtors who argued that while it was perhaps difficult to sell the houses closest to the squatter settlement than further away, there was no evidence that its presence had any negative effect on the overall property market in Milnerton (see Saff 1996b).

In Kenya, real estate prices have more than doubled in the past few years (Majtenyi, 2010) and the demand continues to outweigh the supply (Masika, 2012). The real estate property market has been booming due to factors such as increased availability of financing through mortgages with favourable rates (Masika, 2012). For example, 60% of the pension fund goes to the real estate sector through purchases or investment and pensions also act as security for the mortgages (Okumu, 2010).

Methodology

An attempt was made to identify factors influencing property value in Harare. This was done through the use of secondary sources of data thus it is not first-hand information. The sources include published research papers, reports from different organizations, results from interviews carried out by other researchers. There are no series of steps used during the collection of data.

Results

In buying a property, people jointly purchase a wide variety of services in a particular location. These include the size of living space, a particular structure type and quality, an address, accessibility to their employment (CBD), a neighbourhood environment and a diverse collection of public services including schools, waste collection and police protection (Alonso, 1964).Holding the physical characteristics (for example size, age and construction materials) of a property constant, the literature on land and housing values indicates that environmental attributes can also increase or decrease property value (Nelson *et al.* 1992).These attributes include noise level (especially from vehicles, rail,), air quality and perceived general landscape conditions. With reference to a proposed project by Zimre Property Investment (ZPI) in 2012, in which they wanted to construct 80 cluster housing in Marlborough to curb the housing shortages in Harare, they faced objections from the residents of the adjacent neighbourhood. The objections were supported with reasons such as that there were water and sewer problems already occurring in that area, increase in the crime rate and high traffic especially in Gilchrist road. Furthermore, it was a low-density suburb and they wanted to build a high-density suburb in it, thus being a threat to the property values of that particular area. Public objections are a characteristic of the phenomenon NIMBY which makes it difficult for the planners to make decisions.

Currently, the Zimbabweans are suffering an economy meltdown which has emerged from different reasons. The current economic state has affected the property market as it is volatile in nature. The economy is largely characterised by the informal sector, without payments of rentals and rates to the local authorities, the public just locate anywhere they feel they can realize profits within the central business district and it is so much congested. Due to this, property owners are suffering high occupational voids and default payments of those renting their premises. They cannot afford to practice maintenance on their properties, therefore when they want to sell their properties, they would not get much because of poor condition of their properties for the buyer will have to incur cost of renovations. The quality of a building influences the value of a property if it is to be sold or leased. Also, punitive mortgage rates being charged by the building societies affect property values. Building societies are there to provide funding to those who want to carry out large projects like house construction. With the unstable economy, they are now charging high rates for their mortgages. There will be at risk considering time value of money which they will receive after a long period of time like 10 years. However, they have tried to venture into projects of housing schemes to provide affordable housing considering the shortage of housing in Harare. For example, the National Building Society (NBS) established a housing project in Budiriro but they did this without prospective buyers and some houses where left unsold.

Zimbabwean property market is also being grossly affected by the three-tier pricing system. This was revealed by the real estate agents that this system has lowered the values of property (Makuwaza, 2018). Land is being sold at different prices depending on the payment method which is to be used by the buyer, hence the property values are increasing. Property prices are changed when using plastic money and the current bond notes. The three-tier system began at the end of November 2016. Shortage of cash in circulation was the cause, especially the US dollar. Dawn property general manager, said during an interview that this system has affected the real estate market and gave an example to support this by referring to stands in Mt Hampden which were being sold for $40 per square metre but when one uses swipe or bond notes to pay for the transaction the price will increase to $64 per square meter. She also said that "this has certainly affected the real estate market. When you look at your commercial properties there is a function of the rentals that you realise through an investment, but as we speak, the current rentals are depressed and we have a situation where rentals and capital values are not related at all, which is an abnormal situation." The agents also commented on other factors that affect value which can be rental values and market values. Dawn property manager also said "Market values for residential properties are a function of what similar properties have recently sold at, aspects like location, size and quality are also involved. Commercial properties are a function of market rentals and yields."

Case study: Pomona dumpsite

The Pomona Dumpsite which is located 12 km to the north of the CBD was created in 1984. The site is an open dump which is not lined. Statutory Instrument 6 of 2007 Environmental Management (Effluent and Solid Waste Disposal) and Regulations 2007 of the Environmental Management Act [Chapter 20:27] stipulates that urban areas should have engineered sanitary landfills. Open dumping of waste does not have monitoring measures to control its operations, as compared to sanitary landfills. Uncontrolled open dumps have no strict environmental regulations; they cause major public health threats and also affect the natural environment. When it was first constructed, waste was being spread in thin layers, compacted and then covered with soil. However, due to poor waste management and maintenance systems, the waste is now left uncovered.

According to The Environmental Management Authority (EMA), the Pomona dumpsite poses a serious threat to the environment and people who live close to it. As stated by EMA (2009), the Harare City Council did not register the Pomona dumpsite under the EMA regulations. Whilst EMA regulations require all dumpsites to be registered to allow the authorities to carry out regular inspections and to limit incidents of pollution and other related health and environmental hazards. Plastic and paper wastes are being blown by the wind, Therefore, littering the area around the landfill because the waste is not covered. There are also fires at the dumpsite and they emit dark toxic smoke into the atmosphere, which constitutes both a health and environmental hazard. For example, the largest fire broke out in October 2013, taking two weeks to extinguish and killed one person (Mupedziswa, 2009). Unlined dumps have increased the rate of contamination of soil and groundwater by leachates. The solid wastes are also hazardous materials and sometimes contain human faecal matter. When it rains the waste is thrown into ground water thus contaminating water sources whereas the residents now depend on water from wells and boreholes due to water shortages. Since 2008, there have been epidemics of cholera and typhoid in the city mainly because of the unsanitary conditions in the residential area and consumption of contaminated water. For example, in 2009, cases of cholera recorded in Harare totalled 19,517 (WHO, 2013).

Currently, town planners are facing challenges when looking for a site to dispose solid waste, generated from industrial and residential areas. This creates serious health and environment problems. With all those effects posed on the people living near dumpsite, no one will be willing to pay a high market value for such properties, even those practicing letting. They would not want to pay high rental values for they are living under poor conditions. Water sources are being contaminated; sewerage may be flowing for more than 100 meters from the main sources, bringing out pungent smells in the neighbourhood. Services offered in a locality influence the values of property in that area. If one has to walk to get a service or has to incur large costs, the property values will be lowered. The local government should try to improve services in such areas.

However, Pomona is not the only area with declining property values. These property values are being influenced by various factors such as locality, availability of services such as schools and police, proximity, age of the property being sold among others. There are areas such as Caledonia. Without serviced stands, in order there was no layout used to subdivide the land, an individual would just build where he feels or thinks his structure can fit. That area is characterised by high unemployment rates, poor water, boreholes and children have to walk a long distance to get to school. The residents of that area are indulging in activities like prostitution and drug abuse. There is a reported large number of crime rates.

Therefore, this will cause a decline in market value of buying land there or in nearby suburbs. For example, in Waterfalls, the values of the properties are decreasing because of the nearby location, Hopely. This is because the properties there are not regularised or properly serviced, therefore are associated with insecurities. The facilities there like roads are not in good condition although there is available of transport. There are also areas such as Tafara and an area called KwaMazai. They suffer from sewerage problems, which flow for a distance more than 100 meters. This is because of overpopulation due to urbanisation, a typical single-family house can be living more than two families and the sewer pipes installed there were not able to withstand such a large number of people, therefore it will burst out because of waste overload. This is not safe for the residents of those areas. They are at risk of health hazards and outbreak of diseases like typhoid and cholera. This same water will be used for irrigation of crops which also not safe.

Discussion and synthesis

As unveiled by the chapter, informal settlements have emerged from increased levels of urbanisation. As noted by SADC, Zimbabwe is the most rapidly urbanising country in Southern Africa. Different factors influence property values either positively or negatively. Non-governmental organisations have been working with those in the slum communities in trying to improve their living standards as there are outbreaks of diseases such as cholera and typhoid. In Harare, the property sector is mainly affected by the economic performance affecting the demand of properties. Locally unwanted land-uses (LULU) developers face objections from the societies but because the views are suppressed, they continue with their developments which are harmful to society. Developing countries especially in Africa are faced with similar problems.

As for the NIMBY phenomenon, it is accused for strengthening itself. The public is expected to reason irrationally and egoistically forcing the risk imposers to keep information secret until it is too late to oppose any plans. This secrecy is claimed to strengthen suspicion among the residents of a chosen society that the risk imposers cannot be trusted, a suspicion that can trigger the NIMBY phenomenon (see e.g., Rabe 1994; Wolsink 1994). Some claim that the NIMBY attitude is a good that comes with democracy whilst others argue that the concept is too simplistic because it disregards that there are a variety of different motives behind resisting a facility (cf. Lober 1996; Sjöberg and Drottz-Sjöberg 2001; Wolsink 1994). The government of Zimbabwe is recommended to venture into Public Private Partnership in housing and social services delivery. The Government, in its new National Housing Delivery Programme (2014-2018) directed that 20% of land for housing development should be reserved for construction of flats.

Conclusion, policy options and future direction

Zimbabwe has a huge national housing backlog. This is because of limited financial capacity, at both central government and local government level. With this, the country has witnessed a slump in housing delivery by the public sector. This has caused the increase in the in formal settlements in different parts of the town, thus affecting property values of adjacent neighbourhoods. The private sector has tried to chip in and cover the void left by the public sector. However, the stumbling block has been lack of, or obsolete off-site infrastructure for water extraction, treatment and transmission, sewerage extraction, treatment and disposal and such infrastructure requires huge capital outlay, which the nation cannot currently access due to the economic sanctions imposed on the country.

With the available space in the vicinity of the Central Business District (CBD) land can be re-zoned and encourage the property owners to consider extending their buildings upwards in high rise buildings in order to accommodate a lot of people per square kilometre. This will as well ease the burden of servicing the land with access roads, sewerage and water reticulation. All that will be required is to increase the water pumping capacity to reach the tallest buildings. To a larger extent, the Government of Zimbabwe should also decentralise local government so as to strengthen local authorities. Local authorities are able to provide and maintain public services and infrastructure using funds generated from the local community through rent and rates charges and sometimes loans, donations and other sources. If the services being provided by the local authorities are of high quality, the property values will increase.

References

Alonso, W. (1964). *Location and Land-use*. Cambridge: Harvard University Press.

Basolo, V. (1999). Passing the housing baton in the U.S: Will cities take the lead? *Housing Studies,* 14(4), 433-52.

California Planning Roundtable. (1993). Myths and facts about affordable housing and high-density housing. Sacramento. California Department of Housing and Community Development.

Chaplin, S. E. (1999). Cities, sewers and poverty: India's politics of sanitation. *Environment and Urbanisation,* 11(1), 145-158.

Chifamba, M. (2016). Zimbabwe: *Majority of urban dwellers living in informal settlements*. Shout Africa.

Cummings, P. M and Landis, J. D. (1993). *Relationships between affordable housing developments and neighbouring property values: An analysis of BRIDGE Housing Corporation developments in the San Francisco Bay Area*. University of California at Berkeley, Institute of Urban and Regional Development.

Dear, M., Taylor, S. M and Hall, G. B. (1980). External Effects of Mental Health Facilities. Annals, *Journal of Association of American Geographers* 70, 3: pp, 342-52.

Ding, C., Simons, R and Baku, E. (2000*)*. The Effect of Residential Investment on Nearby Property Values: Evidence from Cleveland, Ohio. *Journal of Real Estate Research*. 19, pp23–48.

Downs, A. (1992). Creating more affordable housing. *Journal of Housing* 49 (4), pp 174-83.

Fobil, J. N., Armah, N. A., Hogarh, J. N and Carboo, D. (2008). The influence of institutions and organizations on urban waste collection systems: An analysis of waste collection system in Accra, Ghana (1985–2000). *Journal of Environmental Management,* 86 (1), pp262–271.

Government of Zimbabwe, (2011). *Environmental Management Act Chapter 20:27*. Government of Zimbabwe Publications.

Heiman, M. (1990). From "Not in My Backyard!" to "Not in Anybody's Backyard!" Grassroots Challenge to Hazardous Waste Facility Siting. *Journal of the American Planning Association* 56, (3) pp359-62.

Immergluck, D and Smith, G. (2006). The external costs of foreclosure: The impact of single- family mortgage foreclosures on property values. *Journal of Housing Policy Debate,* 17 (1), pp 57-79.

Landis, J. Vicki E and Zook, M. (2002). The new economy and housing market: Fast and furious—but different? *Housing Policy Debates,* 13 (2), pp 233-73.

Lober DJ (1996). Why not here? The importance of context, process and outcome on public attitudes toward siting of waste facilities. *Soc Nat Resour* 9, pp 375–394

Majtenyi, J. M and Witkiewiez, W. (2010). International Evidence on Real Estate as a Portfolio Diversifier. *The Journal of Real Estate Research,* 26, (2) pp 161-206.

Masika (2010). Hedging Housing Risk: *Journal of Real Estate Finance and Economics*

Vol.2, No.4, 2011.

Masocha, M. (2003). Solid Waste Disposal in Victoria Falls Town: Spatial Dynamics, Environmental Impacts, Health Threats and Socio-economic Benefits. *Unpublished Thesis, Geography and Environmental Science*. Harare, University of Zimbabwe.

Michael Dear, (1992). Understanding and Overcoming the NIMBY Syndrome. *Journal of the American Planning Association*, 58:3, pp288-300.

Hochfeld, T., Selipsky, L., Mupedziswa, R and Chitereka, C. (2009). Developmental social work education in Southern and East Africa. *South Africa: University of Johannesburg*.

Okumu, J. M. (2010). Price formation and the appraisal function in real estate markets. *Journal of Real Estate Finance and Economics*, 98(1), pp437- 445.

Owusu, G., Nketiah-Amponsah, E., Codjoe, S. N. A and Afutu-Kotey, R. L. (2014). How do Ghana's landfills affect residential property values? A case study of two sites in Accra. *Urban Geography*, 35(8), 1140-1155.

Owusu, G., Oteng-Ababio, M and Afutu-Kotey, R. L. (2012). Conflicts and governance of landfills in a developing country city, Accra. *Landscape and Urban Planning*, 104(1), 105-113.

Pendall, R. (1999). *Opposition to housing: NIMBY and beyond.* Urban Affairs Review **35** (1), pp 112-36.

Power, M. (1999). *Housing America: A call for heroes.* Builder, pp 74-98.

Practical Action, (2006). *Emerging Issues in Urban Waste Management.* Retrieved from: http://practicalaction.org/docs/region_southern_africa.

Rabe BG (1994). *Beyond Nimby. Hazardous waste siting in Canada and the United States.* The Brookings Institution, Washington, D.C.

Schwab, J. (1991*). Blue-collar Groups Are Saying: Not in Our Backyard.* Planning **57,** (10) pp 8-11.

Shlay, A. B and Whitman, G. (2004). Research for Democracy: *Linking Community Organizing and Research to Leverage Blight Policy.*

Sjöberg, L., and Drottz-Sjöberg, B. M. (2001). Fairness, risk and risk tolerance in the siting of a nuclear waste repository. *Journal of risk research*, 4(1), 75-101.

Skogan, W. (1990). *Disorder and Decline: Crime and the Spiral of Decay in American Neighborhoods.* Berkeley, CA: University of California Press.

Turner, M. A., Popkin S and Cunningham, M. (2000). *Section 8 mobility and neighborhood health.* Urban Institute, Washington DC.

UNFPA, (2007*).* State of world population 2007: *Unleashing the potential of urban growth.* New York, NY.

WHO, (2013). *Zimbabwe cholera and health situation.* Available online: who.int/disasters. [Accessed on 27 June 2018]

Wolsink, M. (1994). *Entanglement of interests and motives: assumptions behind the NIMBY-theory on facility siting.* Urban Studies **31** (6):857–866.

Working Paper 599, ed. University of California at Berkeley, Institute of Urban and Regional Development, California.

World Bank (1999). *Observation of solid waste landfills in developing countries: Africa, Asia and Latin America.* Washington, DC: World Bank. **43**, pp 87-92.

Chapter 15

Urban graffiti: Epitome of place-making, property value enhancement or socio-political resistance

Geraldine Usingarawe, Wendy Tsoriyo and Innocent Chirisa

Introduction

This chapter aims to examine the complex relationship between graffiti and the place- making concept in Zimbabwean urban public spaces. Graffiti as part of the urban fabric in cities has become a worldwide spatial phenomenon which can be considered to be both an art and crime. However, most definitions identify graffiti as a criminal act that causes property damage and thus negatively affects property values of both public and private property. According to Mangeya (2014), what makes graffiti a norm-violating practice, is that the graffiti inscriptions are usually done on both private and public property without the permission of property owners. Graffiti inscriptions cannot be separated from the wide power struggles of use of public space (Zieleniec, 2016). In this light graffiti can be viewed as tool of resistance that is used by an otherwise marginalised and less understood group of the urban society-graffiti artist; to assert their views about the world around them on urban space.

However, more often graffiti carries sociocultural, socio-political and economic messages which local residents can identify with. Apart from the aesthetics value, these messages also portray the local culture which may be of interest to visitors of the city (Fraser 2016). Due to its ability to relay various messages and community matters in urban public spaces, graffiti can be an effective tool for place-making with several beneficial factors. These benefits include; re-use of post-industrial ruins (for example the derelict power stations in Johannesburg, South Africa), bringing about social connectivity within neighbourhoods, giving voice to those who have been unheard and an improved public realm

Although graffiti is normally considered as a criminal nuisance of property vandalism in Zimbabwe, this practice can be viewed as an art. Viewing graffiti as an art has immense potential as a place-making instrument which can increase a sense of identity and attachment among the local users of space, if the local skill and talent of graffiti artist is harnessed. However, both concepts of graffiti as art and the place making concept are fairly novel in the Zimbabwean context. More so, only a handful of studies (Mangeya, 2014) have actually been conducted to understand the nature and existence of graffiti in Zimbabwe.

This study is of use to various stakeholders that include; local governments, policy makers and the private sector to create an enabling environment where graffiti can be used as a place making tool which uses local skill and talent to improve public spaces. These stakeholders are considered as "moral entrepreneurs" (Fraser, 2016:33) who control and determine what can be placed into public spaces in the form of public art. In Zimbabwe, normally graffiti is excluded from the category despite its possible benefits as can be evidenced from the absence of graffiti artist in national art events such as the Harare International Festival of Arts.

The study begins by emphasising the theoretical framework which underpins this study before extensively reviewing global and regional literature, followed by a description of the methodology which the study adopts. Results and discussion of key findings proceeds and lastly conclusions and policy directions for graffiti and place making are provided.

Theoretical underpinnings

The creative cities framework by Richard Florida forms the theoretical underpinning of this study. Florida (2002)'s creative cities framework argues that cities that want to prosper should attract the development initiatives which focus on the 3 Ts of- technology, talent and tolerance. Graffiti artists can be considered as a creative class of talented individuals who can contribute to the success of cities through their creative art (Rabine, 2014; Fraser, 2016). Florida describes the creative class as a group whose lifestyle is characterised by; individuality, self-expression and openness. Often, graffiti artist uses urban public spaces to express their own desires and experiences.

Graffiti is defined as "a drawing or inscription made on a wall or other surface, usually so as to be seen by the public" (American Heritage in Frasser, 2016). Graffiti is usually placed on public property or private property adjacent to public space. Whereas contemporary public spaces under the auspices on neo-liberalism goals are produced and shaped by the government and private players with the intention of creating surplus value which is exchangeable at the market (Lefebvre, 1996; Dikec, 2001). However, the production of space under neo-liberalism infringes on the right to the city of other public space users as it tends to exclude or users such as graffiti artist. Henri Lefebvre 1968's the right to the city theory states that the right to the city of urban dwellers is affected by the urbanisation processes on social production of space. The urbanisation process through capitalism orders urban spaces in a way which eradicates urbanity and deprives urban dwellers of places of social encounter (Lefebvre, 1996). While the city administrative authorities desire a city to be all neat and tidy and only represented by authorised public art; graffiti artists on the other hand reclaim their right to city through graffiti on public spaces to *win* contested urban space and as assertive behaviour, despite several ideological exclusions they are confronted with (Bandaranaike, 2001; Fraser, 2016).

Graffiti exists in many forms and varies according to the skill, motivation and experience of the artist. Serkan and Gülse (2006) categorise graffiti into distinct types as gang graffiti, tagger graffiti, conventional graffiti, expressive graffiti, political graffiti, ideological graffiti and piecing. Graffiti has been viewed in literature from two divergent positions, that is -graffiti as art and graffiti as vandalism (Bandaranaike, 2001). Halsey and Young (in Mangeya, 2016) argue that it takes a lot of skill to produce graffiti and further explain graffiti as art on the three bases of skill, intent and aesthetics. Such a view on graffiti is a precursor of graffiti as a place making tool in urban public spaces while viewing graffiti as vandalism or as a tool of resistance in urban public is a punishable offence.

Traditionally, space refers to something anonymous, whereas a place modern distinctively accounts for the meaningful experience of a given site (Sherry, 1998). Relph (1976) proffers that, places are fusions of human and natural order and are the significant centres of our immediate experiences of the world. Goodsell (2013) defines urban places as appropriated sites where social interactions, sense of belonging, collective memories and shared identities occur. Aljabri (2014) defines place-making as part of wider sustainability and regeneration concepts which promotes the strengthening of the relationship between users and the space itself, by increasing a sense of belonging and attachment. Indeed, it entails a collective process by various stakeholders through which spaces are shaped in order to maximise shared values of a community. Place making is a bottom up approach to planning of public spaces which recognises the importance of active engagement of communities by local governments in order to draw on the assets and skills of a community (Project for Public Spaces (PPS, 2012). Place-making is generally the transformation of spaces into places through attaching a meaning and sense to those spaces (Agnew, 1987, 2011; Tonnelat, 2010). Similarly, graffiti as art is a communication medium which conveys various messages through which meaning can be attached; creates a sense of identity amongst the community and encourages community involvement in decision-making.

Literature review

In order to understand the complex relationships that exists between graffiti and the place making approach, in this section, the researchers review literature on the various experiences and trends of graffiti and place making strategies from global and regional contexts giving references to the various experiences from cities across Europe, Australia, America and Africa.

Urban graffiti is a universal phenomenon which is found in almost all cities around the world. It has gained popularity in North and South American as well as in European countries such as Finland, Germany and Russia. Although graffiti has increasingly been viewed as a growing problem for many cities in industrialised nations, the researchers support Mangeya (2014)'s argument that graffiti offers communities with discursive spaces on which to construct alternative discourses despite operating in an environment where it is largely viewed as a negative in the society.

Graffiti first gained popularity in New York which is popularly known as the capital and cultural centre of graffiti. The graffiti writings in New York were inspired by political mass movements in the 1960s and the post-world war II. Originally, in New York, graffiti was a way the ghetto youths used to portray their social world views. However, it has since evolved and advanced over the years (Serkan and Gülsen, 2006). According to Fraser (2016), the evolving nature of graffiti helps in understanding the changes in social, economic, political structure of society in, urban areas. New York City Government controls graffiti in the city by providing a legal wall where graffiti artist can showcase their artworks. However, the police have a community hotline for the reporting illegal graffiti activity and vandalism (Offler, Thompson, Hirsch, Thomas and Dawson, 2009). A legal wall for graffiti art supports and contributes to the liveliness of a community (Project for Public Space 2012). It is also a platform for showcasing talent of graffiti artist and provides locals and visitors an opportunity to meet and enjoy the city which is an important place- making strategy.

In Toronto, Canada, graffiti is promoted as street art (Fraser 2016). An important strategy in place making is designing of streets as public spaces (PPS, 2012). Street art not only contributes to the aesthetics of the street space, it also relays messages which are engaging for communities. In 2015, The Toronto City Government developed a Graffiti Management Plan, which offers grants to graffiti artist as a way of co-opting graffiti into the discourses of public art.

The City of Worcester, in England unites artist (including graffiti artist) and the community through aesthetic improvements of public spaces. In place making, the involvement of communities in decision-making is a key to success (Agnew, 2011; PPS, 2012; Aljabri, 2014). In Worcester, the Public Art Working Group (PAWG) was created and includes the city government staff, local residents and artists. PWAG conducted a survey in 2013 to gain a better understanding of what the community would like to see created through public art.

One of the resolutions was to support local and regional artists in the development of public art throughout the city. As an example, the Arts Alley showcases various murals that reflect a chosen theme. This creates community cohesion as the community participates in decision-making of the design of their public spaces as well as creates sense of ownership of activities.

In Hiedanranta, Finland, graffiti is celebrated and viewed as a legitimate art form (Ylinen, 2018). In the Cities of Tampere and Spraycankontrol- a street art and graffiti organisation in FinLand has managed various events and activities to celebrate street art in Hiedanranta. Hiedanranta is now reckoned as a significant street art destination. Providing places where people play, work, socialise, rest and learn is another important place-making strategy (PPS, 2012). In Brazil, law was passed in 2011 to decriminalise acts of graffiti when it is practiced with the purpose of valuing public or private heritage through artistic expression provided it is a consented to by the owner. Clearly when graffiti is legalised more value is attainable to the community as a whole as graffiti art would fully explore their potential without fear of being incriminated.

Although some city governments in developed countries are more flexible and tolerant of graffiti, other governments are sterner to this practice. For example, in New South Wales (NSW), Australia graffiti spread at an increasing rate during the 1980s. Since then it has been linked to a form of vandalism that is synonymous with violence, gangs and criminal behaviour and it is considered a punishable offence. As a measure the NSW government passed a law which prohibits the sale of spray cans of paint to persons less than 18 years. However, some scholars (Offler, Thompson, Hirsch, Thomas and Dawson 2009) argue that this form of legislation can only be effective when used in conjunction with an education program. Local councils in Sydney, Australia have moved to a zero-tolerance stance. The councils have introduced the Graffiti Control Act (2008) and formed an anti-graffiti council that oversees the management of urban graffiti.

Los Angeles (L.A) city in the United State remains a contested site for space where graffiti is still an unacceptable social deviation (Fraser, 2016). In this city, graffiti is controlled through placing of close circuit television (CCTV) cameras in public places to encourage people to conform to private interests as they move through urban public spaces. However, the city is more appreciative of other forms of public art such as; monuments, civil depictions of historic events and abstract modern sculptures. Certain forms of graffiti are employed as a means of resisting circumstances and phenomena that arise from legal, political and religious impasse. For example, the prohibitive legal environment in L.A has seen graffiti artists adapting to the use of heavens (high up, hard to reach places like freeway over passes, water towers and billboards) (Fraser, 2016). The use of the heavens is the graffiti artist way of putting their own stamp in an urban environment. In Russia, urban graffiti emerged as a way of resisting the interests of the Soviet authorities.

Crawley (2015: 112) has observed graffiti as a "threat to property values, a scourge on the environment, a disease, an ugly stain and one of the most visible and ugliest forms of crime". Urban graffiti is correlated with criminology, fear and vandalism (Killias and Clerici, 2000). Criminal damage and vandalism to public and private property symbolises urban decay (Gibbons, 2003). This automatically implies an effect on the valuation of property, property costs and tenant occupation. More so, due to the fact that graffiti in itself is correlated to crime and illegality, areas with high crime rates acquire poor reputations, so people, shops and employers usually eliminate those areas when choosing properties to occupy. In the US, crime rates affect property values and properties in areas of high crime rates are prone to low values (Thaler, 1978; Hellman and Naroff, 1979; Lynch and Rasmussen, 2001) Property location is a major consideration to a tenant or a possible buyer when choosing to purchase or rent.

Graffiti at times induces fear of crime and therefore, properties in graffiti sites are left out. Urban graffiti reduces tenant occupation, leaving empty properties. These empty properties are more susceptible to vandalism thereby creating an opportunity to vandalism of those empty properties (Social Exclusion Unit, 2001:7). A research that was done in US indicated that high local crime rates deters new residents and motivates already occupying tenants and to move out to lower-crime rate neighbourhoods (Crawley, 2015). This implies that urban graffiti reduces demand for properties located in graffiti sites and increases demand on properties in graffiti free environments. Due to the market forces of supply and demand which tend to control real estate at times, properties in graffiti free environments are demanded more than they are supplied leading to higher prices for the supply to meet demand and the opposite is true for those in graffiti environments. Graffiti and vandalism may be taken as signals or symptoms of community instability, disorder, lack of social cohesion and neighbourhood deterioration in general and property prices respond to all these factors (Brand and Price, 2000).

Graffiti has an impact on the amenity and beauty of the urban environment aesthetics is also another consideration of property values on the valuation of properties (Department of Transport and Main Roads, 2009). Urban graffiti tends to disrupt and depreciate the aesthetic value of the environment and the properties themselves. Aesthetic value among other improvements is also another value that is added to the cost of properties when selling or when leasing and it increases the value of properties. It induces visual appropriateness and legibility to the environment and this is only if the property is smart and free of vandalism and graffiti disorder. Graffiti leads to vandalism and damage of properties and unrepaired damage to property in the neighbourhood encourages further vandalism, perceptions of community disorganisation, increasing crime rates and diminishing neighbourhood status (Crawley, 2015; Wilson and Kelling, 1982). Graffiti impact property prices if seen as a predictor of neighbourhood decline and precursor of escalating crime rates (Crawley, 2015).

Graffiti is also highly visible in most African cities. In Dakar, Senegal, graffiti can be traced to the *Set Setal* (be clean-make clean) youth movement of the 1980s. In this country, graffiti has never been illegal but has always been considered as an art form that spurs creativity, inspiration and technical ingenuity (Rabine, 2014). Graffiti art is considered a force to cleanse and beautify the disintegrating urban spaces in Dakar. The Senegalese community from the municipal officials, businessmen and community members are supportive of the arts culture from graffiti. In Senegal, graffiti artists of different generations work as a collective group, where they paint a message of inspiration and positivity for the community. Senegal provides lessons for other less developed nations like Zimbabwe that seek constructive uses from the arts culture to prosper a healthy society.

Graffiti in South Africa has become a commonly accepted art form which is gaining corporate backing as public art as a tool for social change. A website, graffiti South Africa showcases graffiti and street art in the country as well as the rest of Africa.

Methodology

A case study approach was used to gather data to examine the relationship between graffiti and the place making concept in the two metropolitan cities in Zimbabwe namely Bulawayo and Harare. Intensive literature review was done in order to draw lessons from global and regional experiences while document review, observations and unstructured interviews with city council officials and the Zimbabwe Republic Police (ZRP) were mostly used to explore the local cases in Zimbabwe. The major findings of the local experiences together with lessons from global and regional literature provided the basis for possible strategies of establishing graffiti as a place making tool in Zimbabwean urban public space. Narrative analysis was adopted for data analysis.

Results

This section presents results from the two metropolitan cities in Zimbabwe namely Harare and Bulawayo. The City of Harare is pursuing the vision of becoming a World class city by 2025, while City of Bulawayo's vision is to become a leader in local governance excellence with a vibrant economy by 2024. Both cities could benefit from better place-making approaches.

It is argued that Zimbabwean graffiti has been influenced by its own distinct socio-cultural as well as a political context. Most graffiti are written on wide surfaces and walls of mostly public buildings, roadside signs, inside toilet surfaces and security walls of both public and private premises (Mangeya, 2014). The Regional Town and Country Planning Act (RTCP Act) (Chapter 29: 12) is silent on its position on graffiti or on street art, hence there are no strategies for or against graffiti in city councils. However, the practice is considered to be a criminal nuisance which is usually a finable offence under the Criminal Law Codification and Reform Act at a local police station. Graffiti is only considered a crime in Zimbabwe if the property owner does not concede with the writings on their property and lodges a complaint to the police. Usually if no complaint is lodged by a property owner, the police assume that there is consent between the property owner and the graffiti writers. Political graffiti seem to be prevalent in most urban public spaces based on this research's observation. It is only when a complaint is lodged to the police about a politically insulting message that a graffiti artist can be charged for contravening the Electoral Act. Generally, the law is not very strict on graffiti offenders. Both the concepts of graffiti as art and place-making are yet to be embraced in the Zimbabwean context.

Harare

In Harare, graffiti is mostly written in Shona and English. The study observed that urban graffiti in Harare CBD was very limited. However, where it exists, for example behind the Main Post Office, it was mostly street protest graffiti which is textural in nature and protestant in tone (see Plate 15.1). In such cases, graffiti is viewed as a tool of resistance, where graffiti artist claim public space to express their dissatisfaction with particular issues facing society, for example non-availability of basic services such as water and inadequate jobs. Some messages in street protests are politically charged, which may be reflective of the artist's personal or community's political. The study also established graffiti artists are not visible in the national art events such as the Harare International Festival of Arts to showcase their art. Although political graffiti is highly visible in most public spaces another common form of graffiti is simply expressive. Plate 15.2 shows a mural found in Mbare high-density suburb in Harare. The city council is facing problem of ownership in Mbare's Matapi and other flats such that graffiti is a common phenomenon on the building walls. These phenomena can be likened to that of New York in the 1960s where ghetto youths would use graffiti to express their feeling and communicate their views about their socio-economic environment. Plate 15.2 expresses the feelings and or aspirations of the graffiti artist for a better community. The mural portrays the artists' aspirations for love, play and dance. In place making, public spaces should be convivial places where the people can live, work and play (PPS, 2012). The role of graffiti as a place making tool in Harare is clearly not visible in the city.

Plate 15.1: Political graffiti on security walls
(http://www.livingzimbabwe.com/politically-charged-graffiti-in-around-harare/)

Plate 15.2: Expressive graffiti (graffitisouthafrica.com)

Bulawayo City

In Bulawayo, textual graffiti in normally a mixture of Ndebele, Shona and English languages, Graffiti writing in Bulawayo is visible on building walls and immobile trains, the most prominent styles being tagging, street protest and political. Similar to the case of Harare, graffiti is mostly being used as a tool of resistance by artists. In Bulawayo city, graffiti is visible the on the walls the grand old architectural building which is opposite the national gallery. Bulawayo city through Amakhosi - a local arts organisation is promoting cultural tourism through preservation of its old historic buildings. Graffiti as art can be used in the city's public spaces to portray the local culture which is also instrumental in promoting the cultural tourism agenda. The stance towards graffiti by the city council has been rather passive as there is no legal provision on how to deal with graffiti. However, the city council has embraced other forms of public art as reflected from the famous Joshua Nkomo statue (see Plate 15:4).

Some graffiti artist in Bulawayo however are becoming more pro-active in ensuring that they dispel the misconceptions that communities have about graffiti (Jeche, 2015). Two graffiti artists engaged on a Free Street Art in the Community Exhibition project in the township of Makokoba whereby they would paint one house in each street. This project was well received by the local community and can be replicated in other areas to encourage social cohesion. However, without a collective effort from other stakeholders such as the business community, non-governmental organisations and the city council, the place making strategy would not be fully accomplished.

Place 15.3: Expressive graffiti in Bulawayo (bulawayo24.com)

Plate 15.4: A public art statue of Joshua Nkomo (Sundaynews.co.zw)

Discussion and synthesis

Graffiti is certainly viewed differently by different city governments. While others view it as a crime and an activity which is harmful to the built environment for example in Los Angeles, USA and Sydney, Australia; in some cities such as Worcester and countries such as Brazil and Darkar, Brazil is legalised as art. According to Fraser (2016) graffiti as an art interrupts the urban architectural facades and offers new interpretations of the city and ways for the public to move through the city. Successful strategies for place-making which were used in other countries are mostly those strategies which support and contribute to the liveliness of a community (Project for Public Space 2012). For example, the legal wall in New York, USA and in Hiedanranta, Finland as well as the as well as the Arts alley in Worcester, England offer platforms for graffiti artists to showcase their talent and provides locals and visitors an opportunity to celebrate public spaces in their cities. Other strategies include funding of graffiti artists activities in the case of Toronto City Graffiti Management Plan and use of a website to showcases graffiti and street art in the country as a marketing tool as in the case of graffiti South Africa.

Usually where graffiti is strictly controlled, artists always find ways of resisting to be controlled as they assert their presence and claim their right to the city. For example, artist in Los Angeles's use of heavens or use of protestant graffiti by local graffiti artists in Harare and Bulawayo show resistance. The role of graffiti as a place making tool in Harare is not recognisable yet. Nevertheless, its recognition can significantly contribute to the city, 2025 vision of becoming a world class city as place-making is one important strategy of a liveable world class city. Political graffiti and expressive graffiti are the most dominant types of graffiti in most public spaces in Harare. As a starting point, the City of Harare council could learn from city of Worcester and begin to engage communities particularly where graffiti is common such as in Mbare high-density suburb and identify how the community can benefit from the local talent. The Public Art Working Group (PAWG) which was created in Worcester city identified various community aspirations which were realisable through public art. Similarly, the City of Bulawayo has not yet embraced graffiti as a place making tool although graffiti has potential to improve cultural tourism. The Free Street Art in the Community Exhibition project can be replicated in other communities as a way of promoting community engagement. However, without a collective effort from other stakeholders such as the business community, Non- Governmental Organisations and the city council, the place making strategy would not be fully accomplished. Successful place making strategies involves all key stakeholders as can be learnt from the case of Darkar, Senegal (Rabine, 2014).

Urban graffiti affects property values as it leads to depreciation of property values. If not properly managed urban graffiti disrupts the visual appropriateness and legibility of both the environment and the property as well. Urban graffiti is connected to crime, violence and vandalism and this induces fear in potential tenants and property buyers leading to a decrease in property prices. From the obtained literature, graffiti environments may be aesthetically displeasing and this tends to affect the behaviour of tenants and potential property buyers. Moreover, urban graffiti is associated with crime, violence and vandalism. This is a threat in the real estate environment as this as well brings fear into tenants and property buyers and in turn leads to less demand of properties within graffiti environments, hence reduction in property prices. Vandalised properties already have less value as valuation is done considering the physical and visual appearance of the property. This implies that non-vandalised properties will have more monetary value than vandalised properties. Graffiti creates disorder within the environment and potential investors and developers always avoid such environments, thereby causing less occupancy in properties thus affecting the real estate environment and functioning. However, orderly urban graffiti in form of art can improve the aesthetic value of properties attracting more tenants and property buyers. An addition of aesthetic value to a property leads to an increase in its monetary value. Therefore, this indicates that if graffiti is conducted in an orderly manner, it can lead to increase in property values. In summation, urban graffiti affects property values in a negative way and in some cases inhibits potential tenants and buyers. Properties prone to urban graffiti are susceptible to low monetary values whereas those in graffiti free environments will have a much higher value. This is because of disorder, ugliness, vandalism and crime rates associated with urban graffiti.

Conclusion, policy options and future direction

This chapter sought to examine the relationship between graffiti and the place-making concept in Zimbabwean urban public spaces. Emerging from the study are three aspects namely: the slow uptake of graffiti as art which can be harnessed to become a useful for place-making tool by city governments; the continued resistance by graffiti artist to exclusionary tendencies of space production in neo-liberalist economies by writing on walls and absence of local strategies to deal with graffiti in public spaces. It is concluded that harnessing graffiti as a place making tool is still in its infancy stages in Zimbabwean urban spaces despite the several benefits that it would bring. However effective place–making requires a collective process which requires various stakeholders' participation to shape public urban spaces through shared values of a community. The legal framework for graffiti needs to be revisited so that what constitute graffiti as art is clearly defined and acknowledged in the urban spaces. The support of the business community in funding graffiti artists' initiatives will further refine their artistic skills and improve their global competitiveness. Further studies in this area should try to assess the interaction between graffiti and other place making strategies, exploring the challenges and opportunities. Future research should as well focus on the implications of urban graffiti in real estate and property valuation in detail. Since most developments in several countries are construction and property oriented, this could be more useful to developers and in property valuers as well. A movement from urban graffiti to street art can as well enhance property values and enhance real estate. Street art and art itself improves the aesthetic value which in turn leads to an increase in the monetary value of that property.

References

Agnew, J. A., Shelley, F. M and Pringle, D. G. (2003). Agnew, JA 1987: Place and Politics: the geographical mediation of state and society. *Progress in Human Geography*, *27*(5), 605.

Agnew, J. (2011). Space and Place. In J. Agnew and D. Livingstone (Eds.), *Sage Handbook of Geographical Knowledge* (Vol. 2011, pp. 316 - 330). London.

Aljabri, H. (2014). The Planning and Urban Design of Liveable Public Open Spaces in Oman: Case Study of Muscat. Doctor of Philosophy in Urban Studies. Heriot-Watt University

Austin, J. (2001). *Taking the train: How graffiti art became an urban crisis in New York City*. New York: Colombia University Press.

Bandaranaike, S. (2001). Graffiti: a culture of aggression or assertion. *The character, impact and prevention of crime in regional Australia. Australian Institute of Criminology, Townsville.*

City of Bulawayo, (2015). Service Level Standards.

City of Harare. (2012). Strategic Plan 2012-2025, Harare.

Dikec, M. (2001). Justice and the spatial imagination. *Journal for Environment and Planning, (33)1785- 1805.* http://dx.doi.org/10.1068/a3467

Florida, R. (2002). *The rise of the creative class and how it's transforming work, leisure, community and everyday life.* New York, NY: Basic Books.

Fraser, A. (2016). Urban Prophets: Creating Graffiti as a Means of Negotiating the Constructs of Urban Public Spaces. Stream: *Inspiring critical thought,* 7(2), 32-42.

Goodsell, C. (2003). The Concept of Public Space and Its Democratic Manifestations. *The American Review of Public Administration,* 33(4)*, 361–83.*

Government of Zimbabwe (1998). Regional Town and Country Planning Act (Chapter 29:12). Government Printers, Harare.

Jeche, N. (2015).Vandalism or Art? Story of a graffiti artist. Zimbojam. Available online www.zimbojam.com.

Lefebvre, H. (1996). Right to the City. In E. Kofman and E. Lebas (Eds. and Trans.), *Writings on cities. Oxford, UK: Blackwell Publishers Limited.*1*(3).*147-159.

Mangeya, H. (2014). A Sociolinguistic Analysis of Graffiti Written in Shona and English Found in Selected Urban Areas of Zimbabwe. Doctor of Literature and Philosophy in African Languages. University of South Africa.

Mann, D. (2016). From Tags to Murals-South African graffiti's move into the accepted public eye. *The Creative Showcase.* South Africa. Available online https//10and5.com

Offler, N., Thompson, K., Hirsch, L., Thomas, M., and Dawson, D. (2009). A review of the literature on social, non-technical deterrents for vandalism in the rail industry. *Brisbane: CRC for Rail Innovation.* CRC Australia.

Project for Public Spaces (2012). *Place making and the Future of Cities.* UN-Habitat.

Rabine, L. W. (2014). "These Walls Belong to Everybody" The Graffiti Art Movement in Dakar. *African Studies Quarterly, 14*(3), 1-11.

Relph, Edward (1976). Place and Placelessness, London: Pion. Reverend Billy (2006), *What Would Jesus Buy?* New York: Public Affairs.

Serkan, G and Gülse, Y. (2006). Understanding Graffiti in the Built Environment: The Case in Ankara, Türkiye. Understanding Graffiti in the built Environment 42nd ISoCaRP Congress.

Sherry, John F., Jr., (Ed.). (1998). *Servicescapes: The Concept of Place in Contemporary Markets*, Chicago: NTC Business.

Tunnacliffe, M. C. (2016). The power of urban street art in re-naturing urban imaginations and experiences. DPU Working Paper 182. Available online http://www.bartlett.ucl.ac.uk/dpu/latest/publications/dpu-papers

www.graffitisouthafrica.com. [Accessed on 29 June 2018]

Ylinen, K. (2018). The Graffiti Storyline and Urban Planning: Key Narratives in the Planning, Marketing and News Texts of Santalahti and Hiedanranta. Available online http://widerscreen.fi/numerot/2018-1-2/graffiti-storyline. [Accessed on 08 June 2018]

Zieleniec, A. (2016). The right to write the city: Lefebvre and graffiti. *Environnement Urbain / Urban Environment,* 4(10), 1-21.

Australian Department of Transport and Main Roads (2009). *Queensland Government Graffiti Management Policy 2008–2011.*

Brand, S and Price, R. (2000). 'Home Office Research Study 217: The Economic and Social Costs of Crime', London, Home Office Research Development and Statistics Directorate.

Crawley, K. (2015). Beyond the War on Graffiti: The Right to Visual Expression in Urban Spaces. *Griffith Journal of Law and Human Dignity.* http://hdl.handle.net/10072/99076

Gibbons, S and Machin, S. (2001). *Valuing primary schools.* Centre for the Economics of Education, London School of Economics and Political Science.

311

Hellman, D. A and Naroff, J. L. (1979). 'The Impact of Crime on Urban Residential Property Values', *Urban Studies*, vol. 16, pp. 105-112.

Killias, M and Clerici, C. (2000). Different measures of vulnerability in their relation to different dimensions of fear of crime. *British journal of criminology*, 40(3), 437-450.

Lynch, A. K and Rasmussen, D. W. (2001). 'Measuring the Impact of Crime on House Prices', *Applied Economics*, 33(1), 1981-1989.

Social Exclusion Unit, (2001). 'A New Commitment to Neighbourhood Renewal', London, Cabinet Office.

Thaler, R. (1978). 'A Note on the Value of Crime Control: Evidence from the Property Market', *Journal of Urban Economics*, vol. 5, pp. 137-145.

Wilson, J. Q., and Kelling, G. L. (1982). The police and neighbourhood safety: Broken windows. *Atlantic monthly*, 127(2), 29-38.

Chapter 16

Resilience and sustainability in the real estate sector

Tinashe Natasha Mujongonde–Kanonhuhwa, Spiwe Mupukuta and Innocent Chirisa

Introduction

The real estate sector has been argued to influence positive development of a nation, if handled properly. This is mainly because the impact of humans on the earth's resources and on climate change can only be reduced when the world adopts an eco-friendly built environment (Warren-Myers, 2012). This indicates that to ensure sustainable development, there is need to blend the soft and hard landscapes to enable the functioning of the economy. The built environment is argued to consume 40% of global energy and release 20% of greenhouse gases (a figure expected to increase by 7% in 2030), whilst there is a projected 56% increase in carbon-dioxide emissions by 2030 (UN, 2016). If not handled properly, the built-landscape can, consequently result in unfavourable and un-habitable human environments due to creation of urban heat islands which may have negative impacts on people's livelihoods and productivity levels which may produce a negative correlation on socio-economic development. Due to the ever-changing urbanisation trends, the growth of real estate in city centres becomes inevitable. 60% of the world's population is projected to live in cities by 2030, which will ultimately lead to growth of the construction industry (UN, 2016).

This phenomenon may present opportunities and threats to various countries, depending on how developments are manipulated to produce unique designs which are more environmentally sensitive than just simple conventional designs. The fast-paced demand for housing as a result of increased urbanisation, has prompted governments of various nations to revise their building standards by prioritising green building and green leasing to encourage the creation of eco-friendly and sustainable liveable environments. The chapter is an appreciative overview to encourage the new way of thinking which has evolved over the past decades to promote mixed uses and compact cities which seem to put less burden on the city by minimising some of the negatives associated such as air pollution and traffic congestion. Unless an exploratory study is done, the environment shall remain at risk of suffering from the undesirable effects caused by the old conventional way of building, inclusive of global warming, high building maintenance costs, reduced environmental aesthetics and unattractiveness of rental property (which may deter investors from renting the property in preference of green-structures). The study remains significant because real-estate remains a major pillar of development in any economy, thus the urgency to seriously plan for it and take it seriously for the benefit of present and future generations.

This study defines real estate as the economy's built up areas and vacant land, usable by governments, firms and / households as places of work or residence (Mouzughi *et al.* 2014). The real-estate sector therefore, forms the greater part of tangible assets of a nation and can reflect the stage of development of a nation. Sustainable development entails harmonising the social, economic and environmental aspects for the benefit of current generation, without compromising ability of future generations to also benefit (Dell'Angelo *et al.* 2017). Sustainability also involves substituting the use of natural resources with renewable ones, recycling of waste and improved building, occupant health, comfort and safety (Kats, 2003 cited in Waren-Myers, 2012). Sustainability touches on many aspects and must essentially be looked at in a holistic manner to fully maximize on benefits and safeguard healthy building. Resilience refers to elimination of long-term risks to people and property from hazards and their effects (Godschalk 2002 cited in Hughes and Healey, 2014). Resilience is driven by three important factors which include disaster prevention, climate change adaptation and sustainable development (Schneider-Roos, 2017). Resilient buildings emphasis is on ability to cope and adapt to harsh environmental conditions. In this case, sustainability and resilience are viewed as intertwined and complementary. This chapter first explores the theoretical underpinnings followed by global and regional trends which have characterized the property sector, and then cascades down to the interpretation of results and trends from the global north. The study then narrows down to the Zimbabwean context by giving reference to selected towns and cities and conclude by giving various policy options as well as future direction to ensuring Resilience and Sustainability (R&S) in Zimbabwe's real estate sector.

Theoretical underpinnings

Sustainable Development (SD) cannot be isolated from the three pillars of SD and governance related issues. In order for SD to become a reality, policies, plans and strategies ought to be in place in guaranteeing uniformity and compliance at global, regional, national and local levels. It is argued that a strong correlation exists between risk, resilience and sustainability (R&S) and that, governance has a bearing on the outcomes of each (Shumba, 2017). Figures 16.1 and 16, 2 are a reflection of how good and bad governance impacts on sustainability.

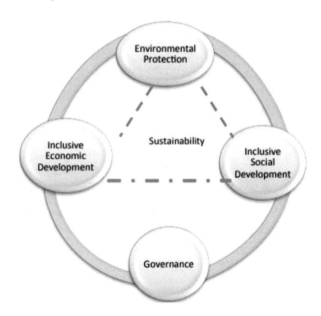

Figure 16.1: Governance and Sustainability (Shumba, 2017)

In ensuring sustainability and resilience in real estate, the three pillars of sustainability (Environment, Economic and Social) must be well balanced. Governance then plays an overall regulatory role of enforcing policies to make sure that standards and procedures are followed in the planning, designing and maintenance stages of development of the built-environment.

Bad Governance   **Good Governance**

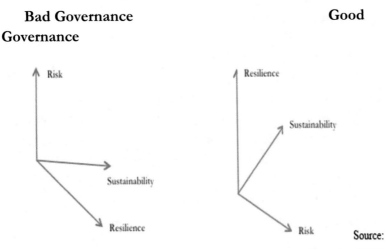

Figure 16.2: Bad Governance vs Good Governance (Shumba, 2017)

It can be concluded that good governance upholds S and R and reduces risk, which in turn reduces the amount of harm caused by man to the environment. Under bad governance, risk is very high and hence the need for proper decentralisation of power, clear plans and procedures, articulation of duties and coordination of stakeholders to promote and enforce coordinated sustainable and resilient building standards. The socio-economic and environmental aspects must be satisfied for much gain, with the main reason being that investors now advocate for green leasing because of the associated lower maintenance and reduced energy costs to trigger improvements in profit levels.

Literature review

At international level, various countries have devised their own means to measure sustainability of buildings according to various certifications as per agreed acceptable standards which may vary from one nation to the other. Switzerland and Australia have adopted the Minergie and Green Star certifications, whilst the USA and the UK have established the Leadership in Energy and Environmental Design (LEED) and Building Research Establishments' Environmental Assessment Method (BREEAM) classifications respectively, as a way to measure and rate buildings according to levels of sustainability (UBS Global Asset Management, 2014). This shows level of seriousness and strictness by different governments as it has become possible to measure level of building compliance to green building standards via the use of well-defined measuring scales.

The Property Sector touches heavily on people's livelihood, especially in the urban centres. 80% of European Union (EU) residents live in and / around cities and improper urban planning practices can have detrimental effects to people's lives (European Commission, 2013). As consequences increased urbanisation and expansion of the built environment also increased to accommodate more users, urban areas have been regarded as the greatest consumers of energy and emitters of GHGs, further characterising urban areas with poor air quality and changing climatic trends (European Commission, 2013). Urban areas must, for that reason, have their own mitigation and adaptive measures to prevent the increased dilapidation of the urban environments as they are regarded as centres of economic activity and development. The United Kingdom have issued the Energy Performance Certificate (EPC) which rates the energy efficiency of a building and those ranked below 'E' will not be able to lease their properties after April 2018 (Deloite Centre for Financial Services, 2014). This stricter regulation by government will definitely encourage landlords (both individual and private developers) to improve existing buildings to be more energy efficient, which would reduce building maintenance costs.

The United States of America (USA) has for over a decade now been concentrating on reaching a level of zero tolerance to use of non-renewable energy in construction of new building structures. This has seen the formation of the Energy Independence and Security Act of 2007, which was established to promote construction of new-zero energy (NZE) buildings by 2030 (UNEP 2016). The setting of targets and regulatory instruments sets the tone for sustainable building. The USA department of Energy has also developed national codes to help states adopt more efficient energy codes, with ENERGY STAR and LEED being the more successful voluntary programs (UNEP, 2016). The LEED system was developed by the US Green Building Council to encourage increased acceptance of green building issues (Rogerson, 2014). This shows seriousness as there is a well-established council to spearhead the exercise. LEED rates buildings according to three classifications which are silver, gold and platinum (UBS Global Asset Management, 2014). These categories rates buildings according to the level of environmental sustainability found in a building, with platinum being the best.

The Australian government established a multiple ranking system which includes energy efficiency for built-up structures such as NABERS and NAtHERS, with NABERS ranking residential and non-residential buildings on a gauge of 0 – 6 stars (with 6 representing an excellent level of resource efficiency and GHG performance) and NAtHERS using a scale of 1-10 stars to rate energy efficiency (UNEP, 2016). This shows advancements in the Australian real-estate markets as measures are put in place to rank buildings according to their levels of sustainability. Sustainable housing reduces heating and cooling costs which contributes to affordability of a housing unit (McKillop, 2013). If a resilient and sustainable building is engraved in the design and building of infrastructure, then structures may become affordable, whilst reducing negative effects posed on the natural environment.

In achieving vision 2030, Bahrain prioritised three areas to meet socio-economic related sustainability and these include; infrastructure, affordable housing and tourism/ leisure; with the latter relying heavily on infrastructure (Mouzughi *et al.* 2014). Infrastructure then forms the basis or foundation for many other activities to perform on, as signalled by work places, residential and areas. Infrastructure also supports recreational activities through the building of stadiums for example. It remains a top priority for government, private developers and individuals to develop the hard landscape in such a way that causes better than harm to the environment.

In Switzerland, buildings with a minimum energy use of zero have now become attainable. In 1975, an average building consumed 22 litres of heating oil per m2 per year, a figure reduced to 3 litres per m2 after 2009 (UBS Global Asset Management, 2014). Evidence therefore indicates that technological advancements and incorporation of nature into urban designs can result in massive reduction of energy consumption by buildings, with some houses reaching zero energy consumption. Sustainable building may be expensive in the short run but very efficient as time progresses as it may result in significant reductions in energy costs.

Regionally, South Africa has established a monitoring system to ensure sustainability of its buildings via SANS 1544, which audits and provides an EPC for government buildings on a three-year basis (UNEP, 2016). This indicates strong government support to spearhead sustainable building issues in promoting a healthy, liveable environment for all. The Green Building Council of South Africa (GBCSA) is responsible for promotion of commercial green-building by playing a facilitative role in handling training sessions and coming up with a ranking system for the level of building sustainability (Rogerson, 2014). This shows acceptability of green building measures by South Africa, Therefore, sustainable development. Several ranking systems exist and examples include the LEED used by the (USA), BREEAM (UK) and Green Star from Australia and South Africa has adopted the Green Star Australian style (Rogerson, 2014). This indicates that S.A has learnt from the developed nations and has adopted standards to also put it on the global map as regards to resilience and sustainable building practices. Another new form of thinking is also to embrace slum urbanism which mostly characterise the African landscape. 62% of Africans are said to live in the slums (UN-Habitat, 2008). The emergency of slums in Africa can negatively affect the face of real estate due to increase of sub-standard structures built by the poor. The number of slum-dwellers is expected to triple by 2050 (UN. 2013). The types of slums differ from region to region and if not properly regulated, some may be devoid of basic services to service the area, resulting in unsustainable development. Major concentration of slums are said to be in Sudan, Niger and Madagascar (Grant, 2015). Cities has since been characterised by urban sprawl resulting in areas being less dense (Weakley and La Mantla, in Todes *et al.* 2015). Sprawl have eaten the greenbelt and developed the land on unequal grounds by eating some of the most important land-uses such as open spaces, which defies the odds of sustainable development. Sustainable cities now call for mixed uses and compact cities to reduce urban sprawl (Weakley and La Mantla, in Todes *et al.* 2015). This combination reduces most of the problems suffered in today's cities such as traffic congestion as people work where they stay.

Methodology

The research used the archival method of data collection by looking at developments at international, regional and local scales. Case studies from Australia, USA and UK where analysed. Cases from the African sphere such as South Africa were also analysed so as to judge on the level of adoption of green issues at a regional level. An analysis of these 'two worlds' was aimed at noting improvements and changes, analysing how issues of sustainability have been tackled in achieving great strides towards SD and resilience building.

Results

Resilience and sustainability come along with the manipulation of building designs and land-uses to accommodate green issues. Early adoptions of well-planned strategies and plans have been argued to save lives and time (Zimbabwe Resilience Strategic Framework, 2015). This calls for strategies and plan to promote green buildings to be well placed and executed in time. Government support becomes critical for sustainability and resilience to become a success. An example is that of America which has made great strides in sustainability issues due to massive government support.

Sustainable building requires high initial investment as compared to simple conventional building, mainly as a result of many standards which developers are obliged to follow, signalled by various standard rankings (UBS Global Asset Management, 2014). Government support is necessary in promoting sustainable building as it can encourage building firms through tax removals, building permit fees and provide financing to encourage firms to embrace green issues when building. This will reduce building costs and encourage firms to practice sustainable building. The USA is a prominent example which has adopted this strategy as a way of encouraging firms and individuals to practice sustainable building. Incentives given by government will encourage firms to invest in sustainable green building at local and national scales. This forms a good example for African nations to copy strategies and workable solutions and strategies to adopt green issues.

Despite being expensive, adoption of green building in the preliminary planning and design stages of settlements and buildings remains essential as more positive gains are attached in the current and future time periods. Resilient and sustainable building have been argued to de-risk and improve financial performance of infrastructure as well as contribute to unlocking of capital needed for investment (Schneider-Roos, 2017). Environmentally friendly buildings also have intangible and tangible financial benefits (UN, 2016). This implies that productivity increases as people blend more with nature in their workplaces (Deloitte Centre for Financial Services, 2014). United Kingdom even introduced stricter measures not to lease properties ranked below the "E" energy efficiency level after April 2018. This shows stricter regulations to force landlords to comply, which is a plus to promoting sustainability.

The construction industry services almost all the other industries and aids in value creation (World Economic Forum, 2016). The property sector therefore, forms a crucial component in the creation of healthy cities which are of great value, Therefore, the need to seriously plan and infuse sustainability ideas in development and maintenance of this sector. The Real Estate Industry has potential to satisfy the social and economic aspects, with all stakeholders having a shared vision (Mouzughi *et al.* 2014). This implies that the sector can be developed in a way that business and societal needs are all satisfied, which gives people peace of mind and increases on productivity levels.

Climate Change Adaptation (CCA) is also another very crucial component in promoting resistance and sustainability. CCA can be protective or opportunistic in nature. Protective aspects deal with how the real estate can respond to changes in climate, thereby minimising the effects, whereas, opportunistic issues involve making positive use of predicted weather changes (Zimbabwe Resilience Strategic Framework, 2015). It then becomes very important to plan even for future settlements by taking the climate change aspect into consideration, as it becomes possible to tune buildings in such a way that they can either positively respond or adapt to temperature changes.

Acceptability of sustainable and resilient building has been widespread in Europe. An example is that of Switzerland where 67% of investors started taking sustainability issues when buying property in 2013, a figure which had increased by 24% from that of 2009 (UBS Global Asset Management, 2014). This indicates a more positive shift to resilience and sustainable building. Despite having high initial construction costs, sustainable buildings can still have high returns in future which make it a worthwhile investment strategy for landlords.

Sustainable development of cities involves provision of infrastructure such as water, sewer, roads, electricity and facilities which include schools, healthcare and transport (UN, 2013). Harare aims to attain world class city status by 2025 and hence the urgency to plan and effectively coordinate its activities among various stakeholders to achieve the common goal. Sustainability has synonymously been used with the term green building (Warren-Myer, 2012). This has seen Harare building sustainable green buildings such as Eastgate and Hurudza house in the CBD as well as, converting some buildings such as Trafalgar Court to accommodate mixed uses.

Design standards can also be manipulated by government to ensure sustainable neighbourhoods. Circular 70 of 2004 have revised building standards to encourage the compact city approach and reduce the unsustainable sprawling of cities. The revised standards accept use of gravel roads in high-density areas and stand sizes have been reduced from 150-300m2 to 70-200m2 (GoZ, 2004). This is a sustainable measure as it reduces sprawl by accommodating a larger number of people in a limited space. However, sustainable development should ensure proper waste management disposal system, which calls for effective Council waste collection services. The legalization of gravel access road as a cost cutting measure may have a negative bearing on air pollution in the area which may have negative health implications to residents as they may breathe dust time and again from unsurfaced roads. The reduction of standards to accommodate the middle to low-income earners may not necessarily end up promoting sustainability as a result of more negatives associated as a result of increased compromise on planning standards, hence the need to be careful in adopting these standards. This has seen in neighbourhoods such as Hopley high-density which does not fully comply with healthy standards as people do not have well defined measures to dispose of their wastes, a situation further worsened by existence of poor roads

The new form of thinking, (UZ Biennial Symposium, 2018) is that people must move from merely thinking that, everyone must occupy a portion of land in their name, to also considering the option of affordable renting where government must also come in to subsidize and also provide sustainable and affordable housing for the low-income earner. Affordability can also be ensured by massive reduction of energy costs in the long-run, which leaves a lot to be desired for the real estate sector to consider issues of green building and green-leasing and also to encourage people to occupy environmentally friendly units at low maintenance cost. Mudehwe *et al.* (2016) acknowledge that a green building now adds value when valuing property as compared to simple conventional building. Green leasing has been associated with reduced water and energy costs through recycling which in turn improves asset value and reduces operational and maintenance costs in the long-run (Mudehwe *et al.* 2016). It becomes the mandate of landlords (in this case, the government and private investors) to make available affordable eco-friendly housing units which may become cheaper to maintain with time. Tenants are also said to pay higher rentals if their energy costs are lower during their occupation period, assuming they would be the ones responsible for their utility bills, lower energy costs would in turn mean more profits for business investors (UN, 2016). Green Building and green leasing, then, becomes a top priority in growing sustainable built landscapes which are able to attract investments and offer employment to its respective residents. It is also important to note that, unstable economic conditions hinder real estate operations, hence the need for a country to be as economically stable as possible.

Mutare has many uses which include administrative and residential. It can also be viewed as a tourist destination area as it has 200 hectares of the Vumba Botanical area which is protected (Zimbabwe Parks and Wildlife Management Authority, 2017). These areas bring in revenue to the country's economic base and their preservation is essential for positive developments in the real estate sector. Sustainable and resilient real estate must respect each region with its diversity and strengths. It must make sure that food security is ensured and minimised by also capitalizing on agro-ecological regions and their strengths. Due to favourable rainfall and temperatures, coffee, tea and potatoes which are cash crops are grown to heavily contribute on the country's gross domestic product (Mugandani *et al.* 2012). This enriches the economic status of a country through employment generation, ensuring food security and also revenue generation of extra revenues through importation, thus supporting the pillars of sustainability, as the economy is enhanced. This reflects the diversified nature of real estate.

Sustainable real estate also respects the existence and preservation of tourist towns. The Victoria Falls (Vic Falls) is a leading tourist destination in Zimbabwe (UNDP, 2012). By virtue of being a town based primarily on tourist areas of attraction, which include the Falls and Wildlife. It has to grow by harnessing its strengths and preserve dilution from other land-uses and cultures. This entails not growing big to dilute its culture and uniqueness, but rather maintaining its growth and purpose of being a tourist town. The Victoria Falls remains an area of much tourist significance to attract a lot of tourists from the international and local scenes. It houses one of the three major international airports in Zimbabwe and has 2340 hectares of Parks and Wildlife Estate Protected areas (ZPWMA, 2017). These areas are protected and maintained as they are which enables them to generate lots of funds from tourism to buttress the country's GDP, further contributing to economic growth. The recently proposed Tourism Master Plan is meant to plan and minimise on areas which are believed to contribute more to the economy than they are already doing. This includes extending activities at the Vic Falls as well as enhances other areas to be more attractive and realize more gains from tourism. The existence of areas of attraction represents sustainability due to the country's ability to identify those areas and capitalize on them to promote diversity, which in turn beautifies the country's landscape. Real estate is diverse as it takes advantage of the natural beauties of an area for financial gain and upliftment of people's standards of living.

The Case of Magunje Growth Point (MGP)

The proportionate distribution of land-uses can facilitate or hinder growth in an area. There is need to proportionately invest in assets which encourage growth of lagging behind regions. Growth points were historically established as development nodes, to lessen the burden on the core, by decentralising activities and services to the marginalized areas of society, thereby lessening the rate of rural to urban migration. The location of MGP was attributed to by various factors which include centrality, Farming and existence of a main road from Karoi (Mannanhaire *et al.* 2009). The Magunje service centre was comprised of 63% shops, 10% recreational area 1% cottage industries and 1% GMB depot (Manyanhaire *et al.* 2009). The presence of 1% industrial area does not fully promote sustainable growth, since industry is the major drive of economic growth, thus the inability of the growth point to grow as expected due to unbalanced land-uses.

It is noted that, lack of much industrial activities and title deeds contributed 23.1% and 9.2% respectively, to the growth point's stagnation and decline. This indicates that, property sector plays an important role in developing an area which requires people to be provided with the required title deeds and that the area should be backed by adequate industrial activity to fuel economic development of the area.

Table 16.1 Constraints to the growth of MGP (Makanhaire *et al.* 2009)

Constraints	Frequency	% Frequency
Lack of Industries	15	23.1
Financial Constraints	5	7.7
Lack of Mineral Resources	7	10.8
Lack of Incentives for Investors	4	6.2
Council Planning Problems	13	20
Uneconomic Rates and Levies	3	4.6
Migration of Commercial Farmers	4	6.2
Lack of Title Deeds	6	9.2
Spatial Dominance by Individuals	5	7.7
A Small Market Population	3	4.6
Total	**65**	**100**

Table 16.2: Housing delivery in Magunje for the period 1982-2006 (Makanhaire *et al.* 2009)

Year	Housing Units Built	Growth Rate (%)
1982	127	
1987	230	81
1992	570	148
1997	622	9
2002	634	2
2006	645	2

Magunje Housing Delivery Trends 1982-2006 housing delivery sectors boosted from 1987 to 1992. The housing delivery growth rate started declining from 148% to 9% between 1992 and 1997 respectively and declined even further to 2% in 2006. This indicates that the housing sector has shrunk indicating a decline in growth rate, Therefore, unsustainability. The decline in housing built-units, from 148% to 2% in 2006 could have been attributed to ESAP (Makanyanhaire *et al.* 2009). This indicates that the real estate sector can suffer from economic recessions and hence a need for government support and promote a stable economic environment which promotes flourishment of the real estate sector.

Discussion and Synthesis

The Global North has made great strides in making sure that well defined standards and measuring parameters are in place to ensure compliance by construction companies and all other interested stakeholders. This shows strictness by international governments which is a positive step towards achieving totality in resilience and sustainable building. This then enables climatic changes to be monitored, thus reducing adverse effects to people and nature. It also becomes necessary to promote issues of affordable green leasing and remove the mentality that everyone must own a stand, which is a number one drive to urban sprawl. It is government's responsibility to fund and subsidize such projects so as to accommodate people of all income groups effectively. Green building, the compact city approach and mixed uses are key drivers to promoting resilient and sustainable cities and these must be engraved in government's regulatory framework to ensure that such green-building practices are acceptable to society and practiced in the design stage of settlements and buildings. The real estate can be applauded for promoting diversity and uniqueness of landscapes, signalled by the existence of tourist towns (such as Vic Falls), administrative centres (Harare) and agro-ecological regions. This is meant to make maximum benefit of naturally given landscape talents in each area.

Conclusion

It can be concluded that, real estate must simply shape and give more meaning to development by harmonising nature with new development in order to give new places meaning without causing more harm to the natural environment. Government support is necessary to enable a favourable economic environment for the operation of the property sector. Government must also promote green-building practices through support and offering incentives in order to promote healthier liveable and working environment. The global world has set a very good pace in promoting S and R building and African countries have followed suit. However, there is need for stricter regulations and well-defined measuring standards in the case of Zimbabwe, in order to ensure uniform development in green building issues in African as well as other international countries.

References

African Development Bank, (2011). Infrastructure and Growth in Zimbabwe: An Action Plan for Sustained Economic Growth. African Development Bank Group.

Dell'Angelo, J., D'Odorico, P., and Rulli, M. C. (2017). Threats to Sustainable Development caused by Land and Water Grabbin. *Current Opinion in Environmental Sustainability* 2017, 26(27); 120-128

Deloitte Centre for Financial Services, (2014). Break Through for Sustainability in Commercial Real Estate. Deloitte Development LLC

European Commission, (2013). Research and Innovation on Sustainable Urban Dynamics. Directorate General for Research and Innovation, European Union.

Grant, R. (2015). Sustainable African urban futures: Stocktaking and critical reflection on proposed urban projects. *American Behavioural Scientist, 59*(3), 294-310.

Global Property Guide, (2010). In MacKillop F (2013). Sustainable as a Basis of Affordable? Understanding the Affordability 'Crisis' in Australian Housing. *Australian Planner*, 50 (1), 2-10

Government of Zimbabwe. (2004). Circular No 70 of 2004. Government of Zimbabwe, Harare.

Hughes, J. F and Healey, K. (2014). Measuring the Resilience of Transport Infrastructure. NZ Transport Agency Research Report 546, AECOM New Zealand Limited.

Klaufus, C. van Lindert: van Noorloos, F and Steel, G. (2017). All Inclusiveness versus Exclusion: Urban Project Development in Latin America and Africa

Manyanhaire, I. O., Mhishi, B., Svotwa, E and Sithole, N. (2009). Growth points or declining points? A case of Magunje Growth Point in Mashonaland West province of Zimbabwe. *Journal of sustainable development in Africa, 10*(4), 506-520.

MacKillop, F. (2013). Sustainable as a basis of affordable? Understanding the affordability 'crisis' in Australian housing. *Australian Planner*, *50*(1), 2-12.

Mouzughi, Y., Bryde, D and Al-Shaer, M. (2014). The role of real estate in sustainable development in developing countries: The case of the Kingdom of Bahrain. *Sustainability*, 6(4), 1709-1728.

Mudehwe, R., Chirisa, I and Matamanda, A. (2016). Green Leasing in Zimbabwe: Lessons from Harare Commercial Property Market. *International Journal of Real Estate Studies*, 10 (2), 13-24

Mugandani, R., Wuta, M., Makarau, A and Chipindu, B. (2012). Re-classification of agro-ecological regions of Zimbabwe in conformity with climate variability and change. *African Crop Science Journal*, 20(2), 361-369.

Rogerson, J. M. (2014). Green Commercial Property Development in Urban South Africa: Emerging Trends Emerging Geographies. *Bulletin of Geography. Socio-Economic Series*. 26(26), 233-246

Schneider-Roos, K. (2017). Infrastructure Financing: The Role of Sustainability and Resilience, Session 2: Infrastructure Investment Trends and the Investment Gap, Global Infrastructure Basel.

Shumba, D. (2017). Risk, Resilience and Sustainability: How Governance in Zimbabwe Countervails this Nexus, Consilience. *The Journal of Sustainable Development*, 17(1), 196-218.

Todes, A. Harrison: and Weakley, D. (Eds) (2015). Resilient Densification Four Studies from Johannesburg, South African Research Chair in Special Analysis and City Planning. University of Witwatersrand, Gauteng City Region Observatory.

UBS Global Asset Management (2014). Real Estate and Sustainability: A future with Yield Potential. Global Real Estate Research and Strategy, Switzerland.

United Nations. (2013). World Economic and Social Survey: Sustainable Development Survey. Department of Economic and Social Affairs, United Nations: New York.

United Nations Development Programme. (2012). Zimbabwe Recovery on Course but Challenges Remain, Argues that Experts: Brown Bag Dialogue Series.

United Nations Development Programme and World Food Programme (UNDP AND WFP). (2016). Overview of Technical Analysis for the Zimbabwe Building Resilience Fund. United Nations Development Framework and World Food Programme, Harare: Zimbabwe.

United Nations Environment Programme. (2016). Towards zero-emission efficient and resilient buildings: Global Status Report. Global Alliance for Building and Construction.

UN-Habitat. (2008). The State of African Cities: a framework for addressing urban challenges in Africa. *In Grant, R. (2015). Sustainable African urban Futures: Stocktaking and Critical Reflection on Proposed Urban Projects*, American Behavioural Scientist Vol 59 (3) 294-310, SAGE Publications

Wolmer, W., Chaumba, J and Scoones, I. (2003). *Wildlife management and land reform in southeastern Zimbabwe: A compatible pairing or a contradiction in terms?* Sustainable Livelihoods in Southern Africa Programme.

Warren-Myers, G. (2012). Sustainable Management of Real Estate: Is it really sustainability? *The Journal of Sustainable Real Estate*, Vol 4, Number 1 pp177-197

World Economic Forum. (2016). Shaping the Future of Construction: A Breakthrough in Mindset and Technology. World Economic Forum: Boston Consulting Group

Zimbabwe Resilience Strategic Framework. (2015). Building Resilience in Zimbabwe: Towards a Resilience Strategic Framework, Zimbabwe Resilience Strategic Framework.

Zimbabwe Parks and Wildlife Management Authority. (2017). Investment Prospectus Zimparks Commercial Services Division.

Chapter 17

Conclusion and the future direction

Innocent Chirisa and Mike Juru

In the present era, many people if not thousands of them from the world at large, are working very hard being backed by billions of dollars to transform the way real estate is being used, operated and traded. Change is very apparent as everyone is working towards achieving a diversified real estate environment (PWC, 2017). When one considers the future of real estate, it might be difficult to visualise the advancements on the cityscapes that would have been brought about by technology. It would be worthy to predict that the underlying driver of the changes that will be brought about in the real estate sector would be the consumers themselves. The users or the occupiers of the properties would demand changes pertaining to the way they want their needs or expectations satisfied and as a result, the developers would have to keep up with such requirements and demands and thus leading to massive transformation in the sector. Real estate is no longer about the buildings, their walls and roofs, it is also about the consumer and as such, the landlords would need to use consumer-centric approaches in order that they may remain competitiveness on the market (KPMG, 2017).

The context and the current situation taking place in the real estate sector in Zimbabwe needs to be understood both on the existing challenges and the opportunities in the sector. This would help get one prepared for the future. Some of the challenges that are faced in the present situation are those of liquidity and unemployment and these an impact on the functioning and the feasibility of the real estate market in the country. For the real estate market in Zimbabwe to far well in the future, both on the local and the international markets, there is need of much greater effort of gathering the financial muscles to keep the sector going. It is first therefore, important to find ways that may revive the economy or the real estate market in the country amidst the existing economic challenges in the country. This is because, the future would be about technology and when there are not enough funds to meet the changes in the market, it would be difficult to attain success in the field as the consumer tastes and preferences would not remain constant but rather are ever changing.

The trends in the real estate environments have been ever changing. Most of the work done in the real estate sector is more quantitative and all the data can easily be found in the government databases. This includes the information on Land Registry, the prices and various transactions that take place. Therefore, to some reasonable extent, the trend in the real estate sector is largely driven by the data or the information available. Also, the trends are also demand driven and due to this, the nature of information and the transactions are likely to increase in the future (Chau, 1998). Various pricing models in the sector may emerge in the verge of liquidity challenges in the country, if ever it is going to increase. Due to the current liquidity challenges in the economy, the volumes of transactions in the real estate sector tend to be lower. The properties involved tend to be heterogeneous thereby increasing the number of independent variables in relation to the number of observations. The choice of tenure which is especially politically related, will continue to be another contributing factor to the changes in the real estate. However, such choices tend to be affected as well by the various government policies that would be existing in the country and these include the monetary and fiscal policies (Chau, 1998).

Any revolution is guaranteed to change the way in which people live and how they use their buildings. Technological changes and digitisation are also to change the real estate as seen and experienced today through posing either a threat or an opportunity to the country. Each property now faces challenges forcing it to adapt to volatility of the environment and technology. Digital connectivity is becoming the major key aspect in any set up compared to the physical connectivity itself. This is enhanced through the invention of shopping centre apps and remote working to automated warehouses and smart homes. There is also an increased need for customer experience as well as personalized services. Everything is moving towards digitisation due to the continuous improvements in technology. Therefore, real estate, both for the present and in the future will not only be about the bricks and mortar. There is now need to provide holistic service by the property owners such that the customer expectations are met and one of the factors is that, it has become a top priority of convenience. As such people require easy delivery of services and this demands a transformation in the retail and logistics sectors. Therefore, the shopping centres need to fit well with the busy lifestyles, thus allowing people to indicate easily their shopping list among many other benefits. Therefore, it is a call to the landlords and the property owners to catch up with the latest technology. There is need for scaling up and be flexible in the real estate footprints as their businesses evolve (Pyle, 2017).

With the trending issue of sustainability in the world, the real estate sector will move towards achieving it. People require safety, wellness as well as comfort in their workplaces and residential houses. Therefore, there will be a rise in the knowledge and understanding of the union between the wellbeing of the work force or the property users with productivity. Because of that, there will arise the need to improve the physical structure of a building in order to promote wellness. This will be done by way of introducing new standards that promote sustainability through encouraging natural ventilation. This would improve even the value of the properties for the real estate (Deloitte, 2017). Every real estate investor should be awake to any possible changes that are prone to take place in the field of real estate in order to catch up with the movement of time. There is a constant increase in the demand for co-working space as well as for smart buildings. As this is gaining popularity even from other countries, it then becomes imperative for the sector to gain a competitive advantage through the use of the Internet (IT), in order to also improve privacy and make cyber risk protection a priority (Deloitte, 2017).

Soon, the real estate will face rapid economic and social change as the built environment will be transformed as well. Due to the highly inflating energy prices, the ongoing climate change and the call for sustainability by the world at large, the same issue will soon become an agenda for the real estate. The valuation of properties will be putting in the factor of sustainability as well. Due to the general increase in population in the cities, this will drive construction up and sustainability being the key driver of value (PWC, 2014). Therefore, there is need for the real estate sector to adapt to the changing technology and social face in order to improve property value as well as satisfy the customers' needs and satisfaction.

The future gives opportunities for practitioners in the real estate sector business to achieve success. Due to the transformation of the operations of the real estate sector and property management operations, the public sector as well has enough opportunity and chance to far well in the business. The public sector and other organisations that are in the field of property management and real estate sector are at an advantage to grab the digitisation and embrace the transforming technological environment in order to improve on their property operations, management and their portfolios and at the same time benefit from the lessons in the private sector. The economic environment as well as the ecological, social and technological environments will, because of their volatility and transformations, change the way people live, work and even their daily activities. All these changes in the future will also impact the already established markets as well as their share of value. When the changes are grabbed on time there will reduce chances of losses as well as obsolescence (Deloitte, 2017).

Many of today's buildings will soon become unfit to stand the test of time. Therefore, it is important that in the present operations, the structures that are being set up become adaptive to any future changes in order to overcome the chances of obsolescence. This should be done by analysing the changes in the patterns of the consumer demands and requirements to integrate them in their properties as well as the emerging technologies. This also means flexing up even in the consumer changes in lease requirements. Overall, this would be of benefit both to the property owner as well as the user. The property owner would benefit from the reliable clients as well as regular rental income from the clients (KPMG, 2017).

However, even though it seemingly shows that the future is full of opportunities for the real estate, there are some notable risk factors that need to be taken into account. In as much as the technologically advanced properties and buildings would help lure in many consumers due to their improved focus on service provision and community spaces, they provide a false sense of security. Because of the fact that any computer or electrical device is vulnerable, it also means that any building or structure that uses the ICT would become vulnerable to cyber-attacks as compared to the usual conventional buildings. When there is failure to provide secure software systems, there are chances that hackers may take over control of the structure or the building's sensitive information and crucial functions. Nothing is 100% security safe and the Internet of Things is certainly battling with the issues of cyber security. Once an attack happens, there will be challenges of culpability and it becomes difficult to solve as it may neither be the landlord's or the occupier's problem. Therefore, there will be conflicts over who is going to underpin the insurance (KPMG, 2017). This analysis is very important to consider in the move towards embracing technology in the buildings and properties.

Rigorous review methods for the current management of the properties need to take place. This would help in providing diversifying solutions to the present challenges in the sector and at the same time meeting the future requirements in terms of operations in the sector. There is need to focus attention in the real estate sector on property management as the sector has received very limited attention even in the top journals of general management in the country (Abatecola *et al.* 2013). There has been and will be an increased growth in the emergence of real estate and property management as an academic discipline. This is because of the increased demand for information pertaining to the real estate markets as they become more accessible even to the international community. With the increase that will be brought in the markets for real estate, there will be need for empirical research. This would include the implications of the political, economic and the social effects that would even raise interest in the academics, the policy makers as well as the practitioners in the field (Abatecola *et al.* 2013).

In conclusion, there is a need for the sector to adapt to the changes in the country. There is or there will be a competition over talent as the local knowledge will be more sought after and as such, that expertise will become very imperative for the success of the companies. Because of the stiff competition that will arise in the future, there will be need for property owners to provide competitive incentives to their tenants and at the same time making them to also adapt to the changing strategies in the sector. However, this would be good when the business is first and well established. This is because, the business in the real estate sector and property management has become, in many parts of the country as well as the world at large, less profitable and this has led to an increased need to have effective cost management methods. Some methods of minimising cost for the property owners include automation through technology. The general fact is that, the real estate information is centred business and as such would best use automation which is a great potential for minimising costs (KPMG, 2017).

The clients need as well to adapt to the changes in the real estate sector and thereby save themselves from exploitation on the market. Realtors and real estate agents are better informed as compared to the clients that hire them and this advantage may be exploited and abused at the disadvantage of the client. The real estate agents know more about the housing and property market than the typical home owner. However, because the real estate agents receive only a smaller percentage or commission from the incremental profit when a property has been sold at a higher value; this may lead them to convince their clients to sell out their properties at a cheaper price too quickly, thus putting the client at a disadvantage or loss (Levitt and Syverson, 2005).

References

Abatecola, G., Caputo, A., Mari, M and Poggesi, S. (2013). Real estate management: past, present and future research directions. *International Journal of Globalisation and Small Business*, 5(1-2), 98-113.

Chau, K. W. (1998). Real Estate Research in Asia-Past, Present and the Future. *Journal of Asian Real Estate Society*, 1(1), 1-16.

Deloitte. (2017). *Building the Future of Real Estate*. University of Oxford, Oxford.

Levitt, S. D., and Syverson, C. (2008). Market distortions when agents are better informed: The value of information in real estate transactions. *The Review of Economics and Statistics*, 90(4), 599-611.

Pyle, A. (2017). Real Estate in the Digital Age. KPMG, UK.

PWC. (2014). Real Estate 2020: Building the Future. Available online: www.pwc.com/realestate. [Accessed on 05 March 2018].

Printed in the United States
By Bookmasters